⌘ H

THE ROLE OF
NATIVE AMERICANS IN
MILITARY ENGAGEMENTS
FROM THE 17TH CENTURY
TO THE 19TH CENTURY

Heritage Books, Inc.

Published 2003 By

HERITAGE BOOKS, INC.
1540E Pointer Ridge Place, Bowie, Maryland 20716
1-800-398-7709
www.heritagebooks.com

ISBN 0-7884-2360-6

A Complete Catalog Listing Hundreds of Titles
On History, Genealogy, and Americana
Available Free Upon Request

TABLE OF CONTENTS

INTRODUCTION

From the landings of the first European colonists to nineteenth century histories to 1950s film westerns, Native Americans have been portrayed with unquestioned prejudice and ugly bias. In the early days of exploration by the English, America's natives were viewed as animals and judged incapable of properly using their land. Virginia Indians were described as creeping like bears and living in houses that were hog styes; the natives were "more brutish than the beasts they hunt[ed]."[1] Ralph Lane confidently reported to Queen Elizabeth that the "savages that possesse the land…know no use of the same" and, consequently, the English saw the New World as empty, unused, and ripe for habitation and improvement by themselves.[2]

Samuel Bowles traveled throughout the American West in the mid-nineteenth century and recorded facts, impressions, and opinions for publication in his book entitled *Our New West* (1869). He is representative of the popular thought of

---

[1] Keith Thomas, *Man and the Natural World: A History of Modern Sensibility* (New York: Pantheon Books, 1983), p. 42.
[2] David B. Quinn and Alison M. Quinn, *Virginia Voyages from Hakluyt* (London: Oxford University Press, 1973), p. 22. And it could not have helped the Native Americans' cause that Martin Luther, in 1530, spurred the English belief that "the possession of private property was an essential difference between man and beast." Thomas, p. 31. Gregory H. Nobles, *American Frontiers: Cultural Encounters and Continental Conquest* (New York: Hill and Wang, 1997), p. 31.

his day regarding Native Americans. As whites expanded across the continent and increasingly violent conflicts between them and the original occupants of the land occurred, Bowles offered a solution to the problem by echoing earlier beliefs about land use: "We know that our right to the soil, as a race capable of its superior improvement, is above theirs." And, he proposed that Indians be treated "just as a father would treat an ignorant, undeveloped child." He described how it was to be done: "Let us say to him, you are our ward, our child...ours to displace, ours also to protect. We want your hunting-grounds to dig gold from, to raise grain on, and you must 'move on.' ... You must not leave this home we have assigned you; the white man must not come hither; we will keep you in and him out; when the march of our empire demands this reservation of yours, we will assign you another; but so long as we choose, this is your home, your prison, your playground."[3] Bowles, like so many of his contemporaries, treated Native Americans as mindless bodies, mere non-entities who took up space on the landscape. To emphasize his point, Bowles quoted General Sherman's succinct policy: "Peace and protection to the Indians upon the reservations; wars and extermination if found off from them."[4]

The Lone Ranger was a typical TV western of the 1950s. It had simple characters and plots but lots of action between the good guys and the bad guys. Running from 1949 through 1957, it was a consistently popular show among children and their parents as well. The Indian Tonto, on the show supposedly a member of the Michigan-based Potawatomi tribe, was played by Jay Silverheels, a part-Mohawk Native American.[5] Tonto was a stereotypical Indian character. He

---

[3] Samuel Bowles, *Our New West* (Hartford: Hartford Publishing Co., 1869; reprinted Bowie: Heritage Books, Inc., 1990), pp. 118-121.
[4] Ibid., p. 159.
[5] "The Lone Ranger," <http://www.skypoint.com/members/joycek19/ranger.htm> (18 March 2003). Mark Largent, "Largent's Lone Ranger Page," <http://www.endeavorcomics.com/largent/ranger/silver3.html> (18 March 2003). The television show grew out of a local radio show that had first aired in 1933.

was the sidekick, the foil against which the Lone Ranger played. He was one of the good guys only because he was associated with the impeccable Lone Ranger. He rode a pinto, or paint, horse, labeled by most Americans as an "Indian pony." And, he spoke garbled English in the way that Americans believed Indians would communicate with whites.

In all of these instances, Native Americans are not considered on their own terms nor is any attempt made to understand their point of view. That is not to say that no one ever tried to do so during the passage of all these years from the first white settlements to the mid-twentieth century, however. As just one example, Colonel Johnson, who would send off the Mariposa Battalion to clear out the local Yosemite Indians in 1851, not only espoused the belief that the native people needed to be removed from the area in order to protect the incoming whites but he also credited the Indians for having reasonable cause for taking retaliatory actions. "While I do not hesitate to denounce the Indians for the murders and robberies committed by them, we should not forget that there may perhaps be circumstances which, if taken into consideration, might to some extent excuse their hostility to the whites. They probably feel that they themselves are the aggrieved party, looking upon us as trespassers upon their territory, invaders of their country, and seeking to dispossess them of their homes."[6]

It would not be until the 1970s that history scholars would begin to seriously demand a change in how Native Americans were viewed and their lifeways studied. They believed that Indians were vital participants who contributed actively to the unfolding of United States history. Francis Jennings was among the first historians to call for a new approach to looking at America's past. In *The Invasion of America: Indians,*

Parents liked the TV show "because of the lack of overt killing and the hero's faultless grammar." "The Lone Ranger."
[6] Johnson quoted in Lafayette Houghton Bunnell, *Discovery of the Yosemite, and the Indian War of 1851, Which Led to That Event,* <http://memory.loc.gov> (29 February 2000), pp. 35, 36.

Colonialism, and the Cant of Conquest (1975), he argued that the record needed to be set straight regarding the myth and reality of European and Indian interactions. He challenged the long-held consensus that Europeans discovered America and that the native peoples were worth no more than a footnote in the history books.[7] In 1980, Karen Kupperman boldly argued that the early English explorers and colonists did not off-handedly dismiss Native Americans or want to dominate them, as early historians had argued, but that the English sought ways to understand the Indians by finding expressions of what they considered essential elements of a civilized society in native society.[8] James Merrell and Richard White are just two of the more recent scholars who present evidence that Native Americans were active manipulators of their world, including how they dealt with the numerous people of European and African descent, and not helpless victims, as so often portrayed by earlier writers.[9]

Although much progress was made in the decades following the 1970s, need for improvement remained and demands for change continued into the 1990s. George Miles, for instance, pointed out in a 1992 article that scholars had not as yet considered how various Native American groups used written language or how Indians and whites endeavored to learn and use each other's languages.[10]

The search for a full understanding of North America's numerous groups of native peoples and their contributions to U.S. history continues. This volume explores the Indian–non-

---

[7] Francis Jennings, *The Invasion of America: Indians, Colonialism, and the Cant of Conquest* (Chapel Hill: University of North Carolina Press, 1975).

[8] Karen Ordahl Kupperman, *Settling With the Indians: The Making of English and Indian Cultures in America, 1580-1640* (Totowa: Rowman and Littlefield, 1980).

[9] James Merrell, *The Indians' New World: Catawbas and Their neighbors From European Contact Through the Era of Removal* (Chapel Hill: University of North Carolina Press, 1989). Richard White, *The Middle Ground: Indians, Empires, and Republics in the Great Lakes Region, 1650-1815* (Cambridge: Cambridge University Press, 1991).

[10] George Miles, "To Hear an Old Voice: Rediscovering Native Americans in American History," *Under an Open Sky: Rethinking America's Western Past*, eds. William Cronon, George Miles, and Jay Gitlin (New York: W. W. Norton, 1992).

Indian interactions from the seventeenth through the nineteenth centuries, with a focus on military encounters.

The essays are arranged in a roughly chronological order, beginning with early contacts in 1609 between the Lenape and Dutch in the Delaware region, and the Mohawks and French in New France. The Wiechquaeskeck of southwestern Connecticut also deal with the Dutch in Governor Willem Kieft's War in the early to mid-seventeenth century. The Abenaki (1694), Shawnee (1791), and the southeastern U.S. tribes (mid-nineteenth century) deal with incursions onto their lands. The final essay looks at the St. Albert Mounted Rifles, a corps of the Canadian Militia, in 1885, which was composed mostly of Metis men.

In these essays, the Native Americans, whether working with the whites or against them, are active participants in constructing their lives under the impact of the early European arrivals and their descendants.

Steven G. Gimber discusses the interactions between the Lenape and the Dutch and Swedes from 1609 until the arrival of the English in 1664. The Lenape had a world view different from that of the foreigners who arrived in their land, Lenapehoking. Reciprocal relationships permeated the Lenape world, whether between one individual and another or between humans and the manitous, their spiritual kinsmen; the Dutch and Swedes had no similar conceptualization of exchange. Understandings of property ownership were less rigid among the Lenape than among the foreigners. Such differences as these led to repeated, and escalating, conflict between the natives and the newcomers, despite several attempts on both sides to resolve their disputes.

Barbara J. Sivertsen addresses the split within the League of the Iroquois that generally placed the Mohawks in a pro-British stance while the other league members remained pro-French or neutral as the British and French empires battled each other for supremacy in North America. Several factors contributed to the Mohawks' turn to the British: the French supplied Mohawk enemies with arms; the Mohawks were geographically located closer to the British settlements than were some of the other league members; and French Jesuits convinced numerous members of the Mohawk tribe to convert to Catholicism and move to Canada.

John Alexander Buckland takes a close look at the war that New Netherland's Governor Willem Kieft waged against the Wiechquaeskeck. Although the West India Company had a generally tolerant and cooperative policy towards the native people, Governor Kieft took a hard stance against the Wiechquaeskeck over the late 1630s and into the mid-1640s. Conflicts arising over cultural differences, population pressures, and other factors eventually escalated and resulted in massacres committed on both sides. The style of governance changed with the arrival of Peter Stuyvesant in 1647, but not before the Wiechquaeskeck had suffered irreparably.

Craig J. Brown argues that the Abenaki attack on Oyster River Plantation (present-day Durham, New Hampshire, and vicinity) in 1694 was not an accident, as some historians claim, but a planned and organized assault. Native Americans burned half of the settlement to the ground, destroyed countless crops, and killed hundreds of head of livestock. They also captured or killed fully one-third of the population. The Abenaki did this to protect their land and way of life, and in disagreement with a small group of disaffected chiefs who had signed the Treaty of Pemaquid.

Harry G. Enoch analyzes the battle of Captina Creek, a little-known but signal battle in the border wars in the early 1790s. After the four Crow sisters were attacked by several Shawnee in May 1791, war arrived in Washington County, Pennsylvania, and Rangers (frontier militiamen) were used to deal with the situation. Drawing from numerous kinds of documentation, the author reconstructs in detail what probably happened during the multi-day Captina Creek affair, an unusually severe contest in which natives and whites both suffered heavy losses.

Rogan H. Moore reviews President Andrew Jackson's Indian removal policies that culminated in the Federal Indian Removal Act of 1830. Jackson's policies can be traced back to the Creek War of 1813-1814. Over the following years, he forced land cessions from the southeastern tribes (Cherokees, Chickasaws, Choctaws, Seminoles, and Creeks), gained much fame as a land negotiator and Indian fighter, and rode the wave of popularity into the White House. Jackson used the Native Americans as pawns and demonstrated no concern for their culture or their welfare.

Cynthia Dunnigan investigates the formation, purpose, and composition of the St. Albert Mounted Rifles in 1885, a corps of the Canadian Militia made up mostly of Metis men. Descendants of First Nation-French unions, these men did not fit within the stereotypical confines upheld by non-Native people: they involved themselves in local affairs and were often leading citizens, they owned property and businesses, and they were astute and proactive with their use of lobbying and other techniques of obtaining what they wanted in order to effect change in their community.

Karen L. T. Ackermann
Managing Editor

CONTRIBUTORS

Craig J. Brown is most interested in the history of the interactions between Native Americans and Europeans during the colonial era. He is the author of numerous articles, including "The Fort William and Mary Powder Raid: Legend Rewritten," that have appeared in several New Hampshire magazines and newspapers. He is currently pursuing a B.S. degree in archaeology and history.

John Alexander Buckland grew up with the lore of the Capilano, Cowichan, and Gitskan First Nations in British Columbia, Canada. He is the author of *The First Traders on Wall Street: The Wiechquaeskeck Indians of Southwestern Connecticut in the Seventeenth Century.* He holds a Ph.D. degree in engineering from the Pennsylvania State University.

Cynthia M. Dunnigan has been involved with the First Nations of Canada in a number of ways since 1992 including archiving Metis Nation documents and researching Metis women's life ways. She was an instructor for the School of Native Studies, University of Alberta, for three years. She is currently the Research Manager of Aboriginal Land and Legal Issues at Aboriginal Affairs and Northern Development. She holds an M.A. degree in anthropology from the University of Alberta.

Harry G. Enoch, a native of Kentucky, is on the board of directors of the Bluegrass Heritage Museum (Clark County) and the Red River Historical Society and Museum (Powell County), and is a founding member and secretary of the Kentucky Old Mill Association. He published a book-length treatment on the battle at Captina Creek in 1999. He is currently Director of Environmental Health and Safety at the University of Kentucky. He holds a Ph.D. degree in biochemistry from the University of Kentucky.

Steven G. Gimber, a member of the Organization of American Historians, is currently an Adjunct Professor in the History Department at West Chester University, West Chester, Pennsylvania. He has made several contributions to www.explorepahistory.com for the Pennsylvania Historical and Museum Commission. He holds a Ph.D. degree in history from American University.

Rogan H. Moore has taught numerous courses in history and related social sciences at several colleges in New Jersey and Pennsylvania. He is the history and geography expert for WLVT TV's "Scholastic Scrimmage" (Lehigh Valley, Pennsylvania, PBS TV). He is the author of *The Bloodstained Field: A History of the Sugarloaf Massacre September 17, 1780*. He holds an M.A. degree in history from Drake University.

Barbara Jean Sivertsen has a long-standing interest in local and family history as well as Native American genealogy and ethnohistory. She is the author of *Turtles, Wolves, and Bears: A Mohawk Family History*. She is currently the Managing Editor for *The Journal of Geology*. She holds an A.M. degree in anthropology from The University of Chicago.

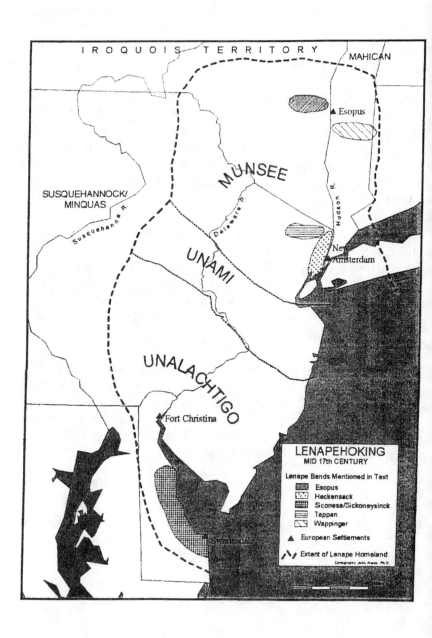

I R O Q U O I S   T E R R I T O R Y   MAHICAN

▲ Esopus

MUNSEE

SUSQUEHANNOCK/
MINQUAS

Susquehanna R.

Delaware R.

Hudson R.

New
Amsterdam

UNAMI

UNALACHTIGO

▲ Fort Christina

Swanendal

LENAPEHOKING
MID 17th CENTURY

Lenape Bands Mentioned in Text
- ▨ Esopus
- ⋰ Hackensack
- ▦ Siconese/Sickoneysinck
- ▤ Tappan
- ▨ Wappinger

▲ European Settlements

〰 Extent of Lenape Homeland

Cartography John Hasse Ph.D.

MISTAKEN MANITOUS IN LENAPEHOKING: CONTACT AND CONFLICT BETWEEN THE LENAPE AND THE DUTCH AND SWEDISH SETTLERS, 1609-1664

Steven G. Gimber

Contact and war with Europeans brought about a major transformation of the Lenape world. The Lenape (also known as the Delaware) were among the first Native Americans to have extensive contact with Europeans. After the arrival of the Dutch in Lenapehoking, the land of the Lenape, in 1609, casual aggression, cultural misunderstanding and greed repeatedly led to hostility that eventually evolved into a number of serious conflicts. Although these battles and the events that led up to them are not well known today, they were very significant at the time and had far reaching consequences for the Lenape and many other Indian people—the Mahicans, the Minquas and the Iroquois.[1] The Swedes, who arrived

---

[1] The Lenape identified themselves by their geographic location in their homeland, known today as southeastern New York, eastern Pennsylvania, New Jersey, and Delaware. The people who lived in the southern part of Lenapehoking, near the bay and the ocean, had the name Unalactigo which is translated as "the people who live near the ocean." Up the river from them were the Unami, "the up river people;" and the Minsi or Munsi were "the people from the stony country," from the northern regions of their homeland. Deeds and documents from the contact period indicate that they further identified themselves by the names they gave to rivers or streams nearby their home villages (e.g.: Esopus, Hackensack, Okehocking, Raritan, and Tappan). The Mahicans were an Algonquin people (related to the Lenape) who, at the time of contact with Europeans, lived in the Hudson River Valley in the area extending from present-day Albany, New York, south to the Catskill Mountains. The Minquas (also called Susquehannocks by the English) were an Iroquoian people who lived in Pennsylvania's Susquehanna River

in 1638, also had some significant hostility and tension in the course of their relationship with the Lenape. As for the Lenape, they must have been frequently puzzled in dealing with the newcomers. It seems likely that none of the Indians could have imagined that by following the example of their deities, whom they called manitous, and welcoming strangers amongst them, could lead to such unfortunate consequences. The Lenape and other Native Americans soon found out that these guests often treated them with astonishing callousness and disrespect; they brought strange, virulent and deadly diseases; and moreover, the newcomers sought to control them or kill them and take their land.

The Lenape And Their World

All the Indian people throughout Lenapehoking knew the importance of the manitous—their supernatural kinsmen. They lived everywhere and controlled everything in the world. The Creator, the greatest of all the manitous, was the primary force in the world and all things came from him. While he contemplated a vision he had about the world he transformed the immense void around him and made the images in his vision a reality. He made the universe and the other manitous in the world by his thoughts. As he created them, he infused them with his spirit and they became his spiritual agents.[2] These lesser manitous, or manitouwuk, appeared as the forces present in all of nature. The relationship between the Creator and the lesser spirits filled the world with life.

The Lenape were totally reliant on the manitous for guidance and support in their everyday lives. They worked with them daily and were an integral part of their lives.[3] Lenape men worked with the Mesingw or "Masked Keeper" to help them find game and women

---

Valley. In the seventeenth century, the Iroquois were comprised of the Mohawk, Oneida, Onondaga, Cayuga, and Seneca (collectively known as the Five Nations). Iroquoia—the land of the Iroquois—is roughly the region of present-day New York from Albany westward to Lake Erie. The Iroquoians were (and still are) unrelated to Algonquin peoples like the Lenape and the Mahicans.

[2] C. A. Weslager. *The Delaware Indians* (New Brunswick: Rutgers University Press, 1991), p. 66; C. A. Weslager, *Magic Medicines of the Indians* (Somerset: Middle Atlantic Press, 1973), pp. 38-39.

[3] Herbert C. Kraft, ed., "Delaware Indian Reminiscences," *Bulletin of the Archaeological Society of New Jersey* no. 35, 1978: 1-17; Weslager. *Magic Medicines*, p. 42.

worked with the Corn Spirit or Corn Mother who cared for plants and assisted in cultivation.[4]

According to Lenape belief, their spirit kinsmen not only worked with them but also appeared to them and provided the people with important, remarkable and sometimes powerful gifts. For example, a vision quest was the first step to adulthood for any Lenape youth and would put the human in direct personal contact with a guardian spirit who would aid and protect the person forever.[5] The guardian manitou might even offer the person a talisman or instruct the person in the creation of one to mark this new special relationship.

Lenape could expect to have encounters with other manitous throughout their lives. Their grandfathers told an ancient story of two hunters who shared part of their food with a young maiden who descended from the sky on clouds.[6] Their thoughtfulness to this stranger, who in reality was an incarnation of the Corn Mother, resulted in the gifts of beans, corn, and tobacco.[7]

The manitous, who gave of themselves to provide for the people, had to be thanked in return through certain prescribed rituals and in sharing with others. Lenape people learned at an early age that it was important to be generous and kind with each other and with strangers. According to their beliefs, this was how the world worked—through a series of reciprocal relationships—and this is how their society operated. Since the Lenape had regular contact with spirit-beings who shared remarkable things with them, it should come as no surprise then that when strange-looking newcomers appeared in the Lenape homeland in 1609, they were considered manitous and were welcomed with gifts and given every courtesy. The strangers, however, did not behave like any other guests the Lenape had had contact with before.

---

[4] Herbert C. Kraft and John T. Kraft, *The Indians of Lenapehoking* (South Orange: Seaton Hall University Museum, 1991), p. 30; Herbert C. Kraft, *The Lenape: Archaeology, History and Ethnography* (Newark: The New Jersey Historical Society, 1988), p. 175; Weslager, *Magic Medicines*, p. 39.

[5] Kraft, *The Lenape*, 178; Gladys Tantaquidgeon, *Folk Medicine of the Delaware and Related Algonkian Indians* (Harrisburg: The Pennsylvania Historical and Museum Commission, 1977), p. 8; Weslager, *Magic Medicines*, pp. 44-45.

[6] M. Cocciardi, "The History of Tobacco," *Retrospect* 1, 2, Summer 1995: 1.

[7] Cocciardi, p. 1.

The Lenape Welcome Manitous Mistaken

On September 4, 1609, Robert Juet, a ship's officer on Hudson's *De Halve Maen* recorded the first extensive contact between the Dutch and the Lenape.[8] Over the next twelve days, the people of two different worlds became acquainted with each other.[9] Both people were interested in trade and both were cautiously curious about each other. Even though they bargained for food and furs from the Indians, Juet wrote that he and his fellow mariners dared not trust them but did not explain why.[10] It seems likely that the Dutch were both wary and worried because they did not know what to expect from these people whom they considered to be "wilden" (a Dutch term meaning savages or wild men). This mistrust and possible mutual misunderstanding or provocation led to open violence just two days after their initial contact.[11] The killing of one of Hudson's crewmen by the Indians led to additional precautions, increased hostility and wariness on the part of the newcomers.[12] Perhaps intending to insure their safety or to intimidate the "people of the Countrey," the strangers kidnapped some of the Lenape but they managed to escape.[13] The voyagers nevertheless sailed northward where they came in contact with more Lenape bands and some Mahicans. After establishing contact with them, the Hollanders sailed south for the return trip.

Again, violence was a feature of their interaction with the inhabitants of Lenapehoking. Following a couple days of peaceful contact, Juet wrote that on the "afternoone" of the first of October,

> one Canoe kept hanging under our sterne with one man in it, which we could not keepe from thence, who got up by our Rudder to the Cabin window, and stole out my Pillow, and two Shirts, and two Bandeleers. Our Master's Mate shot at him, and strooke him in the breast, and killed him. Whereupon all the rest fled away, some in their Canoes, and

---

[8] Robert Juet. *Juet's Journal. The Voyage of the* Half Moon *from 4 April to 7 November 1609*, ed. Robert M. Lunny (Newark: The New Jersey Historical Society, 1959), p. 28.

[9] Ibid., pp. 28-31.

[10] Ibid., p. 28.

[11] Ibid., p. 29.

[12] Ibid.

[13] Ibid., pp. 29, 31, 32.

so lept out of them into the water. We manned our Boat, and got our things againe. The one of them that swamme got hold of our Boat thinking to overthrow it. But our Cooke took a Sword, and cut off one of his hands, and he was drowned.[14]

Still more combat took place the following day:

Then came one of the Savages that swamme away from us going up the River with many other, thinking to betray us. But wee perceived their intent, and suffered none of them to enter our ship. Whereupon two Canoes full of men, with their Bowes and Arrows shot at us after our sterne: in recompense whereof we discharged six Muskets, and killed two or three of them. The above an hundred of them came to a point of Land to shoot at us. There I shot a Falcon [a small cannon] at them, and killed two of them: whereupon the rest led into the woods. Yet they manned off another Canoe with nine or ten men, which came to meet us. So I shot at it also a Falcon, and shot it through, and killed one of them.[15]

Despite the battles involved in these initial meetings, the Dutch government chartered the West India Company to trade with the Lenape with visions of great profits from furs. First, however, the company had to acquire a foothold in the New World.

In 1624 and 1626, the Company sent representatives and a group of adventurers to the region to buy land, establish bases of operations, and engage the native inhabitants in commerce.[16] The problem was that the Lenape had no concept of buying or selling land.[17] The earth was one of the foremost manitouwuk; called Kukna, she was a living island situated on the back of a turtle in the

---

[14] Ibid., p. 35.
[15] Ibid., pp. 35-36.
[16] Ives Goddard, "Delaware" in *Northeast*, vol. 15 of *Handbook of North American Indians*, ed. Bruce G. Trigger (Washington: Smithsonian Institution, 1978), pp. 35-36.
[17] Weslager, *The Delaware Indians*, p. 37.

midst of a great sea.[18] She was the mother of all life.[19] The Lenape believed that the strangers were providing them goods for the right to share the land with them. According to the Lenape way of thinking, they were embarking on a long-term reciprocal relationship with these newcomers—like the one they had with each other and the manitous. The Lenape renewed their relationship with each other everyday through sharing and with the manitous through special rituals, and annually with all creation in a major ceremony called the Gamwing or Big House Ceremony.[20] Thus, it made sense to them that they should receive gifts from the "Swannekins" (the "saltwater people") as a token of appreciation and respect for sharing the land and have a special annual ceremony to renew their reciprocal relationship with them.[21] The idea of exclusive, individual ownership was alien to them.

The Dutch found Lenape concepts and customs equally strange. They did not understand the Native American belief that giving was the greatest good. They also did not comprehend that they entered into a reciprocal relationship with the Indians—one that would require them to regularly share with their hosts and one that would be renewed every year. For the Dutch, their interaction with the Indians was not a relationship of extended kinship that was established and fortified by giving gifts and sharing; it was business and business was conducted for profit. Since they did not fully understand Lenape customs, the Dutch frequently complained that the Indians demanded new goods or "bribes" to maintain their friendship.[22]

---

[18] John Bierhorst, *The White Deer and Other Stories Told by the Lenape* (New York: William Morrow and Company, Inc., 1995), p. 7; Weslager, *The Delaware Indians*, p. 66; also see John Bierhorst, ed., *Mythology of the Lenape* (Tucson: University of Arizona Press, 1995).

[19] Weslager, *The Delaware Indians*, p. 66; Kraft, *The Lenape*, pp. 163-166; also see Birehorst, *The White Deer* and *Mythology of the Lenape*.

[20] Bierhorst, *Mythology of the Lenape*, p. 107; Frank Esposito, "Indian-White Relations in New Jersey, 1609-1802" (Ph.D. diss., Rutgers University, 1976), p. 28; also see Frank G. Speck, *A Study of the Delaware Big House Ceremony* (Harrisburg: Pennsylvania Museum Commission, 1931) and Frank G. Speck, *Oklahoma Delaware Ceremonies, Feasts and Dances* (Philadelphia: The American Philosophical Society, 1937).

[21] For the Lenape name for the Dutch, see Weslager, *The Delaware Indians*, p. 112 n10.

[22] For the Dutch view, see, "Proposals Made to the Esopus Indians and Their Answers," in Barbara Graymont, ed., *New York and New Jersey Treaties, 1609-*

Although the formerly supposed manitous did not regularly give gifts to honor their Lenape hosts, they did provide them goods in exchange for foodstuffs, furs, handcrafts and labor.[23] As Lenape hosts gradually became aware that the Dutch were not manitous, they also, much to their chagrin, came to learn and understand their European guests' concept of exclusive land ownership. The Lenape relationship with the strangers they permitted to stay in their midst had benefits, but it was not an easy one.

Lenape bands throughout their homeland endured ongoing conflict in trade with the Dutch. They provided food and furs to their guests in exchange for manufactured goods such as cloth, copper pots, iron kettles, liquor, and metal tools.[24] According to Isaack de Rasiere, Secretary of New Netherland, the Indians liked the Hollanders' merchandise, the Dutch knew it and knew that the Indians would hunt more diligently to get it.[25] They also knew that they could take advantage of the native peoples and did – even though it was completely against West India Company rules and regulations.[26] When the corporation began its operations in 1623, it instructed the settlers and traders not to offend the Indians but to respect them and honor their agreements with them.[27] Despite the company's directives, settlers and traders regularly engaged in chicanery and employed a variety of dishonest practices to minimize expenses and maximize profits in trade with the Lenape and other Indians.[28] They stretched cloth very tightly before they cut it from the bolt to effectively shorten its length, they cupped their hands tightly when doling out beads or gunpowder, they watered down liquor, they offered trade goods that were often of an inferior quality

---

1682, vol. VII of *Early American Indian Documents* (Washington: University Publications of America Inc., 1979), p. 180.

[23] For Indians as laborers, see "Journal of New Netherland," in Graymont, ed., p. 100; Paul A. Otto, "New Netherland Frontier" (Ph.D. diss., Indiana University, 1995), pp. 213-214.

[24] For European manufactured goods, see, "Letter Of Isaack De Rasiere To The West India Company," dated 23 September 1626, in Graymont, ed., pp. 14-16.

[25] Graymont, ed., pp. 14-16.

[26] Otto, 129; also see Matthew Dennis, *Cultivating a Landscape of Peace: Iroquois-European Encounters in Seventeenth Century America* (Ithaca: Cornell University Press, 1993).

[27] Otto, p. 129; Dennis, pp. 1-200.

[28] Ibid.

and they arbitrarily raised their prices so that it took more furs to purchase desired items.[29]

Although cheating and dishonest trading practices provoked Lenape anger and hostility, the strangers did even more to infuriate them. They often shamelessly abused their generosity and hospitality. The native people were pleased to share everything they had with the "Swannekins;" they shared their homes, their land and even their wives and daughters. It was a duty for the Lenape to share; it was one of the ways they actively lived their faith; this traditional practice honored all involved, the guests, the hosts, their clan and most importantly, the manitous. What the natives expected in return for their courtesy and generosity was some token of appreciation and respect. In dealing with the newcomers, however, often they did not acknowledge or appreciate their hospitality; in many cases it was simply exploited even further.

The Lenape were absolutely critical to the existence and success of the Dutch colonial commercial venture; they not only provided the newcomers with pelts for profits but also supplied then with vital provisions. As more settlers came to the Dutch colony, their requests for staples, especially corn, became greater which was a drain on Lenape food supplies and hospitality. Rather than trade for what they wanted, Hollanders occasionally demanded supplies or plundered what food and furs they wanted in raids or simply stole from those people who came to barter. On the morning of March 5, 1643, at a conference with sixteen chiefs, a Lenape spokesman from present-day Rockaway, New York explained to Dutch settler David Pieterszoon de Vries that since the time the "saltwater people" had arrived in their country, the Indians had provided them with food "and now for a reward they killed their people."[30] Moreover, Dutch settlers and traders also physically and verbally abused the Lenape and others.[31] Even those Indians fortunate enough to be considered the most favored clients of Dutch traders and even allies of New

---

[29] Graymont, ed., pp. 14-16; Otto, p. 1; Weslager, *The Delaware Indians*, p. 117; Kraft, *The Lenape*, p. 198.

[30] See extracts from, "Korte Historiael Ende Journaels Aetyckeninge" in Graymont, ed., p. 86.

[31] Otto, pp. 50-60, 166 n82, 172, 180, 213-214; also see "Propositions of the Mohawks," in Graymont, ed., p. 197. For a general picture of the Dutch aggressive and sometimes violent pursuit of profit in New Netherland, see Matthew Dennis, *Cultivating a Landscape of Peace*.

Netherland—the Mahicans, Mohawks and Senecas—complained of being assaulted, battered, and insulted.[32] This kind of behavior was aggravating and bewildering for the Lenape and other Indian peoples, especially since it came from people who called them brothers. None of the Lenape's other kinsmen had ever treated them in this manner.

While Indians interested in trade suffered cursory indignities at the hands of the Hollanders, some Lenape bands may have endured more significant offenses in the course of their relationship with them, such as the physical and sexual abuse of their women. It is possible that these kinds of incidents may have occurred as a result of the Dutch misunderstanding of traditional Lenape hospitality. Occasionally hosts offered wives or daughters to guests for their sexual pleasure; some Dutchmen might have misconstrued this custom and perhaps abused the privilege or raped Indian women.[33] Recurrent affronts, casual mistreatment, and unresolved cultural misunderstandings led to growing anger, confusion, hostility, resentment and violence. In fact, it is likely that a cultural *faux pas* and abuse of Indian women were probably the causes of one of the first significant open conflicts between the Lenape and the Dutch; this was the destruction of Swanendale.

The Southern Lenape Make Their Displeasure Known: The Destruction of Swanendale

On June 1, 1629, the council of elders of the Sickoneysinck band in southern Lenapehoking, "Aixtamin, Oschoesien, Choqweke, Menatoch, Awijapoon, Menhatehan, Nethatehan, Atowesen, Ackseso, Maekemen, Queskakons and Esanques," met and traded

---

[32] See Graymont, ed., p. 163. Graymont wrote that ordinary Dutch citizens, traders and soldiers abused Indians who crossed them or displeased them. Hollanders treated Native Americans "with the utmost contempt." Also see, other documents in Graymont, ed., "Propositions Of The Mohawks," p. 197; "Mohawk Proposals And Resolutions Of The Dutch," p. 217; "Conference Between Director General Stuyvesant And The Sinnekus," p. 224. Also important on this issue are: Dennis, *Cultivating a Landscape of Peace* and Otto, "New Netherland Frontier."

[33] Donald H. Kent, ed., *Pennsylvania and Delaware Treaties, 1629-1737*, vol. I of *Early American Indian Documents* (Washington: University Publications of America, Inc., 1979), p. 2. I agree with Kent that the place name "Horekill" or "Whorekill" and the destruction of the Dutch settlement Swanendale along "Whore's River" is probably evidence of this.

with Gils Housett, a Dutch adventurer.[34] Acting on instructions
from patroon Samuel Godyn, Housett purchased land from the
Indian sachems, which was to be the site of Godyn's planned
private colony.[35] In the spring of 1631, the ship *De Walvis* arrived
with twenty-eight settlers and a large stock of cattle; the new
arrivals created a small fortified outpost, planted crops, engaged in
whaling, traded with the nearby Lenape and no doubt enjoyed all
aspects of their neighbors' hospitality.[36] Based on the fact that the
strangers named the river near their fledgling settlement "Horekill"
or Whore's River, it seems likely that they misunderstood the local
custom of providing for an honored guest's every desire.[37] It is also
possible that the abuse of that particular privilege led to the
complete destruction of the colony shortly after its founding.[38]

Charred palisades, a ruined brick house, partially bleached bones
of domestic animals and people—the ruins of the Swanendale
settlement—greeted Dutch patroon David Pieterszoon de Vries and
crew as they arrived at the site of the colony in early December
1632.[39] After making contact with the very apprehensive Native
Americans, De Vries sought an explanation regarding the
destruction of the outpost.[40] In answer to his inquiry, a brave
member of the Sickoneysinck band offered a curious yet interesting
tale of mutual cultural misunderstanding. According to de Vries, on
the night of December 8, from the deck of the yacht *The Squirrel*,
the Lenape man showed them

---

[34] "Deed: The Sickoneysinks to the Dutch for Swanendale," in Kent, ed., p. 5. The
Dutch settlement was called Swanendale and was located on the present-day
Delaware Bay, near what is today Lewes, Delaware.
[35] Kent, ed., p. 5; "Patent to Godyn and Blommaert for Land on the Delaware Bay,"
in Kent, ed., pp. 6-7. A patroon was a private investor who was granted a charter
from the Dutch West India Company to establish his own colony; his grant was
confirmed by the government of New Netherland. As a private investor he was
responsible for buying land from the Indians. In granting patroonships, the goal of
the company was to hasten the process of colonization. Swanendale and
Rensselaerwyck were two such ventures.
[36] Albert Cook Myers, *Narratives of Early Pennsylvania, New Jersey and
Delaware, 1630-1707* (New York: Charles Scribner's Sons, 1912), p. 7 n3.
[37] Kent, ed., p. 2; Weslager, *The Delaware Indians*, p. 109. Weslager states that
Dutch-Lenape children were not uncommon.
[38] Kent, ed., p. 2; Weslager, *The Delaware Indians*, p. 109.
[39] Kent, ed., pp. 7-9; Myers, p. 15.
[40] Kent, ed., pp. 7-9; Myers, p. 16.

The place where our people had set up a column, to which was fastened a piece of tin, whereon the arms of Holland were painted. One of their chiefs took this off for the purpose of making tobacco-pipes, not knowing that he was doing [something wrong]. Those in command at the house made such an ado about it, that the Indians, not knowing how it was, went away and slew the chief who had done it, and brought back a token of the dead to the house to those in command, who told them that they wished they had not done it, that they should have brought him to them as they wished to have forbidden him to do the like again. They then went away, and the friends of the murdered chief incited their friends – as they are a people like Italians, who are very revengeful – to set about the work of vengeance. Observing our people at work, that there was not more than one inside, who was lying sick, and a large mastiff, who was chained – had he been loose they would have not dared approach the house – and the man who had command, standing near the house, three of the bravest Indians, who were to do the deed, bringing a lot of beaver-skins with them to exchange, asked to enter the house. The man in charge went in with them to make the barter; which being done, he went down from the loft where the stores lay, and in descending the stairs, one of the Indians seized an axe, and cleft the head of our agent who was in charge so that he fell down dead. They also relieved the sick man of his life; and shot into the dog, who was chained fast, and whom they most feared, twenty-five arrows before they could dispatch him. They proceeded towards the rest of the men, who were at their work and going among them with pretensions of friendship, struck them down.[41]

De Vries and his associates met with local sachems the next day to conclude a firm peace and assuage any lingering anger and resentment over the annihilation of the settlement.[42] They exchanged gifts and the Indians left happily convinced that the strangers had forgiven their offence and they would never recall it

---

[41] Myers, pp. 16-17.
[42] Ibid., p. 17.

again.[43]   The Dutch gave them that impression even though the Indians did not mollify them.[44]   Their earnest, secret desire was to punish the Lenape "for causing [such] a serious loss" but "[they] saw no chance of revenging it as they dwelt in no fixed place."[45]

The destruction of Swanendale was a turning point for the Dutch and the Lenape.   This was probably the first indication the Hollanders had that the native peoples of the region were not as docile and manageable as expected.   The southern Lenape no doubt quickly learned that although the newcomers gave them remarkable items in trade, they were very demanding, difficult to please, often wanted more from them than they were willing to provide, and treated them poorly and lied.   Lenape bands throughout their homeland soon learned that the Hollanders would often say one thing and mean another.   By 1643, a Munsee (northern Lenape) sachem informed de Vries that he and his people believed that most Hollanders were liars.[46]   The Sickoneysinck and other southern Lenape bands found that after their meeting with de Vries, the Dutch did not come to trade as often as before.   As a result of the Swanendale disaster, the Dutch lost a significant investment and rather than venture another settlement in the southern region of their colony, they decided to focus their attentions on more profitable operations in the north.

A Steady Decline

However, by the end of the 1630s, the over-hunting of beaver and other fur-bearers meant that the Lenape living near New Amsterdam were bringing in fewer valuable pelts which translated into a decline in profits for the Dutch commercial enterprise.   In fact, by that time, beaver in the Lenape homeland "had been hunted to near extinction."[47]   Since the Lenape were not bringing in sufficient quantities of high-value pelts, the Hollanders viewed them with contempt and disregard which led to increasing anger, frustration, and hostility.   Lenape-Dutch relations began to

[43] Ibid., p. 17.
[44] Ibid.
[45] Ibid., p. 18.
[46] "Extracts From Korte Historiael Ende Journaels Aetyckeninge by David P. De Vries, 1633-1643 (1655)," in Graymont, ed., p. 87.
[47] Gregory Evans Dowd, *The Indians of New Jersey* (Trenton: New Jersey Historical Commission, Department of State, 1992), pp. 35-36.

deteriorate significantly after September 15, 1639, when the new Director-General Willem Kieft ordered a tax levied on all Indians living around the area of New Amsterdam.[48] The tribute was to be collected in "peltries, maize or wampum."[49] According to the edict, if there was any tribe that would not "contribute" it was to be induced to do so "by the most suitable means."[50] Ostensibly to defray the expenses incurred in defending the northern Lenape bands from their enemies, the tax really was an effort by the Dutch leadership to make the Lenape more productive and valuable to their commercial venture.[51] While the Director-General thought this policy was fair and just, it incensed the nearby native people who felt it was the height of rudeness for guests to make such demands of their hosts. The Lenape living at "Tappen" (present-day Tappan, New York) told patroon David Pieterszoon de Vries that it surprised them that the governor "dare exact" such a tribute from them.[52] The patroon further recorded that they told him that "he [Kieft] must be a very mean fellow to come and live in their countrey without being invited by them, and now wish to compel them to give him their corn for nothing[.]"[53] De Vries observed that the new policy "began to cause much dissatisfaction among the savages." [54]

Another part of the Dutch effort to boost declining profits from their commercial enterprise was to make their settlement more self-sufficient. To do this they began to diversify and expand operations by creating more agricultural settlements near New Amsterdam.[55] This policy also further agitated and alienated Lenape bands living

---

[48] "Resolution to Exact a Tribute From the Indians in Maize, Furs or Wampum," in Graymont, ed., p. 56. New Amsterdam was located on the southern end of Manhattan Island, present-day New York City.
[49] Graymont, ed., p. 56. Wampum is beads made of polished shells strung in strands or belts. The Indians made it; for them it was a powerful, sacred item that served various functions. For further information, see Lynn Ceci, "The Effect of European Contact and Trade on the Settlement Pattern of Indians in Coastal New York, 1524-1665: The Archaeological and Documentary Evidence" (Ph.D. diss., City University of New York, 1977) and Wilbur R. Jacobs, "Wampum, the Protocol of Indian Diplomacy," *William and Mary Quarterly* 6, no. 4, October 1949: 596-604.
[50] Graymont, ed., p. 56.
[51] Ibid.; Otto, p. 178.
[52] Graymont, ed., p. 83.
[53] Ibid.
[54] Ibid.
[55] Ibid., p. 57.

around the area of Manhattan.[56] More farms meant the purchase of more land, the arrival of more settlers and more domestic animals— all of which resulted in more contact and more conflict between the two peoples.[57]   Particularly vexing to the Lenape was the newcomers' style of animal husbandry.

Dutch settlers established their farms near Indian villages and let their chickens, cows, goats, horses, pigs, and sheep roam free. Although having free-roaming farm animals might seem odd today, this was not unusual in seventeenth and eighteenth century colonial America.[58]   Rather than keep their animals in fenced-in pastures, many early European settlers preferred to enclose their cultivated land instead. Unrestrained by fences, the domestic animals not only competed with deer for forage but many of them made their way to Lenape gardens where they gorged themselves and trampled crops.[59] Irritated Indians defended their garden patches by killing (and occasionally capturing and keeping) trespassing domestic fowl, kine and swine.[60]   The loss of livestock angered Europeans, who demanded compensation and suggested that the Native Americans either fence in their gardens or relocate. Obnoxious neighbors not withstanding, very few Lenape were interested in leaving their homes; it was their land—the Swannekins were guests.

The Lenape relationship with the "saltwater people" also brought them something else that was a major problem: liquor.   The Dutch were happy to supply alcoholic beverages if the Lenape had pelts to buy it. By the 1640s, brandy and rum had become common trade items with the Indians in New Netherland. When they could get it, they often drank to excess and became rowdy and malicious, sometimes injuring themselves and others.[61]   Drunken Native Americans in the fortified hamlet of New Amsterdam were considered a dangerous public nuisance, and, in 1643, the colony's

---

[56] Ibid.

[57] Otto, p. 167.

[58] In July 1712, the Lenape and other Indian groups settled at "Conestoga" complained to the Pennsylvania Provincial Council in Philadelphia that nearby settlers' cattle, horses and pigs damaged their crops. See "Council of Gov. Gookin and Council with Chiefs of Delaware and Schuykill Indians," in Kent, ed., pp. 111-112.

[59] Charles A. Stansfield, Jr., *An Ecological History of New Jersey* (Trenton: New Jersey Historical Commission, 1996), pp. 36-37.

[60] Graymont, ed., "Resolution to Attack Raritan Indians," p. 66; Otto, p. 171.

[61] Otto, p. 176.

governing council outlawed the sale of liquor to Indians.[62]   The
penalty for breaking this ordinance the first time was twenty-five
guilders.[63]   Although there were no recorded violations of the law,
officials renewed it in 1645 and increased the fine to 500 guilders
which seems to indicate that the practice continued.[64]   While some
Indians opposed the sale of alcoholic beverage and abstained from
drinking it, there were many others who wanted liquor very much;
there were just as many Europeans in the Dutch colony who wanted
to sell it to them, despite the risks.   In fact, officials recorded two
cases regarding the violation of the 1645 ordinance.[65]   Eventually,
the Hollanders passed additional special laws which they designed
to stem the flow of liquor to the Lenape in 1647, 1648, 1654, 1656,
1657, and, lastly, in 1663.[66]   The new statutes increased fines and
prescribed such punishments as jail sentences and even banishment,
but the problem continued unabated.   Liquor flowed freely to the
Lenape and other Indians.[67]   While Dutch officials could pass any
laws they wanted, settlers would have to enforce and follow them;
the same people who found themselves nonplussed by legislation
curtailing their opportunities to make money by providing strong
drink to the Indians.

Pursuit of the Almighty Guilder

An aggressive, energetic, individualistic pursuit of profit fostered
a belligerent disdain for both Indians and the law in New
Netherland.[68]   The colony was a place of illegal commerce and the
people exhibited a general disregard for law and order.[69]   Colonists
were concerned neither with the West India Company's profit
margin nor the legislation designed to preserve and protect it.   They
paid little attention to laws restricting their activities; they were
simply interested in making as much money as possible.[70]   Despite
ordinances to the contrary, many settlers engaged in the fur trade

---

[62] Ibid., p. 105.
[63] Ibid. A guilder was the basic Dutch monetary unit, like the dollar in the United
States.
[64] Ibid.
[65] Ibid.
[66] Esposito, p. 179-180.
[67] Ibid.
[68] Dennis, pp. 123-124, 136, 142, 145, 147-151, 172.
[69] Ibid., pp. 123-124.
[70] Ibid., p. 145.

illegally and probably smuggled pelts out of the colony to avoid the payment of taxes on furs they acquired by honest or dishonest trade with the Lenape and other native peoples.[71] It seems that many Europeans in the Delaware and lower Hudson River valleys behaved in a less civilized manner than they would if they had been in Holland; perhaps they reasoned that living in the American wilderness gave them license to simply do what they wanted.[72] Indeed, the larger pattern of life in the colony can be described being one of frolic and profit.[73] New Netherland officials noted daily occurrences of armed robberies, thefts and the shooting of livestock.[74] European scofflaws also drank to excess and engaged in public revelries, mischief and violence.[75] Citizens committed adultery, slander and murder.[76] The situation was such that Dutch patroon Van Rensselear complained that settlers in his colony violated his laws regularly and he described their behavior as covetous, licentious, unfaithful and wanton.[77] The all-consuming desire for profit even led Hollanders to cheat each other in the most subtle ways. Some unscrupulous Dutch bakers sold bread to their fellow settlers with a less or poor quality flour and reserved better flour to make cakes and sweets to sell to Native Americans, probably at exorbitant prices and perhaps in exchange for furs.[78]

Kieft's War
    The Lenape resisted Kieft's tax as well as the increasing mistreatment and expanding Dutch settlement through individual acts of revenge and violence: in 1639 they killed a number of hogs on Staten Island and attempted to steal a yacht; in the following spring, the Raritans threatened and physically abused several Dutch traders.[79] Contrary to direct orders, Dutch troops retaliated by killing four Lenape, and by kidnapping and torturing the brother of the Raritan chief.[80] In September 1641, the Lenape exacted their

---

[71] Ibid., p. 136.
[72] Ibid., p. 172.
[73] Ibid., pp. 147-151.
[74] Ibid., p. 172.
[75] Ibid., pp. 123-124.
[76] Ibid., p. 172.
[77] Ibid., p. 142.
[78] Ibid., pp. 147-151.
[79] Graymont, ed., pp. 82-90; Otto, pp. 167-168; 179-185.
[80] Ibid.

revenge by attacking the farm of patroon David Pieterszoon de Vries where they killed four workmen and then they burned his house.[81] Ignoring the fact that Dutch provocations were at the heart of these reprisals, the Director-General and other Hollanders were livid and anxious to launch an all-out attack on those Indians they felt were responsible.[82] Perhaps acting on Kieft's orders, the Mahicans (Dutch allies) launched an attack on northern Lenape bands in February 1643. The survivors fled to nearby Dutch settlements where they apparently aroused considerable hostility and suspicion in the already very tense atmosphere.[83] Following the raids, on February 25, 1643, Director-General Kieft, long anxious for a fight with "the River Indians," authorized a surprise attack on the Munsee refugees and other Lenape bands living adjacent to Manhattan in an area the Dutch called Pavonia (present-day Hoboken and Jersey City, New Jersey).[84]

The Hollanders attacked and killed 120 men, women, and children, and took thirty prisoners.[85] When the Lenape retaliated, what the Dutch began as an attempt to punish "brazen," "insolent" Native Americans broadened into a long, brutal war.[86] Eleven Munsee bands declared war on the Dutch and over the next seven months they attacked all settlements outlying Manhattan and destroyed everything they could in the way of animals, crops, fodder, grain, homes, and people.[87] A newly formed militia and a company of English mercenaries were virtually ineffective against the Native Americans.[88] Many Dutch settlers fled their plantations for the security of fortified New Amsterdam.[89]

---

[81] Graymont, ed., pp. 82-90.

[82] Graymont, ed., pp. 82-90; Otto, pp. 167-168; 179-185.

[83] Otto, p. 185.

[84] "Petition of Maryan Adriaensen and Others for Leave to Attack Indians at Corlear's Hook, with Kieft's Commission," in Graymont, ed., pp. 72-73; "Resolution for Surprise Attack Against Indians, with Authorization to Maryan Adriaensen and Sergeant Rudolf," in Graymont, ed., pp. 73-73; "Resolution to Continue Attacking Indians," in Graymont, ed., pp. 74-75.

[85] Graymont, ed., pp. 72-73.

[86] Otto, p. 186.

[87] "Letter of Eight Men at Manhattan to the Assembly of the XIX Asking Aid Against the Indians," in Graymont, ed., pp. 78-80; Otto, p. 186.

[88] The militia was formed by a resolution passed in 1643, see Otto, p. 198, n9; for English mercenaries, see Otto, p. 190 and "Letter of the Eight Men to the Amsterdam Chamber of the West India Company," in Graymont, ed., p. 94.

[89] Otto, p. 138; Graymont, ed., pp. 78-80.

While the Lenape bands on Long Island and "the River Indians" brokered peace agreements with their attackers in the spring of 1644, those living near Manhattan continued to fight well into the following year.[90] The devastation of the ongoing conflict was so great and so surprising that a group of citizens wrote the West India Company in Amsterdam and their "High Mighty Lords," the States-General, explaining their wretched situation and requesting the assistance of both the company and the national government.[91] The guerilla warfare practiced by the Indians frustrated the Hollanders who found no safe place outside of the fort at New Amsterdam.[92] On August 30, 1645, through the efforts of the Dutch allies and friends, the Mahicans and Mohawks, warring northern Lenape bands and the Hollanders came to a peace agreement that finally settled six years of ongoing hostility.[93] In keeping with the traditional Indian diplomatic custom, to assuage the Indians' grief over the loss of kinsmen and actually make peace, Kieft presented token gifts and promised many more presents.[94] However, many Lenape still felt dissatisfied; they believed that the offering was insufficient, and that the goods were too few and of too little value to make just compensation to the individuals who had been wronged.[95] The scope of the conflict was such that they felt additional restitution was necessary. Since the Dutch did not deliver the promised trade goods, the Indians near Manhattan grew "restless and dissatisfied."[96] Those northern Lenape, who still found themselves angry and disgruntled, continued to engage in violent reprisals and hostile threats, and attempted, without success, to incite another war against the Dutch.[97]

---

[90] "Council Minute: Arrival of the River Indians at Samford to Sue for Peace with the Dutch," in Graymont, ed., p. 90; "Minute of the Appearance in Council of the Sachem of Matinnekonck, Long Island to Sue for Peace," in Graymont, ed., p. 91; Otto, pp. 186-187.

[91] Graymont, ed., pp. 91-96.

[92] Otto, p. 191.

[93] "Articles of Peace Concluded in Presence of the Mohawks Between the Dutch and the River Indians," in Graymont, ed., p. 97-98.

[94] "Resolution to Send Van Tienhoven to Hemstead," in Graymont, ed., pp. 107-108.

[95] Otto, pp. 188-189.

[96] "Presents to Secure the Indian Peace," in Graymont, ed., pp. 108-109.

[97] "Journal of New Netherland," in Graymont, ed., pp. 99-106; Graymont, ed., pp. 107-108.

A New Dutch Governor And A New Relationship

Under the administration of a new Director-General, the Dutch began an official policy to improve relations with the northern Lenape bands living around Manhattan. In 1647, Willem Kieft was relieved and replaced by Peter Stuyvesant.[98] With the approbation of the company, Stuyvesant attempted to cultivate cordial relations with the Lenape.[99] It was a practical solution. If fear and resentment between the Dutch and the Lenape remained the *status quo* then the colony, its people and the company's profit margin were in grave danger. Nevertheless, while the government of the colony embarked on pacification efforts, lingering hostility between the two peoples occasionally erupted into acts of sporadic violence and, eventually, full-scale war.

Immediately upon taking office in late August 1647, Director-General Stuyvesant sent the nearby Lenape sachems gifts in the name of the West India Company as "renewal and continuation of the ancient alliance and friendship" between the two peoples.[100] Moreover, he wanted to inform them that he was Kieft's replacement and that the new administration was not responsible for the past hostilities between them; Stuyvesant wanted to live in peace with them as "good neighbors."[101] The directors of the company approved and encouraged this new policy of lenience and reconciliation with the Indians.[102] Part of this new policy was to respond to Lenape demands; the most insistent one was for firearms.[103] While other native peoples who dealt with the Dutch had access to weapons in trade, there were laws in New Netherland prohibiting the sale of guns to the Lenape. It is logical to assume that these laws were designed primarily to protect the inhabitants of New Amsterdam. Dutch officials may have been reluctant to provide the nearby Indians with weapons in sufficient quantities that might shift the balance of power in favor of the Munsee (northern

---

[98] Graymont, ed., pp. 107-108; "Presents to Secure the Indian Peace," in Graymont, ed., pp. 108-109.

[99] Graymont ed., pp. 107-109.

[100] Ibid., pp. 108-109.

[101] Ibid.

[102] "Extract of a Letter From Directors of the West India Company to Stuyvesant Recommending a Lenient Indian Policy," in Graymont, ed., p. 112.

[103] Ibid.

Lenape) who might destroy them. Local Lenape did have some firearms which they got through trade with other Indians or people from other colonies, or by taking them in raids; however, they wanted more of them and regular access to them. Fearing more bloodshed if they did not provide more firearms, the corporation authorized the limited sale of weapons to the Lenape through its own agents, not through private individuals.[104]

The new policies notwithstanding, both Dutch and Lenape individuals continued to engage in violence for plunder and revenge. In keeping with the new spirit of tolerance, European inhabitants of the Dutch colony were encouraged to overlook any wrongs committed against them by the Lenape. The murder of Symon Walingen van Bilt in March 1649 was an incident that provoked a great deal of anxiety and fear on both sides. The dead man's arrow-pierced body was brought to New Amsterdam from his farm in Pavonia. A general commotion ensued as both Europeans and Indians viewed the body and learned the story of how he was found dead outside of his home, and his house, which had been ransacked and the valuables stolen. As tempers flared and rumors spread, Governor Stuyvesant and his council issued an official resolution calling for all inhabitants to let the matter rest for the good of the colony. They prohibited any acts of revenge, which seems to indicate that the Dutch understood the Lenape concept of limited retaliation that governed the incident and that they knew that an ever-expanding cycle of revenge killings would lead to full-scale conflict.[105] Although there were more murders in the early 1650s, tensions rose but they did not result in war.[106]

Part of the pacification program included improving communications with the Indians. To that end Stuyvesant met with the Lenape bands living around Manhattan on July 19, 1649. At this meeting, chief spokesman for the Native Americans, Pennekeck, explained that he and the several representatives of other bands assembled had come to establish friendship with the Dutch at the request of the "Southern Minquas." He also apologized for the unauthorized activities of an Indian named "Mechgackamic," who recently caused what the sachem referred to

---

[104] Ibid.
[105] "Resolution for Moderation Toward the Indians," in Graymont, ed., p. 114.
[106] Otto, p. 215.

as "mischief." To indicate their sincerity, they presented gifts of beaver pelts to the Director-General. Stuyvesant accepted their apology, presents, and overtures of friendship, and expressed his desire "to live in neighborly friendship and intercourse." Additionally, he urged them to come to him if they had any complaints and he gave them gifts to show his sincerity.[107]

This meeting between Stuyvesant and the Lenape sachems is a very important event. It marks a major departure in Lenape-Dutch relations. Rather than attempt to destroy the Lenape as his predecessor Kieft tried to do, Stuyvesant embarked on a policy of peaceful coexistence. He opened the lines of communication and made himself the point of contact for aggrieved Indians. By doing so he obviously hoped that discussion would solve their difficulties and maintain a mutually beneficial business relationship.

Also worthy of note in this meeting is the influence of the Minquas on the native peoples living near Manhattan. It was at their behest that the Lenape sachems came to talk and make a firm peace with Stuyvesant. What degree of authority, if any, the "southern Minquas" may have had over the northern Lenape is uncertain, but their influence apparently brought the two parties together. It is possible that the Minquas, who were the Hollanders' most valuable trading partners in the southern region of New Netherland, were acting on their own or at the urging of the Dutch. There are several possible motivations for the Minquas to bring their influence to bear in reestablishing a friendly relationship with the Swannekins. Firm peace and open communications were in the best interests of all people; it was likely that any unresolved conflicts could develop into a major war which would disrupt Minqua trade with the Hollanders. Additionally, although Dutch traders had contact with the Minquas, they lived far away from them, thus it is likely that the Lenape acted as middlemen in the trade between the two parties and the Minquas wanted to maintain their sure access to goods they wanted from Manhattan.[108] Another possibility is that the Minquas had hegemony over those Lenape bands and used their dominance over them to prompt them to settle with the Hollanders. Whatever the motivation, the event illustrates

---

[107] "Propositions by Chiefs Living About the Manhattans," in Graymont, ed., pp. 118-119.
[108] Myers, pp. 157, 162-163.

the importance of European trade goods and the great influence of the Minquas on the Lenape, which also might suggest some form of tributary relationship between the two Indian peoples.

While enacting his pacification policy, Dutch governor Stuyvesant also embarked on a course of territorial acquisition. He undertook to buy new lands from the Lenape to bring about several important, long-term results. Geographic expansion of New Netherland in the late 1640s and early 1650s was focused primarily in areas where Lenape bands had been hostile to the Dutch presence. Although there was an official peace, there still were occasional outbreaks of violence in different areas of the colony, particularly around New Amsterdam. Thus one of the goals in purchasing land from the Indians was to establish clear and firm title from the native inhabitants; this would end any imagined or real disputes with them over Dutch claims in the area and enable peaceful expansion of the colony. The effort to bolster ownership and secure new territory by deeds and documents from the Lenape brought the Hollanders in conflict with other European people living within the scope of their colonial commercial enterprise, the Swedes.

In 1638 the Swedes had established their own colony in the southern regions of New Netherland. This was the area the Dutch had abandoned after the destruction of Swanendale. Although the Swedes and Finns settled with the permission of the local Lenape sachems, relationship between the natives and the Scandinavians was not the best.[109] In fact, in 1644 Swedish Governor Johan Printz requested that his government send soldiers to kill all the Indians in the colony.[110] Official peace notwithstanding, thinly veiled hostility characterized the relations between the Lenape and Swedes, both of whom used each other yet viewed each other as mere nuisances. The Dutch, too, were eventually affected by the Swedish colony. However, without a permanent Dutch presence in this part of the province and far away from the Hollanders' colonial capital at New Amsterdam, New Sweden was small and initially did not pose much of a threat to the Dutch operation to the north. However, this situation changed in the late 1640s when the Swedes embarked on buying land from the Lenape in the "Zuydt River" (the Dutch name

---

[109] Note: at the time, Finland was under Swedish rule. Many Finns settled in the Swedish colony on the Delaware.
[110] Myers, pp. 103-104

for the present-day Delaware River) at the same time that Stuyvesant was engaged in a similar undertaking in the same region.

The Lenape, Dutch, Swedes, and Colonial Expansion

The efforts of both competing European powers in attempting to develop their commercial ventures further led to conflict between them. In the process they labored to cajole representatives of different Lenape bands to support their opposing claims which caused conflict and dissention within native groups.[111]   For the Lenape, these negotiations were a continued part of sharing their land with the newcomers; by signing deeds and documents they were agreeing to permit them to stay and in return for their generosity they received, and were to continue to receive, gifts from strangers. In keeping with their manner of thinking, both the Dutch and Swedes were welcome to share their territory, provided they continued to be appreciative, respectful guests, which meant that they must abide by their hosts' customs and honor the Lenape by providing them gifts.

The Scandinavians in southern Lenapehoking just barely met their hosts' expectations of the proper behavior of good guests. However, according to the Swedish commercial colonial policy, since the Lenape were not providing them with furs of sufficient quality or quantity, the Indians just barely met their expectations of good trading partners.   To remedy this situation, the Swedes attempted to establish a permanent trading post with the Minquas.[112] The Minquas, advised by their more valued trading partners the Dutch, rejected their overtures.[113]

Realizing that the Swedes were beginning to pose a serious threat to their quest for continued commercial success and domination of the region, the Dutch began an effort to significantly limit the Scandinavian enterprise.   In 1648, Stuyvesant sent representatives to the southern reaches of the colony to buy land from the Indians.[114]   The Lenape sachems Mattehooren, Sinquees, Alebackinne, Mechecksouivebe, Quirkehouck, Kauke and Wacpacvack "fully and irrevokably" sold all their lands on the western side of the "Zuydt River," and those along one of its larger

---

[111] "Peter Stuyvesant's Interviews with Two Minquas Chiefs," in Kent, ed., p. 15.
[112] Ibid.
[113] Ibid.
[114] "Deed of Mattehoorn and Other Indians for Arent Corson," in Kent, ed., p. 16.

tributaries the Dutch called the "Schuykill."[115]   Governor-General
Stuyvesant also ordered the construction of a fort (Fort Beversreede)
just north and west of the main Swedish trading post to increase the
Dutch physical presence in the area and effectively cut off much of
the trade coming to the Scandinavian interlopers.[116]

Swedish trade with the Indians fell off and several Dutch
families settled on lands around or in the new trading post.
Stuyvesant's official peace policy notwithstanding, the Hollanders'
aggressive pursuit of profit and the occasional ensuing physical and
verbal abuse of the Native Americans throughout their colony
continued virtually unabated. The governor's official policy and
laws were easily skirted or not rigorously enforced in New
Netherland. Independent Dutch traders and even soldiers stationed
in the colony beat, dragged, poked, prodded, punched, and smacked
Native Americans to get the all-desired furs. It seems that many
Dutch settlers regarded the Indians as inferior and clearly believed
that it was easier to bully and plunder the "wilden" rather than to
negotiate and trade fairly with them for pelts. The competition for
furs throughout the wilderness of New Netherland was so
aggressive and fierce that it often quickly degenerated into
violence.[117]   Probably the best description of life in the Dutch
colony is that it was a mad scramble for money.

With their own colonial commercial venture in jeopardy by the
aggressive   Dutch,   Swedish   authorities   enacted   several
countermeasures. Swedish Governor Johan Printz ordered that a
blockhouse be constructed "close to and in front of" the new Dutch
post, and, to lure more Lenape and Minqua trade, offered more
Swedish manufactured goods in exchange for furs.[118]   More
importantly, he sent representatives to the region to bargain with the

---

[115] Kent, ed., p. 16. The Schuykill River is in Philadelphia, Pennsylvania.
[116] "Positions of the Mohawks," in Graymont, ed., p. 197; "Mohawk Proposals and
Resolutions of the Dutch," in Graymont, ed., p. 217; "Conference Between
Director General Stuyvesant and the Sinnekus," in Graymont, ed., p. 224.
"Beversreede" is the combination of two Dutch words meaning "beaver road." For
more about Dutch and Swedish Forts, see C. A. Weslager, *Dutch Explorers,
Traders and Settlers in the Delaware Valley 1609-1664* (Philadelphia: University
of Pennsylvania Press, 1961).
[117] Dennis, pp. 1-200.
[118] Stellan Dahlgren and Hans Norman, *The Rise and Fall of New Sweden:
Governor Johan Risingh's Journal 1654-1655 in its Historical Context* (Uppsala:
Almqvist & Wiksell International, 1988), p. 72.

Lenape for a deed to the contested territory.   Although the
Hollanders already had a deed for the land, the Swedish position
was that the document was flawed and therefore worthless even
though it bore the mark of "Peminacka," the sachem of the Lenape
people in that region.[119]   Operating under the assumption that the
Dutch deed was invalid, the Swedish mission was to get a document
from those they believed were the true owners of the contested
ground.

On July 3, 1651, Printz's agents procured title from the "heirs of
the deceased Sachem Mitatsimint," his widow, his son, and two
younger children.[120]   According to the Swedish confirmation deed,
the signatory of the Dutch deed had no right to sell the lands in
question; Peminacka only had had the right to hunt on them.[121]   The
question was, of course, who really owned the land—the deceased
man's widow or the new sachem, a man who was probably a
kinsman of the deceased?   Clan ties and leadership among the
Lenape descended through the maternal line so Peminacka might
have been a brother or maternal uncle of Mitatsimint and thus the
new sachem of the band. Mitatsimint's wife, according to Lenape
custom, was a member of her own clan and the children of their
marriage were also members of her clan. So it depended on whose
customs (Lenape or European) were followed as a basis for
acquiring, understanding, and validating the deed.   The clear
implication was that, according to European custom, the Hollanders
did not have legal title to the parcel of territory in question. While
the document established, to the satisfaction of the Swedes at least,
their rightful claim to the lands on which they settled, it also
confirms something more important. It shows that some Lenape
chose to break with their traditional beliefs regarding property,
inheritance, and hunting territories, and assert their own view of
how they should utilize their territory. Not all the Lenape agreed,
however, and disagreement among them increased.

The Indians also reconfirmed earlier Dutch and Swedish deeds
and documents which the Europeans used to support their
competing claims of Indian-approved, rightful ownership to the
same parcels of the Lenape homeland. In July 1651, Stuyvesant met

---

[119] "Confirmation Deed From Indians to Swedes," in Kent, ed., p. 17.
[120] Ibid.
[121] Ibid.

with sachems "Mattehoorn, Pemenetta and Sinquez" from the western side of the "Zuydt River" and discussed their land sales to the Swedes; he wanted to understand their reasoning behind their actions and the extent of the lands they sold to the Scandinavians. The Lenape chiefs explained to the Dutch governor that "all Nations coming in the river were welcome."[122] They revealed further that with the exception of the ground that comprised the Swedish Fort Christina (near present-day Wilmington, Delaware), they did not consider any of the lands on the western side of the river sold to the Swedes or any other nation.[123]

Despite the fact that the Scandinavians lived on the territory and had a number of deeds to support their claims, in the Lenape mind Swedish "ownership" had lapsed; they did not keep up with the native custom of annually renewing their right to use the lands by providing symbols of their appreciation in the form of some trade goods. Following repeated pointed questioning about the territory, the Lenape chiefs sought to please their demanding, inquiring friend. The chiefs perhaps neither completely understanding the European concept of exclusive ownership nor fully grasping the geopolitical complexities of their actions, presented "the Great Sachem" with the lands as a gift.[124] Thus, in a confirmation deed dated July 19, 1651, practically half of New Sweden became the personal property of Stuyvesant.[125] However, he would have to take possession of this most generous gift. He was content to wait and did not come to claim the territory for another four years.

The Downfall And Destruction of New Sweden

It is not certain if the Swedes had any knowledge of the fact that they had a new landlord. However, between 1651 and 1655, the small colony continued to survive, but just barely. New Sweden suffered from a lack of new supplies from the homeland. The last supply ship from Sweden arrived at Fort Christina in 1648.[126] The

---

[122] "Peter Stuyvesant's Meeting with Mattehoorn and Other Indians," in Kent, ed., pp. 18-21.
[123] Ibid.
[124] Ibid.
[125] Ibid.
[126] C. A. Weslager, *New Sweden on the Delaware* (Wilmington: Middle Atlantic Press, 1988), p. 125; Esposito, p. 159. Also see Dahlgren and Norman, *The Rise and Fall of New Sweden*.

lack of supplies and energetic Dutch commercial activities in the region hurt the Indian trade; it also profoundly affected their relations with the Lenape, who no longer received the quantity or quality of goods they had come to expect as part of the Swedes' annual gifts to them.[127] Moreover, many of the colonists in New Sweden were not self-sufficient. Repeated poor harvests and the lack of supplies from the home country meant that they became increasingly reliant on English and Dutch traders from neighboring colonies and the nearby Indians to supply them with staples.[128]

From the Lenape point of view, the Swedes were wearing out their welcome. They were rude guests, poor friends, and almost worthless trading partners; they did not keep up with their obligations involved in the reciprocal relationship they had established long ago with their hosts. While the Lenape still generously permitted them to occupy the land, the "saltwater people" provided very little in return to show their continued appreciation to them. To make matters worse, the Swedes wanted even more from their Lenape neighbors; they repeatedly requested staples, like beans and corn, plus other foodstuffs, and provided in return things that both people considered only insignificant trinkets.[129] Additionally, in 1651, a ship arrived with more Swedes and with it came a strange evil "Manitho," an unidentified epidemic disease that caused a great deal of sickness and death among the Indians.[130] The effect of what the Lenape considered to be a malevolent force was so catastrophic that it devastated entire villages in some places.[131]

Although the Swedish-Indian relationship seemed reasonably good on the surface, since the two people did not engage in open

---

[127] Weslager, *New Sweden*, p. 125; Dahlgren and Norman, pp. 74-79.

[128] Ibid.

[129] Weslager, *New Sweden*, p. 125; Dahlgren and Norman, pp. 74-79. Things that were probably considered trinkets were clay pipes, combs, cloth caps, glass beads, mouth harps, spoons, and tin cups. Items that were highly prized by the Indians included such things as blankets, brass and copper kettles, cloth, firearms, gunpowder, iron tools, knives, lead, and liquor. However, considering the lack of re-supply missions from the mother country these valued trade goods were scarce in New Sweden.

[130] Dahlgren and Norman, p. 72; "Treaty Between the Swedes and the Indians at Tennakonck," in Kent, ed., p. 25; Peter Lindestrom, *Geographia Americae* (Philadelphia: The Swedish Colonial Society, 1925), pp. 126-128.

[131] Dahlgren and Norman, p. 72; Kent, ed., p. 25; Lindestrom, pp. 126-128.

warfare, in reality interaction between the peoples can be characterized as having been generally poor. Despite the fact that the Lenape provided them with food, the Swedes treated them with thinly veiled contempt and suspicion since the Indians brought in few of the highly valued beaver pelts. The native peoples considered this to be inappropriate behavior for guests, and since it continued they became angry, frustrated and resentful. They expressed their anger and dissatisfaction through acts of violence. They pulled down fences, destroyed crops, and captured or killed livestock.[132] Hostilities grew to the point that in 1654, a Lenape council, led by the sachem Mattahorn, seriously considered the extermination of all the Swedes in Lenapehoking.[133] However, discussion in a special meeting of sachems and elders of one or several bands led to a postponement of a general war against the burdensome and rude strangers.[134] A contributing factor to the council's decision to delay the attack was the fact that they had heard the news that the Swedes were expecting the arrival of new ships laden with "costly wares."[135]

In May 1654, the anticipated Swedish vessels arrived with trade goods, settlers, soldiers, and a new colonial governor, Johan Risingh. Risingh faced a bleak situation and busied himself to improve conditions in the colony as quickly as possible.[136] Under his direction, a force of Swedes captured the most immediate and visible threat to the province, another new Dutch installation called Fort Casimir (near or within the bounds of present-day New Castle, Delaware) located just a few miles south of New Sweden's capital, Fort Christina.[137] He also worked to improve relations with the Indians. On June 17, 1654, he met with ten Lenape sachems from throughout the river valley colony and distributed a generous

---

[132] Kent, ed., p. 25.
[133] "Swedish Purchasing of Land From the Indians," in Kent, ed., pp. 9-10.
[134] Ibid.
[135] Ibid.
[136] Dahlgren and Norman, p. 92.
[137] Dahlgren and Norman, pp. 92-93. Modern-day Wilmington and New Castle, Delaware (Swedish Fort Christina and Dutch Fort Casimir respectively) are located about seven miles apart. Fort Casimir was built in 1651. When the Swedes took the post on Trinity Sunday, 1654, they renamed it Fort Trefaldighet (Trinity). For more information about Dutch and Swedish forts in the region, see C. A. Weslager, *Dutch Explorers, Traders and Settlers* and *New Sweden on the Delaware*.

amount of promised trade goods to them.[138] During the course of this meeting the Indians apologized for their past transgressions.[139] To show their sincerity, they reconfirmed all of their previous land sales to the Swedes, stating that they desired "to be as one body and one heart" with Risingh and his people. Furthermore, they invited them to make a new settlement at "Passajungh," the site of their main village.[140] Moreover, while that meeting was taking place, the new governor's representatives were in the southern reaches of the colony, at "Horn Kill" (the place the Dutch called "Horen Kill" or "Whore's River") to present gifts to chief Hvivan and his people and reestablish Swedish ownership of lands along the bay.[141] Additional meetings with other Lenape village chiefs took place in early July 1654, which affirmed the Lenapes' desire for closer ties and increased trade but also increased Swedish dominion over additional large parcels of their homeland on the western side of the river.[142]

After Risingh reestablished good relations with the nearby Indians and received several deeds from them, he was fully confident in his nation's clear and undisputed possession of the entire territory and began to expand and secure the colonial commercial enterprise.[143] He reopened trade with the Minquas; he directed settlers to rebuild and strengthen old defenses; they also erected new forts; he distributed land to new arrivals and people established new settlements.[144] In 1655, the new governor also expanded the size of the colony significantly through a purchase of land from the Minquas and planned to establish, at their request, a permanent trading post in their country.[145] The Minquas specifically requested Swedish craftsmen to make and repair firearms and bullet makers to provide ammunition for them.[146] They wanted a Swedish presence in their territory to counter English designs on their

---

[138] Kent, ed., pp. 25-27.

[139] Ibid.

[140] Ibid.   The Indian village was no doubt located in the Passyunk neighborhood of present-day Philadelphia, Pennsylvania.

[141] Dahlgren and Norman, pp. 106-107.

[142] "Confirmation of Deed to the Swedes for the Sandhock," and "Deed to the Swedes for Land Up the River," in Kent, ed., pp. 27-28.

[143] Dahlgren and Norman, pp. 92-93.

[144] Ibid., pp. 92-93, 108-111.

[145] Ibid., pp. 108-111; Myers, 159-160.

[146] Ibid.

lands.[147] They also may have hoped that the Scandinavians would
provide them with even greater military assistance in their ongoing
conflict with their enemies from Maryland and Virginia.[148]
Moreover, by terms of this very generous agreement with the
Minqua sachems, they became the Swedes' protectors. To aid the
settlers of the colony, Risingh planned to establish schools and a
system of poor relief.[149] The new governor operated with great
energy to transform the small struggling outpost into a vigorous
colonial commercial venture.[150]

However, despite Risingh's best efforts, a series of calamities
plagued New Sweden. According to the governor's journal, the
crops failed due to heavy winter and spring frosts.[151] The poor
harvest and the very limited food stored meant that provisions
would have to come from other sources which translated into a loss
of profits and an accumulation of debt.[152] English and Dutch
merchants furnished grain and other supplies on credit or in
exchange for valuable pelts.[153] The Lenape bartered for foodstuffs
in return for trade goods, but the amount of trade goods was
exceedingly limited and Risingh intended to trade them for furs
from the Minquas.[154] Another problem was that a number of settlers
fled the difficult and rugged conditions of New Sweden for better
prospects in the more developed colonies of Maryland, New
Netherland, and Virginia.[155] Worse yet, within a year, relations with
the Lenape significantly deteriorated.[156] Risingh recorded that they
regularly threatened to kill the Swedes, end their commerce with
them and ruin their trade with the Minquas.[157] This anger was due,
in part, to the continued drain on their resources and the meager
goods the Swedish colonial government provided in exchange for
vital foodstuffs.[158] While grappling with these serious setbacks, the

[147] Ibid.
[148] Ibid.
[149] Dahlgren and Norman, p. 101.
[150] Ibid.
[151] Ibid., pp. 100, 231.
[152] Ibid.
[153] Ibid.
[154] Ibid., pp. 116, 171, 173, 181, 231, 251; Myers, 107.
[155] Dahlgren and Norman, pp. 73, 93, 100, 118 n130, 171, 231.
[156] Ibid., p. 105 n144.
[157] Ibid.
[158] Ibid.

Swedish outpost faced a more dangerous yet subtle threat to its survival since four years earlier Lenape sachems had given the territory that made up at least half of the colony to Peter Stuyvesant. The Dutch Governor-General arrived in the late summer of 1655 to claim his gift.

Fueled by information that came from English merchants and Lenape Indians who traded at New Amsterdam, rumors of an impending Dutch military conquest were rife in New Sweden.[159] Risingh fully expected some retaliatory reaction from Styuvesant after the capture of Fort Casimir.[160] The reply came a little more than a year later in the form of an invasion. On August 27, 1655, a fleet of seven ships with more than three hundred Dutch soldiers and a company of seamen sailed into the bay to forcibly take possession of the territory.[161] The conquest of New Sweden took place in a piecemeal fashion as the Hollanders sailed up the bay and into the "Zuydt Rivier" (Dutch meaning South River, the Delaware River today) and captured Swedish installations and villages along the way.[162] Squadrons of Dutch soldiers landed near Fort Christina and burned and pillaged farms up and down the western side of the river; they stole or wantonly destroyed anything and everything.[163] They attacked settlers, beat them and even robbed them of the clothing off their backs.[164] Embattled Swedish governor Risingh wrote that Dutch troops plundered or ruined all crops, fodder, homes, livestock, personal possessions and stores of food.[165] By mid-September, nearly half of New Sweden was a scene of utter devastation. On September 15, 1655, with the permission of the council, Risingh negotiated a settlement with Stuyvesant for the surrender of Fort Christina and all of New Sweden.[166] After offering very generous peace terms the Dutch immediately left the region to return to New Netherland to deal with an emerging crisis

---

[159] Ibid., pp. 112-113 n168.
[160] Ibid., pp. 111-113.
[161] Ibid., p. 113.
[162] Ibid.
[163] Ibid., p. 115.
[164] Ibid., p. 253.
[165] Ibid., pp. 115, 253, 263.
[166] Ibid., p. 115.

when Stuyvesant received a message that the Lenape had launched an attack on New Amsterdam.[167]

The Nadir of Lenape-Dutch Relations:
The Peach War and Its Aftermath

Stuyvesant's peace policy prevented full-scale warfare between the Dutch and the Lenape for just a little over fifteen years. In that time, the Indians had endured casual aggression, chicanery, physical and verbal assaults, thefts, and occasional acts of violence from their supposed brothers, the "Swannekins."[168] They also were irritated that the Hollanders did not sell them more firearms and that more and more Europeans were coming to their country and taking up their land.[169] The Dutch also complained of Lenape abuse, insults, threats, thefts, and random violence.[170] Although an official peace existed between the Hollanders and the Lenape that the Dutch dutifully maintained by regular gifts of trade goods, suspicions and tensions between the two people became very high.[171]

Very early in the morning on September 15, 1655, with Stuyvesant and a Dutch army and navy far to the south conquering New Sweden, a massive force of five hundred Lenape warriors landed at Manhattan.[172] Two hundred Munsee (northern Lenape) joined the initial force of five hundred; they all ran riot through New Amsterdam and broke into peoples' homes.[173] Even though they explained that they were searching for enemy Indians, legend has it that the incursion and ensuing violence was to avenge the death of a Lenape girl killed by a Dutchman for taking peaches from his orchard.[174] Thus the conflict that grew out of the incident has since

---

[167] Ibid., pp. 14-15, 115-116.

[168] Otto, pp. 50-60, 90, 91, 166, 172, 180, 214-216; Graymont, ed., pp. 163, 197, 217, 224.

[169] "Intelligence From a Tappan Indian," in Graymont, ed., p. 120; "Remonstrance of Petrus Stuyvesant and the Council of New Netherland to the States General Regarding Indian Hostilities," in Graymont, ed., p. 139-142; "Propositions Submitted by Director-General Petrus Stuyvesant to the Council at the Meeting of 10 November 1655," in Graymont, ed., pp. 142-145; "Response of the High Council to the Foregoing," in Graymont, ed., pp. 145-149.

[170] Graymont, ed., pp. 120, 139-149.

[171] Ibid.

[172] Graymont, ed., p. 140; Weslager, *New Sweden*, p. 173.

[173] Ibid.

[174] Otto, pp. 216-217.

been called the Peach War.[175]   It is possible that several factors motivated the Munsee: the killing of the girl, the quest for enemy Indians, and the desire for long overdue revenge.[176] As the Lenape warriors tore through the town, tensions grew and the Hollanders strengthened the guard.[177]   Tempers flared between the two peoples.[178] They threatened each other with physical harm.[179]   An arrow wounded one Dutchman which resulted in "a great outcry and noise was made and some of the citizens [shot] at the savages."[180] In the ensuing skirmish "a few were killed on either side."[181] Although the Lenape left New Amsterdam proper, they began a three-day rampage, attacking settlements on Manhattan, Staten Island and outlying areas.[182]   They burned homes.[183]   They destroyed twenty-eight farms.[184] They ruined crops in the fields and harvested grain.[185] They captured, drove off, and killed hundreds of cattle and other livestock.[186]   They killed about fifty European settlers and captured over one hundred, mostly women and children.[187] Survivors feared that the Indians would totally destroy New Amsterdam and wrote to the government of the "Fatherland," the States-General, for assistance.[188]

Stuyvesant returned from New Sweden to assist in the defense of the beleaguered town and discussed an appropriate response to the attack with the council.[189]   By November, the Hollanders had decided not to embark on a retaliatory strike against the Indians for fear of escalating the conflict into a full-scale war even though the Lenape had violated a 1645 peace treaty.[190] The Director-General and the council expressed concern that the Indians might kill the

---

[175] Ibid.
[176] Ibid.
[177] Graymont, ed., p. 141.
[178] Ibid.
[179] Ibid.
[180] Ibid.
[181] Graymont, ed., p. 141; Otto, pp. 216-217.
[182] Ibid.
[183] Ibid.
[184] Ibid.
[185] Ibid.
[186] Ibid.
[187] Ibid.
[188] Ibid.
[189] Graymont, ed., pp. 142-149.
[190] Ibid.

captives.[191] Therefore, rather than inflame the situation, Stuyvesant
negotiated for the release of the Dutch hostages.[192] Although the
Lenape probably intended the captive Europeans taken to replace
their deceased family members, they released most of them.[193]
Responding to the governor's overtures, the sachem of the
Hackensack band, Pennekeck, released the Hollanders his people
had taken as a gesture of good will; through the assistance of the
Hackensack chief, other bands released their captives in return for
items they needed such as gunpowder and shot.[194]

While they returned most of the captives to their own people,
both the Lenape and Dutch settlers engaged in violent reprisals.
The Munsee bands who attacked New Amsterdam and the
newcomers never established an official peace to end the ongoing
conflict between them. In order to prevent this from happening
again, Stuyvesant embarked on an effort to nullify the potential
threat from the Indians living near Dutch settlements. He and his
representatives negotiated the sales of new lands from Lenape bands
throughout greater New Netherland, from Staten Island all the way
to the Schuylkill region and presided over ceremonies to confirm
previous sales.[195] In the case of the Indians of Staten Island, a
defensive alliance was incorporated into the deed of sale.[196] In
order to secure full cooperation and banish any doubts the Native
Americans may have had about the Hollanders or land purchases,
the buyers provided generous amounts of trade goods.[197] Moreover,
the Dutch made an effort to inform the Indians of the consequences

---

[191] Ibid.

[192] Otto, pp. 217.

[193] Ibid., pp. 223-224. It was not uncommon for many eastern Native American
tribes like the Lenape and Iroquois Five Nations to capture European women and
children and adopt them to replace deceased family members. Narratives about
Europeans and colonial Americans being taken captive by Indians abounds. Native
Americans also captured Indians from other tribes and adopted them. For more
information see James Axtell, *The Invasion Within: The Contest of Cultures in
Colonial North America* (New York: Oxford University Press, 1985); John Demos,
The Unredeemed Captive: A Family Story From Early America (New York: A. A.
Knopf, 1994).

[194] Otto, pp. 217-218.

[195] "Indian Deed to Land on the Schuylkill," "Treaty with Takapoush and Long
Island Indians," "Indian Confirmation of the Sale of Hempstead in 1643," "Indian
Deed for Staten Island," in Graymont, ed., pp. 150-160.

[196] "Indian Deed for Staten Island" in Graymont, ed., pp. 158-160.

[197] Ibid.

of selling their land.[198] The Hollanders told them that because of the documents they signed and the goods they received the land no longer belonged to them.[199] They would have to leave their homes and relocate since the Dutch would no longer share the land with the Lenape.[200] After Stuyvesant secured the territory of the colony more firmly, part of his agenda in the wake of the Peach War involved changing the settlement pattern in the outlying areas near Manhattan.[201] Under his direction, scattered plantations that already existed became concentrated into more defensible fortified hamlets.[202] In this fashion, Stuyvesant established new communities as more settlers came to the colony.

The Esopus Wars

Other original inhabitants of Lenapehoking did not welcome growing Dutch settlement and all that it brought in the form of increased casual violence, disrespect, mistreatment, and the creation and cultivation of more farms. The Esopus (a Munsee or northern Lenape band) reacted by attempting to make the newcomers understand their displeasure and irritation at the Dutch presence. Several incidents in May 1658 expressed their frustration.[203] They killed a Dutch settler, burned several homes and threatened to destroy more, in addition to physically and verbally abusing settlers.[204] Drawing on this information from the letters of European inhabitants at Esopus, the Governor-General and the council decided to send a military expedition to the region.[205] After a day's voyage up the "Noordt Rivier," (the "North River" today known as the Hudson River) Stuyvesant and sixty soldiers arrived in the area to investigate the situation.[206] After meeting with the settlers and listening to their complaints, he explained that their desire to use direct military force against the Indians would only make matters

---

[198] Ibid.

[199] Ibid.; Otto, 224.

[200] Ibid.

[201] Otto, p. 278.

[202] Otto, p. 226.

[203] "Resolution that the Director-General Proceed to Esopus," in Graymont, ed., p. 167.

[204] Ibid.

[205] Ibid.

[206] "Journal of Director Stuyvesant's Visit to the Esopus," in Graymont, ed., pp. 168-169.

worse and held that the settlers should make defensive preparations.[207] He explained that they should adopt his plan of a fortified village settlement and offered carpenters and troops to assist in the great undertaking.[208] Lastly Stuyvesant also met with fifty or more of the Esopus to hear their side of the story and make peace yet at the same time make them fully aware of the dangers involved if they continued to molest Dutch settlers.[209] After the completion of the newly fortified hamlet, the crisis at Esopus seemed over. He settled this first conflict with this Lenape band with minimal bloodshed.

However, tensions remained high between the two peoples and sporadic violence continued for more than a year.[210] In October 1659, anger, animosity, and fear induced colonists to shoot into a rowdy, late night Lenape drinking party that occurred in the woods near the settlement.[211] They captured one reveler, killed another, and wounded several others.[212] The Esopus response was a deadly seven-day attack on the European village.[213] This time, the violence grew into a general war. Although there was an armistice brokered through the efforts of Dutch allies, the Mahicans and Mohawks, and a Lenape band called the Catskills, the war continued through June 1660 when the Esopus and the Dutch finally settled a peace.[214]

---

[207] Ibid.

[208] Ibid.

[209] Graymont, ed., pp. 171-172.

[210] "Proposals Made to the Esopus Indians and Their Answers," in Graymont, ed., pp. 180-183; "Proposals of Esopus Indians and Dutch Responses," in Graymont, ed., pp. 188-189; "Complaints and Proposals Made by the Esopus Indians," in Graymont, ed., pp. 189-190.

[211] "Declaration of Certain Catskill Indians Regarding Provocation of the Esopus War," in Graymont, ed., pp. 195-197.

[212] Ibid.

[213] Ibid.

[214] "Letter From Ensign Smith to Director Stuyvesant Regarding Armistice with the Esopus Indians," in Graymont, ed., p. 199; "Resolution to Declare War Against the Esopus Indians, to Begin in the Fall," in Graymont ed., p. 202; "Proclamation of War Against the Esopus Indians," in Graymont, ed., p. 206; "Conference Between Director Stuyvesant and Chiefs of Hackensack and Havestraw, an Armistice Granted to Esopus Indians," in Graymont, ed., pp. 212-213; "Letter From Director Stuyvesant and Council to Ensign Smith Concerning Peace with the Esopus Indians," in Graymont, pp. 214-215; "Resolution That Director Proceed to Esopus and Conclude Peace with the Esopus," in Graymont, ed., pp. 215-216; "Extract From a Letter of the Council of New Netherland to the Directors in Concerning Peace with the Esopus Indians," in Graymont, ed., pp. 216-217; 227.

Official peace between the Esopus and the Hollanders only lasted three years. Mutual mistrust and suspicion plus the continuing factor of expanding Dutch settlement, aggression, physical and verbal abuse, the liquor trade, and the Esopus desire for revenge renewed the bloodshed between the two people.[215] Hostilities recommenced in June 1663 and lasted a year.[216] This confrontation with the Esopus grew much wider than the previous two. Despite the fact that the Esopus received assistance from the Wapping or Wappinger Indians, Stuyvesant successfully isolated them from other Lenape bands.[217] In fact, during the course of the war, the Dutch received military assistance from Lenape and other Indian allies from eastern Long Island.[218] The Esopus attempted to make an alliance with the English settlers at Westchester to fight the Hollanders and broaden the scope of the war even further.[219] In their negotiations, the embattled Lenape band found that the English had no interest in taking up arms and fighting against Stuyvesant.[220] Reeling from military defeats and under pressure from Dutch allies, the Mahicans, Mohawks and other Indians, the Esopus had little choice but to make peace with the Dutch.[221]

---

[215] Graymont, ed., p. 232.

[216] "Director Stuyvesant to the Magistrates at Fort Orange, More Trouble at Esopus," in Graymont, ed., pp. 242-244; "Resolution to Make War on the Esopus," in Graymont, ed., p. 244-245; "Report of the Magistrates at Wiltwyck on the Attack by Esopus," in Graymont, ed., pp. 245-249; "Council Minute. The Chief of the Wecquaesgeeks Reports a Rumor that the Esopus Indians are Coming," in Graymont, ed. pp. 249-250; "Instructions for Lieutenant Van Couwenhoven and Party to Seek a Renewal of Peace with the Esopus Indians," in Graymont, ed., p. 254; "Council Minute. Wapping and Esopus Indians Coming to Conclude Treaty," in Graymont, ed., pp. 264-266; "Conference with Chiefs of Hackensack and Staten Island Indians Concerning Armistice with Esopus," in Graymont, ed., pp. 268-272; "Report Made by P. W. Couwenhoven of Information Respecting Intrigues of the English with the Wappings and Esopus," in Graymont, ed., pp. 277-278; "Articles of Peace, Made with the Esopus Indians," in Graymont, ed., pp. 282-285.

[217] "Proposals to Chiefs of Hackensack and Staten Island with Their Response," "Proposals Made to Sachems of the River and Staten Island Indians and Their Answers," in Graymont, ed., pp. 247-249.

[218] "Long Island Indians Pledge Support Against Esopus," in Graymont, ed., p. 253; Otto, pp. 229-230.

[219] Graymont, ed., pp. 277-278.

[220] Ibid.

[221] "Articles of Peace With The Espous Indians," in Graymont, ed., pp. 282-285.

They settled the matter at a formal treaty conference held in the Council Chambers in New Amsterdam on May 15, 1664.[222]   An impressive array of Dutch and Lenape dignitaries assembled there to meet the defeated Esopus and Wapping chiefs.[223]   The Esopus and their allies faced "his Noble Worship Director-General Petrus Stuyvesant," the full Council of New Netherland, the two "Burgomasters" of the city of New Amsterdam, a host of other civil and military officials of the town and from one nearby settlement, two interpreters and the sachem representatives of eight Lenape bands, the Kightewaugh, the Havestraw, the Wiechquaskeck, the Hackensacky, the Tappen, the Marsepingh and the chief of the "Staten-Island and Nayack Savages."[224]   The victors were not generous in framing the terms of peace. While they permitted the Esopus to harvest their crops already planted at the site of their new "fort," the Dutch confiscated all their lands—including those of their new village.[225]   Any further contact between the two peoples was to be strictly limited; the Esopus were to avoid all farms and hamlets and only trade at designated forts.[226]   Included in the agreement were other provisions which governed future behavior and one that specified the return of all captives.[227]   All parties agreed to renew this treaty annually at New Amsterdam, and furthermore Oratam, sachem of the Hackensacks, and Manetto, chief of the Staten Island and Nyack bands, both cosigned the document.[228]   Lastly and most importantly, if the Esopus broke the peace, the Hollanders and their aforementioned Lenape allies would join together and fight against them.[229]

The Loss of the Dutch Business Venture

With the Esopus completely crushed, the Dutch continued their quest for corporate and personal gain virtually unfettered by any

---

[222] Ibid.
[223] Ibid.
[224] Ibid. Note: "Burgomaster" is the Dutch term for the principal magistrate of a town or city, comparable to a mayor.
[225] Graymont, ed., pp. 282-285.
[226] Ibid.
[227] Ibid.
[228] Ibid.
[229] Ibid.

significant Indian resistance.[230] Their relations with other native peoples of their colony, the Mahicans, Mohawks, Seneca and others were friendly and profitable.[231] The fur trade continued to expand, new settlers arrived, bought more land and established new farms.[232] Much to the delight of settlers and colonial and corporate officials, the commercial enterprise of New Netherland thrived and operated with great vigor. Although not without some risks, the colony continued to promise boundless opportunity and profit. However, the Dutch West India Company's full enjoyment of their reinvigorated overseas business venture did not last long. In the late summer, a flotilla of English ships with 450 soldiers arrived in New Netherland and conquered the colony quickly and without any loss of life.[233] On September 8, 1664 Peter Stuyvesant surrendered the entire province to the invaders.[234] All the Indian and European peoples of the Hudson and Delaware River valleys had new landlords.[235]

Conclusion

The Dutch relationship with the Lenape was based on misunderstanding and a desire to dominate and take advantage of the Indians who the Dutch thought were inferior, savage people. War was the inevitable result of this relationship. The Hollanders almost insatiable desire for pelts and the Lenape desire for trade goods led to a rapid decline of the fur trade in the greater Delaware Valley. Thus when the Lenape ceased to be a significant source of profit and when they resisted Dutch colonial expansion by defending their homeland, major wars ensued. In the decades that followed the conquest of New Netherland, the Lenape and the English would embark on their own reciprocal relationship with each other. Unlike many Dutch settlers, some of these newcomers

---

[230] "Proposal of Sweckenamo, One of the Esopus Sachems, to Have Some Provisions Sent to Their Country Beyond Havestraw," in Graymont, ed., pp. 293-294.
[231] Weslager, *The Delaware Indians*, p. 109; Graymont, ed., pp. 163, 197, 217, 224.
[232] Ibid.
[233] Graymont, ed., pp. 293-294.
[234] Ibid.
[235] Although the Dutch recaptured the colony in 1673, it was returned to the English by the treaty of Westminster, 1674.

from the British Isles—the Quakers—made a major effort to understand their hosts. [236]

Bibliography

Axtell, James. *The Invasion Within: The Contest of Cultures in Colonial North America.* New York: Oxford University Press, 1985.

Bierhorst, John (ed.). *The Mythology of the Lenape.* Tucson: University of Arizona Press, 1995.

—. *The White Deer and Other Stories Told by the Lenape.* New York: William Morrow and Company, Inc., 1995.

Ceci, Lynn. "The Effects of European Contact and Trade on the Settlement Patterns of Indians in Coastal New York, 1524-1665: The Archaeological and Documentary Evidence." Ph.D. diss., City University of New York, 1977.

Cocciardi, M. "The History of Tobacco." *Retrospect.* 1, 2 (Summer 1995): 1, 4-5.

Dahlgren, Stellan and Hans Norman. *The Rise and Fall of New Sweden: Governor Johan Risingh's Journal 1654-1655 in its Historical Context.* Uppsala: Almqvist & Wiksell International, 1988.

Demos, John. *The Unredeemed Captive: A Family Story From Early America.* New York: A. A. Knopf, 1994.

Dennis, Matthew. *Cultivating A Landscape of Peace: Iroquois-European Encounters in Seventeenth Century America.* Ithaca: Cornell University Press, 1993.

Dowd, Gregory Evans. *The Indians of New Jersey.* Trenton: New Jersey Historical Commission, Department of State, 1992.

---

[236] "William Penn's First Letter To The Indians," in Kent, ed., p. 55.

Esposito, Frank. "Indian-White Relations in New Jersey, 1609-1802." Ph.D. diss., Rutgers University, 1976.

Goddard, Ives. "Delaware." In *Northeast*, Vol. 15 of *Handbook of North American Indians*. Ed. Bruce G. Trigger, Washington: Smithsonian Institution, 1978.

Graymont, Barbara. *New York and New Jersey Treaties, 1609-1682*. Vol. VII of *Early American Indian Documents*. Washington: University Publications of America, Inc., 1979.

Jacobs, Wilbur R. "Wampum, the Protocol of Indian Diplomacy." *William and Mary Quarterly* 6, no. 4 (October 1949): 596-604.

Jennings, Francis P. *The Ambiguous Iroquois Empire*. New York: W. W. Norton and Company, 1984.

—. "Miquon's Passing: Indian-European Relations In Colonial Pennsylvania, 1674-1755." Ph.D. diss., University of Pennsylvania, 1965.

Juet, Robert. *Juet's Journal. The Voyage of the* Half Moon *from 4 April to 7 November 1609*. Ed. Robert M. Lunny. Newark: The New Jersey Historical Society, 1959.

Kent, Donald H. *Pennsylvania and Delaware Treaties, 1629-1737*. Vol. I of *Early American Indian Documents*. Washington: University Publications of America, Inc., 1979.

Kraft, Herbert C. "Delaware Indian Reminiscences." *Bulletin of the Archaeological Society of New Jersey*. no. 35 (1978): 1-17.

—. *The Lenape: Archaeology, History and Ethnography*. Newark: The New Jersey Historical Society, 1988.

— and John T. Kraft. *The Indians of Lenapehoking*. South Orange: Seaton Hall University Museum, 1991.

 Mistaken Manitous

Lindestrom, Peter. *Geographia Americae*. Philadelphia: The Swedish Colonial Society, 1925.

Myers, Albert Cook. *Narratives of Early Pennsylvania, New Jersey and Delaware, 1630-1707*. New York: Charles Scribner's Sons, 1912.

—. *William Penn's Own Account of the Lenni Lenape or Delaware Indians*. Somerset: The Middle Atlantic Press, 1970.

Otto, Paul A. "New Netherland Frontier." Ph.D. diss., Indiana University, 1995.

Speck, Frank G. *Oklahoma Delaware Ceremonies, Feasts and Dances*. Philadelphia: The American Philosophical Society, 1937.

—. *A Study of the Delaware Indian Big House Ceremony*. Harrisburg: Pennsylvania Museum Commission, 1931.

Stansfield, Charles A., Jr. *An Ecological History of New Jersey*. Trenton: New Jersey Historical Commission, 1996.

Tantaquidgeon, Gladys. *Folk Medicine of the Delaware and Related Algonkian Indians*. Harrisburg: The Pennsylvania Historical and Museum Commission, 1977.

Weslager, C. A. *The Delaware Indians*. New Brunswick: Rutgers University Press, 1991.

—. *Dutch Explorers, Traders and Settlers in the Delaware Valley 1609-1664*. Philadelphia: University of Pennsylvania Press, 1961.

—. *Magic Medicines of the Indians*. Somerset: Middle Atlantic Press, 1973.

—. *New Sweden on the Delaware*. Wilmington: Middle Atlantic Press, 1988.

MOHAWK MILITARY ENCOUNTERS WITH NEW FRANCE, 1609-1760

Barbara J. Sivertsen

Although the central idea of the League of the Iroquois was peace, or more accurately a consensus of ideas on important issues, from the beginning of the seventeenth century the Five Nations of the Iroquois carried out intermittent warfare with New France and its Indian allies, a series of hostile encounters that lasted until the surrender of the French garrison at Montreal in 1760. Of all the members of the Iroquois confederacy, the Mohawks were engaged most frequently against French Canada, often when other tribes of the League remained neutral or even supported French interests.

Territorially the Mohawks occupied the "Eastern Door" of the extended Iroquois longhouse, a strategic location that conferred both advantages and disadvantages. Even before the coming of Europeans, the Mohawks were exposed to attacks from the east, north, and south, a situation that only worsened when the French began to supply some of the Iroquois's traditional enemies. On the other hand, the Mohawks' proximity to English and Dutch trading centers gave them considerable influence with the other tribes of the League (the Oneidas, Onondagas, Cayugas, and Senecas) through the seventeenth century, despite a greater decline in their overall population and number of fighting men. This proximity, however, made for an increasingly pro-English policy (the Dutch were replaced by the English in New Netherland in 1664) on the part of the Mohawks, and, after 1689, they frequently found themselves caught up in the power struggle between Britain and France.

The French, who established the colony of New France about five years after Samuel de Champlain's first expedition up the St. Lawrence River in 1603, soon formed trading alliances with several

Algonquian-speaking tribes and with the Iroquoian-speaking Hurons, supplying them with iron for weapons that were then used in raids against the Mohawks. The Mohawks retaliated by ambushing their enemies' trade convoys as they returned from the French posts, laden with European goods. To alleviate this threat to their Indian trading partners, the French first intervened in 1609, when Champlain and several other Frenchmen accompanied sixty of their Indian allies down the lake that now bears his name into Mohawk territory. The French and northern Indian force defeated two hundred Iroquois, presumably Mohawks. An even more decisive battle the next year also resulted in another Mohawk defeát. In 1615, however, Champlain and ten other Frenchmen led a large force of Hurons, Algonquins, and Susquehannocks against a strongly palisaded Iroquois (probably Oneida) town and suffered a resounding defeat.[1]

Mohawk trade with the Dutch along the Hudson River, particularly at Fort Orange (present-day Albany, New York) started in the second decade of the seventeenth century. With the commencement of this safer and more accessible source of European goods, Mohawk raids against New France decreased during this period. Only in 1621 is there a report of a Mohawk raiding party that attacked the Recollect convent just outside Quebec and the next year of the capture of a priest by Mohawk raiders. Early in the 1620s, however, the Dutch traders began to favor the neighboring Mahicans, and, possibly in response to this change of policy, the Mohawks initiated a brief peace between themselves and the French in late 1622.[2]

With their northern flank thus secured, the Mohawks launched an all-out attack on the Mahicans and succeeded in pushing them from the vicinity of Fort Orange. By 1628 the Mohawks became

[1] Marcel Trudel, *Histoire de la Nouvelle-France II: Le Comptoir 1604-1627* (Montreal: Fides, 1963), pp. 164-171, 219-223; Samuel E. Morrison, *Samuel de Champlain: Father of New France* (Boston: Little Brown, 1972), pp. 107-110, 117-120.

[2] Daniel Richter, "Ordeals of the Longhouse: The Five Nations in Early American History," *Beyond the Covenant Chain*, eds. Daniel Richter and James Merrell (Syracuse: Syracuse University Press, 1987), pp. 19-20; Daniel Richter, *Ordeal of the Longhouse: The Peoples of the Iroquois League in the Era of European Colonization* (Chapel Hill: University of North Carolina Press, 1992), p. 55; Trudel, *Histoire de la Nouvelle-France II*, pp. 368-369; Morrison, *Samuel de Champlain*, pp. 179-180.

the principal trading partners of the Dutch and also positioned themselves as middlemen for the rest of the League. With a secure hold on the Fort Orange trade, the Iroquois resumed their raids against the northern tribes, this time intercepting fur convoys before they reached French trading centers. The captured northern pelts, thicker and more valuable than those available in the Iroquois country, were then carried to Fort Orange and exchanged for guns, powder and shot, iron kettles, and other metal tools that soon became necessities for the Native Americans. Despite these raids, the weaknesses of the French (New France was in English hands from 1629 to 1632) and the Mohawks (in 1633 a smallpox epidemic ravaged Mohawk country) worked to prevent direct conflict between these two adversaries for over a decade.[3]

By the early 1640s the Iroquois had depleted the beaver in their own country and began to replace their sporadic raids against New France's Indian allies with large-scale attacks on the Huron confederacy, the principal trading partners of the French at their reinvigorated settlements of Quebec, Trois-Rivières, and Montreal. In the west the Senecas and other western Iroquois attacked an outlying Huron village in 1642, and in 1643 scores of Mohawks and Oneidas blockaded the St. Lawrence, capturing large numbers of people and furs. The Mohawks concluded a peace with the French, the Hurons, and the Algonquins at Trois-Rivières in 1645, which lasted through 1647. During this period they secured fire-arms, powder, and lead for four hundred men. In the fall of 1648 an army of one thousand Mohawk and Seneca warriors invaded the Huron homeland north of Lake Ontario and the next year wiped out many of the Huron villages. The Iroquois brought back hundreds of Huron captives to replace through adoption the large numbers who had died from war or disease. By the mid-1660s, Jesuit missionaries estimated that as many as two-thirds of the Iroquois were adopted war captives.[4]

---

[3] Richter, *Ordeal of the Longhouse*, pp. 55-57; Marcel Trudel, *Histoire de la Nouvelle-France III: La Seigneurie des Cent-Associés, 1627-1663. Part 1* (Montreal: Fides, 1979), p. 45; David Hawke, *The Colonial Experience* (New York: Bobs-Merrill, 1966), p. 170; R. J. Jameson (translator), "Narrative of a Journey into the Mohawk and Oneida Country, 1634-1635," *Narratives of New Netherland, 1609-1664*, ed. R. J. Jameson (New York: Scribner's, 1909), p. 141.

[4] Richter, *Ordeal of the Longhouse*, pp. 60-65; Richter, "Ordeals of the Longhouse," p. 22; Barbara Graymont, *The Iroquois* (New York: Chelsea House,

After the defeat of the Hurons, the Iroquois confederacy made peace with the French in order to trade with them, while at the same time continuing to attack rival tribes to the west. For the Mohawks, this peace lasted until the early 1660s, when they again began to raid along the St. Lawrence and Ottawa Rivers, provoking a strong military response by the French—a thousand royal troops of the elite Carignan-Salieres Regiment were sent to Canada in 1665. Faced with this threat, the western Iroquois made peace with the French, but the Mohawks, embittered by their years of warfare, did not. The French governor, de Tracy, led five hundred troops against the Mohawk settlements in January 1666, but they failed to reach the Indian towns. A brief Mohawk peace effort in July was unsuccessful, and in the fall another French expedition devastated the Mohawk country. Although the Mohawks themselves fled to the woods, the French and their Indian allies destroyed all three principal Mohawk settlements, the Lower, Middle, and Upper Castles, and all of the Indians' stored crops.[5]

The next year (1667) the Mohawks rebuilt their towns and sued for peace with the French. As part of their peace settlement, they agreed to welcome Jesuit missionaries into their villages for the first time, particularly to Caughnawaga, the Lower Castle just outside Fonda, New York. Despite opposition from traditionalist Mohawks,

---

1988), pp. 61, 63-67; Bruce G. Trigger, *The Children of Anahaentsic*, Volume 2 (Montreal: McGill-Queen's University Press, 1976), pp. 725-792; *The Jesuit Relations and Allied Documents, Travels and Explorations of the Jesuit Missionaries in New France, 1610-1791*, Volume 49, ed. Reuben Thwaites (Cleveland: Burrows, 1896-1901), p. 233; *The Jesuit Relations and Allied Documents, Travels and Explorations of the Jesuit Missionaries in New France, 1610-1791*, Volume 51, ed. Reuben Thwaites (Cleveland: Burrows, 1896-1901), p. 187.

[5] Graymont, ibid., pp. 68-73; William Fenton, "Problems Arising From the Historic Northeastern Position of the Iroquois," *Smithsonian Miscellaneous Collections* 100 (1940), pp. 207-208; Richter, *Ordeal of the Longhouse*, pp. 17-18, 102-104; Thwaites, Volume 51, pp. 81-85. Mohawk towns, often called "castles" by contemporary Europeans, were in fact clusters of wooden, bark-covered Iroquois longhouses surrounded by wooden stockades or palisades. These stockades were constructed of closely spaced upright tree trunks stuck into the ground, with bark and smaller branches filling in gaps; sometimes a platform was built on the inside where defenders could stand and shoot at attacking enemies. Most towns had several lines of these palisades—the Oneida town attacked by the French and Indians in 1615 had four.

many Huron captives and many Mohawk women were receptive to conversion by the Jesuits. In 1673 the Jesuits began to encourage their converts to resettle in Canada, near religious institutions and away from their friends and relatives who still practiced paganism. Because of the traditional role that women played in choosing new living sites when old agricultural fields became unproductive, women converts and adoptees were instrumental in moving their families to the new Iroquois settlements in Canada.[6]

Although begun by Oneidas in the late 1660s, the settlement of La Prairie just outside of Montreal soon acquired a majority of its inhabitants from the converts originating in the lower and middle Mohawk villages. In 1676 this Mohawk settlement moved upriver to Sault St. Louis to form the core of what would become the new Caughnawaga Mohawk settlement. Throughout the 1670s and early 1680s the tribe lost much of its population to this and other settlements set up in Canada by the priests. By 1677 one English observer estimated that the Mohawks had only about three hundred fighting men in their four Mohawk Valley castles. The separation of the Mohawks between those remaining in their ancient homeland and those living in Canada would have important consequences in the following years, as Mohawks of different religious persuasions would ally themselves with either the English or the French—and end up fighting each other.[7]

Ties between the Mohawks and the Dutch—and English, after New Amsterdam had become New York in 1664—at Albany strengthened after the late 1670s when enforcement of new trading regulations eliminated the worst of the abuses previously practiced by the Dutch. By 1680 Mahicans and remnants of other New England tribes had been settled at Schaghticoke (North Albany) on the Hoosic River twenty miles northeast of Albany under the protection of the governor of New York and of the Mohawks. In reality, they served as a buffer against the French. In the mid-1680s French influence among the Iroquois was on the wane and a new

---

[6] Richter, ibid., pp. 124-129.

[7] William Fenton and Elisabeth Tooker, "Mohawk," *Handbook of North American Indians: Volume XV, Northeast*, ed. Bruce G. Trigger (Washington, D.C.: Smithsonian Institution, 1978), pp. 469-470; Fenton, p. 208; Richter, ibid., pp. 119-120; *Documents Relative to the Colonial History of New York* [hereafter *DRCHNY*] Volume 3, eds. E. B. O'Callaghan and B. Fernow (Albany: State of New York, 1853-87), p. 250.

pro-English faction began to exert its political power, particularly among the Mohawks. The last Jesuit left the Mohawk village of Tionnontaguen (Tiononderoge) in 1681, and warfare over access to beaver hunting grounds recommenced between the western Iroquois and the French in the middle years of that decade.[8]

King William's War, begun in 1689 between France and England, only intensified the French-Iroquois conflict. In June of that year an Iroquois raiding party attacked and destroyed the village of Lachine in Canada, killing a number of the inhabitants and burning many houses. The possibility of retaliation by the French and their Indian allies, a group that included a sizeable number of Catholic Mohawks, was now very real and caused the League to seek help from the British authorities in Albany. Where previously they had acted independently in war, after 1689 the Five Nations would find themselves having to choose either neutrality or alliance with one or the other European power.[9]

After the Glorious Revolution of 1688 in England, a dissident group of New Yorkers had overthrown the royal governor and ruled the colony in his place. The rebel leader, Jacob Leisler, sent his future son-in-law, Jacob Milborne, to Albany to try to secure that town for his government. Most of the citizens of Albany supported Leisler, but the mayor, Peter Schuyler, did not. Schuyler holed up in the fort just outside the town. Milborne marched to the fort on November 15, 1689, with a company of armed men. He thrust his foot inside the fort's gate; Schuyler and his men thrust him out. Milborne retreated to the town walls, where his followers loaded their guns and prepared to attack the fort.[10]

---

[8] Richter, ibid., pp. 136-138, 142, 144; Thomas Donohue, *The Iroquois and the Jesuits* (Buffalo: Catholic Publishing Co., 1895), pp. 187-188; *Documentary History of the State of New York* [hereafter *DHNY*] Volume 2 (folio), ed. E. B. O'Callaghan (Albany: State of New York, 1849-1951), p. 95; *DRCHNY* Volume 3, p. 713 n1; Neal Salisbury, "Toward the Covenant Chain: Iroquois and Southern New England Algonquins, 1637-1684," in Daniel Richter and James Merrell, eds., *Beyond the Covenant Chain*, p. 71.

[9] Richard Aquila, *The Iroquois Restoration: Iroquois Diplomacy on the Colonial Frontier 1701- 1754* (Detroit: Wayne State University Press, 1983), pp. 44-45.

[10] Jerome Reich, *Leisler's Rebellion: A Study of Democracy in New York 1664-1720* (Chicago: University of Chicago Press, 1953), pp. 1, 55-58, 64-66, 81-83; C. Colden, *History of the Five Indian Nations*, Volume 1 (New York: A. S. Barnes, 1904), pp. 108-111; *DHNY* Volume 2, p. 73.

These antics were watched by a company of Mohawks who stood upon a nearby hill. They had come to Albany for English assistance in their war with the French. Instead they found themselves the deciding voice in this internecine struggle. The Mohawk interpreter, Hilletie van Olinda (herself part-Mohawk), was with them, and she probably explained the significance of these actions to the Indians. The warriors wanted no part in a citizens' revolt. They needed military help from the English, and that help, they knew, was at the fort, not in the town. Hilletie relayed the Mohawks' message to the fort: the Mohawks were bound by a Covenant Chain to the mayor and the gentlemen at the fort, which was built for "our and there Defence, Desyred yt ye said Hille should tell them if any of those men came without ye gates to approach ye fort they [the Mohawks] would fyre upon them." To emphasize this point while the message was being delivered, the warriors loaded their guns. For the time being, the fort remained closed to the rebels; only later did the people of Albany accept Leisler's commissioners, chiefly for protection against the French.[11]

The Mohawks' need to protect themselves became even more evident when a party of French troops and their Indian allies, including Caughnawaga Mohawks, attacked the Dutch village of Schenectady in the early morning hours of February 8, 1690. Sixty persons were killed, the town was burned, and twenty-seven people were taken prisoner. A hastily gathered party of whites from Albany marched to overtake the raiders; they were reinforced by 140 Mohawks and River Indians (i.e., Mahicans) led by the Christian Mohawk war chief Lawrence. This rescue party, while not recapturing the prisoners, killed about twenty-five Frenchmen and took ten more prisoner.[12]

While the relief party tried to catch up with the French and Canadian Indians, eight Mohawk sachems went to Albany to condole with the magistrates and mayor, Peter Schuyler, for the death of the people of Schenectady.   Sinerongnirese

---

[11] *DHNY* ibid.; Peter Christoph, ed., *The Leisler Papers 1689-1691* (Syracuse: Syracuse University Press, 2002), p. xxi; O. P. Chetwood, *A History of Colonial America* (New York: Harper & Row, 1961), pp. 226-227.

[12] C. Colden, *History of the Five Indian Nations* Volume 1, pp. 139-142; *DHNY* Volume 1, pp. 186, 191, 193-194, Volume 2, p. 91; Lawrence Leder, ed., *The Livingston Indian Records 1666-1723* (Gettysburg: Pennsylvania Historical Association, 1956), pp. 158-160.

(Sinnonquirese), a sachem of the Bear clan, was the speaker. The senior sachem (in age) was probably Rode of the Turtle clan from the first or easternmost castle of Cangnewage (Cahaniaga). He was followed by Saggoddiochquisax, another Turtle clan sachem, from the second castle or Canagere (Canagora) and Oquedago or Aquedagoe, Tosoquatho, another sachem of the Bear clan, Odagerasse, who may have been Thodorasse, a sachem of the first castle, and Aridarenda and Jagogthare. The translator was Hilletie van Olinda, who was allied to the pro-English element of the tribe.[13]

Born of a Mohawk or part-Mohawk mother and a Dutch father, Hilletie van Olinda left the Mohawks to live with the Dutch 'at Schenectady in 1663, where she learned the Dutch language and later converted to Reform Protestant Christianity. In 1667 she married Daniel van Olinda, a tailor, and in 1680 appears in the journal of a visiting Protestant as a devout Christian living a morally upright life. As one of the few people who had a comprehensive, adult-level understanding of both the Mohawk and Dutch languages, and of Mohawk and Dutch religious beliefs, Hilletie was ideally qualified to convey nuances of meaning on both political and religious matters. In the decade that followed she became the interpreter for the Dutch minister, Dominie Dellius, and in the words of the Mohawks themselves, "the mouth and ears" of her mother's people.[14]

Mayor Schuyler's response at the conference in February, 1690, convinced the Mohawks that the English would offer real assistance against the French. The tribe's leaders decided to send another party of warriors, again under Lawrence, to accompany a force of New York and New England men to French Canada that summer. With them went some of the principal women of the tribe, a few of their children, the Dutch minister, and Hilletie. In a gesture both political and religious, three of these women, three men, and four children were baptized by Dominie Dellius at North Albany—or Schaghticoke—on July 11, 1690, while the Indians and New Yorkers were awaiting the arrival of the New England troops.[15]

---

[13] Barbara Sivertsen, *Turtles, Wolves, and Bears: A Mohawk Family History* (Bowie: Heritage Books, 1996), p. 280 n33.

[14] Sivertsen, pp. 1-3, 7-9.

[15] *DRCHNY* Volume 3, p. 752; Holland Society, *Yearbook for 1904* (New York: Knickerbocker Press, 1904), p. 51.

Most of these Mohawk converts were members of one extended family beginning with Dekarihokenh, the first and foremost of the Mohawks' League sachems. Also baptized was Karanondo, Dekarihokenh's mother, the chief woman of the Turtle clan and, because the Turtle clan was considered the first of the Mohawks' clans, arguably the most prestigious woman of the tribe. By the very nature of their status, Karanondo and her relatives represented a traditionalist position. Earlier, the traditionalists had resisted the French and Jesuit influences among the Mohawks; now some of them were allying themselves with the people of Albany.[16]

The expedition against the French in the summer of 1690 foundered for want of more men from Massachusetts, but a small group of New Yorkers and Indians went up Lake Champlain and managed to kill about twenty-eight French and burn sixteen houses. The next year a new royal governor, Henry Slaughter, landed in New York, put down the rebellion, and met with the leaders of the Five Nations in May. At this conference the Mohawks told the governor that they had gone to Canada and tried to make peace with the French governor and the "praying Indians of Canada," their close kinsmen the Caughnawaga Mohawks. Governor Slaughter was not happy with this peace initiative and it came to nothing.[17]

That summer another raiding party of 260 men led by Peter Schuyler, including ninety-two Mohawks and sixty-six River Indians, went up to Canada. Schuyler claimed to have killed two hundred French and Indians on the raid, but the real result was negative, since it made enemies of the Caughnawaga Mohawks.[18]

Another raid, in December of that same year, ended with the killing of fifteen Mohawks and Oneidas, including Caristase (Cristagie), one of the leaders of the summer raid, the Mohawk chief sachem of Trenondoge (Tiononderoge), his son and brother, and "several other of the best Indians very well known amongst us." It was also reported that "most of our praying Indians are now killed, 15 we have lost this summer whom we could most confide in." By December, 1691, the Mohawks and Oneidas had lost ninety men in

---

[16] Holland Society, ibid.; Richter, *Ordeal of the Longhouse*, pp. 107-108, 133-161.
[17] Christoph, *The Leisler Papers,* p. xx; *DRCHNY* Volume 3, pp. 751-753, 771-780.
[18] *DRCHNY* Volume 3, pp. 800-805. One of the leaders of the River Indians, Eetowacamo (Etowaucum), would join three Mohawks on a voyage to England to be presented to Queen Anne in 1710.

two years of warfare, and the Mohawks were said to have only 130 men left.[19]

On February 13, 1693, almost exactly three years after the burning of Schenectady, a French army of nearly six hundred regular soldiers, Canadian militia, and Indian allies attacked the Mohawks' three principal towns, taking three hundred Mohawks prisoner and burning the towns to the ground. Only a pursuing party made up of whites and western Iroquois, led by Peter Schuyler, made the French give up most of their prisoners. The Mohawks returned to the ashes of their homes and their destroyed stores of food. The entire tribe spent the winter on Tribe's Hill overlooking the Mohawk River.[20]

Britain signed a peace treaty with France in 1697, but this did not end hostilities for the Mohawks. In the spring of 1698, New York's new governor, the Earl of Bellomont, sent Dominie Dellius and Peter Schuyler to Quebec to notify the French governor, Count Frontenac, of the peace and get him to stop French incursions into the Iroquois country. Their mission was unsuccessful, since Frontenac refused to admit that the Iroquois were covered under the peace treaty. The French governor demanded that the Iroquois negotiate a separate peace with him. With the Iroquois specifically left out of the treaty of peace between England and France, morale among the entire Five Nations was low, and more defected to the Mohawk settlements in Canada, following the urging of the French priests. By 1700, two-thirds of the Mohawks had left their homeland.[21]

In the summer of 1701, delegates from all five Iroquois nations journeyed to Canada and made peace with the French. At the same time the League also sent delegates to a conference with the lieutenant governor of New York, John Nanfan, at Albany. The Iroquois realized their need for protection both against the French, who were building outposts around the Great Lakes, and from various western tribes, who were attacking Five Nations' hunting parties. Because of these dangers the sachems at Albany signed a deed turning over their western, "beaver" hunting grounds to the

---

[19] *DRCHNY* Volume 3, pp. 814-818 (quotes from pp. 816, 817); Sivertsen, p. 282 n20.

[20] *DRCHNY* Volume 4, pp. 17-19.

[21] Richter, *Ordeal of the Longhouse*, pp. 187-188, 191-192, 356; *DRCHNY* Volume 4, pp. 340-341, 347-351, 648, 730-731; Aquila, pp. 45-47.

king of England, in expectation of English assistance in return. These two treaties signaled a major shift in Iroquois policy—Iroquois attacks against the New France and its Indian allies would now be replaced by a neutrality that the League could choose to exercise when dealing with the two rival European powers. Although not always adhered to, neutrality would remain a viable option for the League through much of the first half of the eighteenth century, one that nicely balanced the confederacy's pro-French factions (chiefly in the western Iroquois tribes), with the pro-English ones (chiefly the Mohawks). For the Mohawks, it would allow the establishment of peaceful communications between those living in the ancestral homeland and those who had moved to the new settlements near Montreal.[22]

War between England and France recommenced in May of 1702, but the Five Nations remained neutral. On July 23, 1702, the Mohawks asked the new New York governor, Lord Cornbury, for permission to send Awanay, one of their sachems, and Brant (probably a war chief) to Canada to exchange prisoners with the Canadian Indians. His lordship refused, but the Mohawks ignored him, sending four sachems to Canada in the late summer/fall of that year.[23]

As the war dragged on in Europe one Boston merchant, Samuel Vetch, formed a plan to rid the North American continent of the French. He sailed to England in 1708 with his scheme for a two-pronged attack against Montreal and Quebec. One arm of the attacking forces would sail down the St. Lawrence and the second would march north from Albany to Montreal. Queen Anne agreed to the plan for the next year, 1709. A fleet sailing from England would bring some regular British forces while two American forces would gather, one near Wood Creek north of Albany and a second in Boston to await transportation to Quebec.[24]

In preparation for the attack, two pro-English Mohawks, "the most trust[ed] and most secret Indians you can get"—Ezras Kanneraghtahare and Cornelius Thaneghwanege (Tanechwanege)—agreed to go to Montreal to spy out the fortifications, and three River Indians went to Quebec with the same mission. In July, 1709,

---

[22] Aquila, pp. 55-69, 124-125; *DRCHNY* Volume 4, pp. 655, 896-911.

[23] *DRCHNY* Volume 4, p. 994; Leder, *Livingston Indian Records*, pp. 185-186.

[24] Hawke, p. 332; Richmond Bond, *Queen Anne's American Kings* (Oxford: Clarenden Press, 1952), pp. 22-24.

Governor Ingoldsby of New York managed to persuade all of the Iroquois except the Seneca to contribute forces to the overland expedition. The Mohawks would supply the largest contingent, 150 warriors. With forces and supplies for the second thrust assembling at Boston, five Iroquois leaders were invited to that city in August to see this gathering of British might. One of them was Brant, almost certainly the Brant Saquainquaragton who would go to England the next year.[25]

The colonial army gathered in New England in the summer of 1709, eagerly awaiting the arrival of the English fleet. As they waited, sickness and desertions thinned their ranks. Word finally came that the fleet, essential to the invasion of Canada, was not coming—it had been diverted to Portugal! The Iroquois contingent, who were waiting at Wood Creek with the second group of colonial troops, went home in disgust.[26]

By that fall the New York commanders, Francis Nicholson, Peter Schuyler, and others, knew that they had to do something to repair the damage caused by the failure of the summer's expedition because the Iroquois were more than ever opposed to intervening to aid the English. Thus, in October, the commanders wrote to a group of colonial governors meeting in Newport, Rhode Island, suggesting that representative sachems of the Iroquois should be sent to England to be impressed with British power and affluence, in an attempt to sway them from neutrality. On October 14 the governors passed a resolution to this effect.[27]

The four "kings" (as they were immediately called in England) sailed from Boston on February 28, 1710, and reached England at the beginning of April. On the nineteenth of that month, after being suitably applauded by wondering crowds and clothed in European dress, they had an audience with Queen Anne. Their spokesman was Hendrick Tejonihokarawa ("Open the Door") a sachem of the Wolf clan who had been baptized at North Albany on July 11, 1690. Born in 1660, this Hendrick would be active in Mohawk affairs until 1735. In his speech to the Queen, Hendrick stressed the

---

[25] Leder, *Livingston Indian Records*, pp. 202-206; Aquila, pp. 85-87; Bond, pp. 27-29.
[26] Hawke, p. 332; John Garratt, "The Four Kings: An Historical Essay," in John Garratt, ed., *The Four Kings* (Ottawa: Public Archives Canada, 1985), p. 6; Bond, p. 34.
[27] Bond, pp. 31-33, 35, 113.

Mohawks' need for security and protection from the French, mentioned the nefarious influence of French priests, and requested that English priests be sent to the Indians to instruct them.[28]

The English finally sent an expedition to conquer New France in 1711, but it, like the previous one, failed to reach Quebec, reinforcing the idea among the Iroquois that neutrality was their best option. In 1713 the two warring European powers signed the Treaty of Utrecht, in which France recognized the Iroquois as subjects of the English crown and agreed not to interfere with them. By this time the Mohawks and the other members of the Iroquois confederacy were more interested in warring with tribes to the south of them than with the French.[29]

In mid-September 1713 the central League council at Onondaga prepared to decide whether to help their kindred Iroquoian tribe, the Tuscaroras, to attack European settlers in North Carolina. A group of five hundred Tuscaroras had come north and settled near the Oneidas some years previously. Possibly as early as 1710 (when Hendrick referred to the Six Nations in his speech to Queen Anne) and certainly by 1714, the Tuscaroras were admitted into the League of the Iroquois under Oneida leadership. Henceforth the League was usually referred to as the Six Nations. In the September meeting, two white commissioners from Albany, accompanied by several Mohawk war chiefs, succeeded in persuading the confederacy not to join the Tuscaroras in their war.[30]

A minor ripple on the calm waters of Six Nations neutrality came in the early 1720s when Massachusetts entered into a struggle with the Abenaki tribes of Maine, known as Father Rasle's (or Rale's) War. The boundaries of Acadia, ceded to Great Britain under the Treaty of Utrecht in 1713, had been left undefined, and what is now Maine was claimed by both New England and New France. Massachusetts' settlement in this area was resisted overtly by the local Abenaki Indians and surreptitiously by the French in

---

[28] Bond, pp. 1-2; Garratt, "Four Kings," p. 8; Holland Society, p. 51; Peter Wraxall, *An Abridgement of the Indian Affairs Transacted in the Colony of New York* (Cambridge: Harvard Historical Studies 21, 1915), p. 191; J. Lydekker, *The Faithful Mohawks* (Cambridge: Cambridge University Press, 1938), pp. 27-28.
[29] Hawke, pp. 332-333.
[30] Lydekker, *Faithful Mohawks*, p. 28; D. Landy, "Tuscarora among the Iroquois," in Bruce Trigger, ed., *Handbook of North American Indians, Volume XV, Northeast*, pp. 518-524; *DRCHNY* Volume 5, pp. 372-376; Sivertsen, pp. 89-90.

Canada. By early 1722 the Abenakis had "captured a number of English at Different places, burned Brunswick, and continued their depredations under the direction of Father Rasle [a French Jesuit priest]. He as their religious leader had acquired almost unbounded influence over them, and his political and religious zeal combined to inflame the Abenakis against English and Protestant aggression."[31]

By September of that year both the Abenakis and Massachusetts tried to draw the Iroquois into the war. During a conference between the Iroquois and the governors of Virginia and New York, Governor Burnet of New York told ten Iroquois sachems (two from each of the original Five Nations), that the Abenakis had broken the peace with the English. He gave them the present sent by the governor of Massachusetts, who wanted the Iroquois to go to war against the eastern Indians. The Mohawk sachem Hendrick Tejonihokarawa replied for the others that the Abenakis had sent them a black wampum belt a year and a half earlier to try and get their help but that the Mohawks had stifled it. Governor Burnet, seeing the Iroquois' reluctance to get involved in the fight, suggested instead that they try to stop the war. An Iroquois delegation that included Hendrick and another Mohawk sachem, Taquayanont, did go to Boston in October to mediate between the English and the Abenakis, but the Bostonians did not encourage their efforts. The sachems were feasted and then presented with guns in the Council Chamber at Boston, hardly an appropriate gesture to a peace delegation. The Iroquois delegates were kept at Boston while only one, Taquayanont, and a Massachusetts officer were sent (on October 3) to the Abenakis at Norridgewock. They returned without finding any Abenakis, and the delegates went home. During two more conferences, in Albany in June, 1723, and at Boston in August, Massachusetts representatives sought to get the Six Nations to declare war against the Eastern Indians. The sum result was two Iroquois volunteers.[32]

In early 1724 Massachusetts established a fort near present-day Battleboro, Vermont, named Fort Dummer. On April 3 Hendrick and Ezeare (probably Ezras Kanneraghtahare) signed up to help garrison the fort. Despite the generous rations allotted to the

---

[31] George Sheldon, *History of Deerfield, Massachusetts*, Volume 1 (Deerfield: E. A. Hall & Co., 1895), pp. 389-392 (quote from p. 392).

[32] Leder, *Livingston Indian Records*, pp. 231-233; Sheldon, pp. 400, 404; Bond, p. 64.

Indians, only a few Schaghticokes under their sachem Apaumeet and six other Mohawks under Hendrick (and three Oneidas) joined them. In August, 280 New Englanders and three Mohawks—Christian, his son Christian Jr., and Isaac, Christian Sr.'s brother—attacked Father Rasle and the Abenakis at Norridgewock. One of Father Rasle's Indian companions killed Isaac, only to be killed in turn by Christian Sr., who also burned the town after the New England officers had left. Hendrick and Taquayanont (and Ezras) seem to have been the only Mohawk leaders who favored involvement in the struggle, which ended with the Abenakis' defeat in 1725.[33]

After more than three decades of peace, war between England and France again broke out in the spring of 1744, but the Six Nations wished to remain neutral. For the Mohawks, usually the most pro-English of the League, this decision in part reflected their fears that the Albany city fathers had designs upon their land. Pennsylvania's interpreter Conrad Weiser, coming to the Mohawk country in July, 1745, found the Mohawks bitter and hostile against the Albany people. In that summer the Mohawks joined the other Iroquois on a visit to Canada.[34]

Because of their distrust of the Albany-based Commissioners of Indian Affairs, the Mohawks turned instead to an Indian trader from Ireland named William Johnson. Johnson volunteered to supply the British post of Oswego on Lake Ontario, and because of his influence with the Mohawks was made Colonel of the Six Nations at a 1746 Albany conference. A proposed British thrust against Fort St. Frederic later that year never materialized, but a French counter thrust against Schenectady was turned aside by the Caughnawagas, who did not wish to fight any of their Mohawk relatives who might have been in the town. By the spring of 1747 Johnson had begun to supply parties of Mohawks going out to fight against the French. A

---

[33] Sheldon, pp. 409, 422-423, 426-427, 435; James Baxter, *The Pioneers of New France in New England* (Albany: Munsell, 1894), pp. 237, 241-242; Records of the First Church in Albany in the New York State Library vault: Church Records SC 17568, Box 1, volume 2; New York Historical Society Collections, Henry Barclay, Register Book, Fort Hunter 1734/5 (photocopy in Montgomery County Archives, Fonda, New York), pp. 7, 17.

[34] P. A. Wallace, *Conrad Weiser 1696-1760, Friend of Colonist and Mohawk* (Philadelphia: University of Pennsylvania Press, 1945), pp. 227-230; *DRCHNY* Volume 6, p. 293.

war chief of the Bear clan, Hendrick Peters Theyanoguin (often confused with the earlier Wolf clan sachem Hendrick Tejonihokarawa) went on a supposed peace mission to the French governor in the fall of 1746, but on the way home he raided a group of French in present-day Vermont. Though once reluctant to fight, Hendrick Theyanoguin now supported Johnson's efforts to arm his tribe and the next May led a raiding party of Mohawks, Senecas, Oneidas and whites up to Montreal. However, it was ambushed by a French force on June 15 and only Hendrick and a few others returned home safely. The Wolf clan Canajoharie sachem Nickus Peters Karaghtadie and fourteen other Mohawks were captured by the French.[35]

Throughout 1747 and early 1748 William Johnson armed numerous bands of raiders, chiefly Mohawks, headed for Canada. For these efforts he was made sole Indian Commissioner by Governor Clinton in 1748, and when the war ended in the summer of 1748 Johnson was appointed to arrange for the exchange of prisoners. There was little problem repatriating the white prisoners, but the French would not release the Mohawks until 1750. The French governor requested that the Indians themselves arrange for the release of these men, kept in chains under conditions so severe that three of them died. The English authorities demanded that the Iroquois, as subjects of England's king, be exchanged through them. Faced with this impasse, the French governor released the prisoners of his own accord in the summer of 1750 after encouraging them to believe that the English were responsible for the delay and that they were once again conspiring to destroy the Mohawks.[36]

William Johnson's management of Indian affairs during and after King George's War had proved effective, but expensive. From his

---

[35] M. Hamilton, *Sir William Johnson, Colonial American 1715-1763* (Port Washington: Kennekat Press, 1979), pp. 43-44, 54, 56-57; C. Colden, *History of the Five Indian Nations* Volume 2, pp. 218-221; Wraxall, p. 248 n1; J. Sullivan, A. C. Flick, and M. Hamilton, eds., *The Sir William Johnson Papers* [hereafter *JP*] Volume 9 (Albany: State University New York Press, 1929-65), p. 18; Ian Steele, *Betrayals: Fort William Henry and the "Massacre,"* (New York: Oxford University Press, 1990), pp. 20-21; *DRCHNY* Volume 6, p. 512; M. Hamilton, "Theyanoguin," in Francess G. Halpenny, genl. ed., *Dictionary of Canadian Biography* Volume 3, 1741-1770 (Toronto: University of Toronto Press, 1974), p. 623; Isabel Kelsay, "Karaghtadie," *Dictionary of Canadian Biography* Volume 3, p. 322; C. Russ, "Louis La Corne," *Dictionary of Canadian Biography* Volume 3, p. 331.
[36] *DRCHNY* Volume 6, pp. 512, 589-90; *JP* Volume 1, p. 168.

appointment as Indian Commissioner in 1748 to 1750-1751 he spent nearly six hundred pounds, and there was no provision for its payment by the governor or assembly of New York, or by the Crown. Moreover, Johnson's accounts for the supply of Fort Oswego during the 1744-1748 war had only been partly paid, leaving a balance of over seventeen hundred pounds. Frustrated by his unsuccessful efforts to get his expenses paid, Johnson resigned his position as Commissioner in May of 1751.[37]

By now Mohawk leadership was solidly behind William Johnson, and new Indian commissioners, appointed in late 1752, had no influence with Mohawk leaders. The new commissioners were seen as being in league with the purveyors of false deeds and crooked surveys, individuals who again sought to steal Mohawk land. Hendrick Peters led a Mohawk delegation to Governor Clinton in New York in June, 1753 to complain: "When we came here to relate our Grievances about our Lands, we expected to have something done for us, and we have told you that the Covenant Chain of our Forefathers was like to be broken, and brother you tell us that we shall be redeemed at Albany [by the Commissioners], but we know them so well, we will not trust to them, for they are no people but Devils, so we rather desire that you'l say, Nothing shall be done for us. Brother, by and by you'l expect to see the Nations [come] down which you shall not see, for as soon as we come home we will send up a Belt of Wampum to our Brothers the Five Nations to acquaint them that the Covenant Chain is broken between you and us. So, brother, you are not to expect to hear of me any more, and, Brother, we desire to hear no more of you." With that Hendrick stalked out, followed by the other Mohawks.[38]

This ostensible severing of ties between the Iroquois and the English drew a quick reaction in London, where government officials were keenly aware of the importance of the Iroquois League in holding the western frontier of North America. Intelligence of a French expedition in the upper Ohio Valley two years before had been followed that very spring by news of a large French force that sailed down the St. Lawrence and across Lake Ontario, and then established Fort LeBeuf at present day Erie, Pennsylvania. The British ministers knew that another war with

---

[37] Hamilton, *Sir William Johnson*, pp. 63-65.
[38] *DRCHNY* Volume 6, pp. 781-788 (quote is from p. 788).

France was in the offing and that it was the worst time to lose Indian allegiances. Because of Hendrick's action they directed seven of the colonial governors to appoint delegates to a conference between the colonies and the Iroquois.[39]

At the conference, held in Albany in the early summer of 1754, Hendrick excoriated the English commissioners for their lack of preparedness against the French, saying "look at the French, they are Men, they are fortifying everywhere–but, we are ashamed to say it, you are all like women bare and open without any fortifications." Hendrick's brother, Abraham Peters Canostens, used the occasion to ask for the reappointment of William Johnson as Indian Commissioner.[40]

While the Six Nations were meeting in Albany a force of Virginians under George Washington had been meeting with a French force at Fort Necessity in what is now western Pennsylvania. Inexperienced and outnumbered, Washington was forced to surrender and leave the Ohio country in the hands of the French, who had recently built Fort Duquesne at the Forks of the Ohio River.[41]

The government in London, determined not to leave this vital area in French hands, directed Governor Shirley of Massachusetts and Sir William Pepperell of that colony to raise regiments of one thousand men each and also sent several regiments of British regulars under the command of General Braddock to Virginia the following spring. Braddock met with the governors of New York, Massachusetts, Virginia, Pennsylvania, and Maryland on April 14, 1755, to plan the overall strategy for the summer campaign. Three major thrusts were to be made against the French: one against Fort Duquesne on the Ohio, one against Fort Niagara at the western end of Lake Ontario, and one from Albany north against the French fortress of Crown Point on Lake Champlain. Braddock would command the first expedition, Governor William Shirley of Massachusetts the second, and William Johnson the third.[42]

---

[39] Hamilton, *Sir William Johnson*, pp. 100-101.

[40] Hamilton, pp. 104-105, 348-349 n29; *DRCHNY* Volume 6, pp. 869-871.

[41] Fred Anderson, *Crucible of War* (New York: Knopf, 2000), pp. 47-49, 52-66, 78.

[42] Hamilton, *Sir William Johnson*, pp. 114-117; James Flexner, *Lord of the Mohawks: A Biography of Sir William Johnson* (Boston: Little, Brown, 1979), pp. 124-125; Hawke, p. 388; Anderson, pp. 87-88.

The English commander-in-chief had already been directed to appoint Johnson as sole superintendent of the Indians. At the April conference, which Johnson attended, Braddock also gave Johnson a commission as Colonel of the Six Nations. The governors of New York and Massachusetts made him a major-general of their militia, because he was to command levies raised mostly from the New England colonies in the thrust up Lake Champlain. Shirley, the Massachusetts governor, was to command mostly New York troops. Both expeditions would assemble and set out from Albany, William Johnson's force heading north and Shirley's west through Mohawk and Oneida country to Fort Oswego on Lake Ontario, and from there by boat to Niagara.[43]

It was a situation made for confusion and rivalry as both Shirley and Johnson vied for men, supplies, and Indian auxiliaries. Johnson was supposed to take the bulk of the Six Nations warriors with him, but Shirley would need Iroquois guides through the Six Nations country. Perceiving that Johnson would not be helpful in this matter, Shirley turned to John Henry Lydius, a Dutchman with longstanding ties to the Mohawks and an adopted Mohawk, to aid his recruiting efforts among the Iroquois.[44]

At a conference with the Six Nations at his home in June, 1755, Johnson told of his new appointment as sole manager of Indian affairs and relayed General Braddock's message to them. In opening the conference, Johnson asked the Iroquois leaders that "you will take care that no snake may creep in amongst us or anything which may obstruct our harmony." He was probably referring to French spies. John Henry Lydius was present at the conference to recruit for Shirley but was forbidden to carry out further recruitment. Lydius then shifted his efforts to Canajoharie, where he asked Hendrick Peters Theyanoguin and his half-brother Nickus Peters Karaghtadie to accompany Shirley. Nickus referred the matter to his wife, Elizabeth, an action which, since she was the head woman of the Turtle clan—Lydius's clan—was perfectly proper. Elizabeth was the adopted daughter of Rebecca Kowajatense, who was in turn the daughter of Karanondo baptized at North Albany in 1690. Elizabeth's response to Lydius's request must have been negative, because the Peters brothers and most of

---

[43] Hamilton, *Sir William Johnson*. pp. 117-118.
[44] Sivertsen, pp. 53, 56, 313 n5.

the other Canajoharies, including the head Turtle clan war chief at Canajoharie, ended up accompanying William Johnson.[45]

After assembling near Albany in July and August, Johnson's forces headed northward along the Hudson to Lydius's house, where the portage to Lake St. Sacrement began. Here Johnson directed that a fort be erected and a road built across the portage to Lake St. Sacrement, which he renamed Lake George. The troops were to pass along the road to Lake George, then embark in bateaux up the lake, make another portage to Lake Champlain, and go on to Crown Point. While the troops were constructing walls around Lydius's original house the first of the Six Nations warriors joined them on August 23. Abraham Peters Canostens led this advance contingent, and two days later Hendrick Theyanoguin came with two hundred more. By the time the army was ready to march two hundred to three hundred Indians had assembled to accompany the three thousand troops. Leaving five hundred militia at the Lydius fort (soon renamed Fort Edward), Johnson and his men advanced along the newly-made road to the south end of Lake George in early September. Here they cleared an expanse of trees and prepared to build another fort as a base for their boat trip up the lake.[46]

In the meantime a sizeable French force—two hundred French regulars, six hundred Canadian militiamen, and about six hundred Caughnawagas and Abenaki Indians—were marching south from Crown Point to attack the Lydius fort. Led astray by his Caughnawaga Mohawk guides (who also refused to attack a fort), the French general, Baron Dieskau, turned his men around and set out to attack Johnson's main force, now at Lake George. On the morning of September 8, after discovering that Johnson was sending a relief force from Lake George to Fort Edward, the French waited in ambush along the road their enemies had just built.[47]

Johnson had been sending out scouting parties to warn him of any French movements. On the afternoon of September 7, Thick Lawrence and two other scouts reported to Hendrick and Johnson at Lake George that about six hundred men were headed from Lake Champlain's South Bay to the Carrying Place (Fort Edward).

---

[45] *DRCHNY* Volume 6, pp. 964-989; *JP* Volume 9, pp. 193-203; Hamilton, *Sir William Johnson*, pp. 133-135; Kelsay, "Karaghtadie," p. 322; Sivertsen, pp. 23-25, 119-120.

[46] Hamilton, ibid., pp. 145-149, 152, 157.

[47] *DRCHNY* Volume 10, pp. 316-321.

Johnson called a council of war, and the New England officers proposed sending five hundred men to the South Bay to destroy Dieskau's boats and five hundred to relieve Fort Edward. When asked, Hendrick is reported to have said of the relief force: "if they are to fight they are too few, if to they are to be killed they are too many." He took three sticks and showed how together they could not be broken, but that separated each could be broken.[48]

With this graphic advice Johnson decided to send all one thousand troops led by Colonel Ephraim Williams, Jr. of Massachusetts and two hundred Six Nations warriors to the relief of Fort Edward. Mounted on horses, Williams and Hendrick, old acquaintances from Stockbridge, led the van. All three sections of the relief force—van, center, and rear—had their own contingent of Six Nations Indians.[49]

Two or three miles down the road they were ambushed by the French force. The French regulars were drawn up onto the road itself, while the Canadians and their Indian allies lay hidden along both flanks. Supposedly a whispered conversation between Hendrick and a Caughnawaga concealed in the bushes precipitated the Caughnawaga and Abenaki Indians' fire before Johnson's force was entirely in the trap, but British and Six Nations loses were heavy. Colonel Williams was killed as were many other officers. Hendrick slipped off his horse and made his way through the skirmish line into the woods on the left only to meet the French Indian baggage party composed of women and children. The old chief, too stout to run, was killed and scalped by the women and children. William Tarraghioris, chief Turtle clan warrior of Canajoharie, was also killed, along with one of Nickus Karaghtadie's sons. Other Mohawks killed were Waniacoone, Skahijowio, Onienkoto, Thomas, and Scaroyady's son Nica-awna. Cayadanora, a Tuscarora, was also slain. In all, thirty-two of Johnson's Indian allies were killed or missing and twelve wounded. British colonial casualties were even worse, with 120 killed, 801 wounded, and sixty-two missing by the end of the day. These

[48] Hamilton, *Sir William Johnson*, pp. 157-159; Claus Papers, Public Archives of Canada MG19, ser. F1, volume 23, pp. 31-32; *JP* Volume 2, pp. 16-17; W. L. Stone, *Life and Times of Sir William Johnson, Bart.*, Volume 1 (Albany: Munsell, 1865), pp. 512-513.

[49] Hamilton, ibid., p. 159. For Hendrick's connection with Stockbridge, see Sivertsen, pp. 144-150.

figures include the afternoon battle, which occurred after the surviving British militia and Six Nations warriors fled back to the camp at Lake George, pursued by the French. Within the camp, Johnson managed to rally his forces despite receiving a bullet in his thigh; and after several hours of fighting the French retreated, leaving their wounded commander Baron Dieskau on the field. Both sides were too exhausted to continue their campaigns that year.[50]

Although the British heralded the Battle of Lake George as a victory to match the defeat of General Braddock on July 9—and rewarded William Johnson with a baronetcy—to the Mohawks it was a disaster. Not only had they lost their greatest speaker and another influential war chief, but in all twelve of their principal men had fallen in the battle. They had also involved themselves in war with their Caughnawaga relatives, a war which would become increasingly bloody in the years to come.[51]

Braddock's defeat on the banks of the Monongahela in July caused great unease among the Mohawks. In November they asked William Johnson to build a fort at Canajoharie and man it with white troops. This fort, and the increased number of troops at Fort Hunter (adjacent to the Mohawk's Lower Castle), led to conflicts between the garrisons and the Indians. Two years later the Wolf clan chief Abraham Teyorhansere reported how soldiers from Fort Hunter had attacked him in his own stable because he found them stealing his horses. Other soldiers from the fort encountered the wife of one of the sachems and attempted to ravish her. Fortunately she had been out cutting wood and successfully defended herself with her ax.[52]

British attempts to counter French attacks in the following years generally met with disaster. The most notable failure was in the summer of 1757 when, despite the arrival at Fort Edward of Sir

---

[50] Hamilton, ibid., pp. 159-166; Hamilton, "Theyanoguin," p. 623; *DRCHNY* Volume 10, pp. 317, 321-322, 342; Claus Papers, Public Archives of Canada MG19, ser. F1, volume 23, pp. 35-37; *JP* Volume 9, pp. 238, 357.

[51] A. H. Young (compiler), "Letters from and Concerning the Reverend John Ogilvie, M.A., D.D., Written to the Society for the Propagation of the Gospel in Foreign Parts, 1747-1774," *Papers and Records* Volume 22 (Toronto: Ontario Historical Society, 1925), p. 316; *DRCHNY* Volume 6, p. 1020; *JP* Volume 2, pp. 343-348.

[52] *JP* Volume 2, p. 293, Volume 9, pp. 546-548, Volume 13, p. 105.

William Johnson with fifteen hundred colonial troops and two hundred warriors, the fort's commander, General Webb, refused to go to the aid of the besieged Fort William Henry. The latter fort surrendered on August 9, and over fifty British and colonials were killed by France's Indian allies. When the survivors of this slaughter arrived at Fort Edward the colonial troops mutinied and the Iroquois went home on stolen horses to the Mohawk Valley. Released into Johnson's fields, the horses damaged a great many crops. Later the Mohawks apologized.[53]

In the summer of 1758 Johnson again led a contingent of about 450 warriors against the French at Ticonderoga, but British General Abercromby refused to use them. Without waiting for his heavier artillery to come up from the rear, Abercromby marched his regular troops against the massive French fortifications only to have his men slaughtered. Having been ordered to the top of nearby Rattlesnake Mountain (Mount Defiance) where they could play no part in the battle, Johnson and the Mohawks watched in horror and disgust at such a wanton waste of life. According to one source, after the battle the Mohawk sachems told the British general that "his army had fine limbs but no head and that he was an 'old Squah' and had better 'go home and make sugar!'"[54]

Despite the failure of British generals to use large bodies of Indian auxiliaries during these years, Sir William Johnson was able to send numerous small raiding parties north to Lake Champlain. In 1757 one such raiding party led by Moses, probably the Mohawk war chief Moses Nowadarika, met with disaster and "Moses was made a sacrifice of by the enemy"—he was captured by enemy Indians and tortured to death. At the Upper Mohawk Castle of Canajoharie, Hendrick Peters's son Paulus Peters Saghsanowano was so active in organizing war parties that he neglected his duties as schoolmaster and had his salary stopped.[55]

While war captains were leading their men northward, Johnson's deputy George Croghan was holding a series of conferences in

[53] Flexner, pp. xi-xiii; 181-182.

[54] *JP* Volume 2, pp. 852-853, 870-872, 885-886, Volume 9, pp. 936-939, 941; *DRCHNY* Volume 10, pp. 725, 739-741, 797-798; Isabel Kelsay, *Joseph Brant 1743-1807: Man of Two Worlds* (Syracuse: Syracuse University Press, 1984), pp. 62-63 (quote).

[55] *JP* Volume 9, p. 820; Young, "Letters from ... the Reverend John Ogilvie, M.A., D.D.," p. 319.

Pennsylvania to try to regain the allegiances of the Delawares and Shawnees. Sir William sent a Mohawk delegation to John Harris' Ferry (Harrisburg, Pennsylvania) in April-May of 1757 to meet with the Delaware leader Teedyuscung. The delegation consisted of the Bear clan chiefs Jonathan Cayenquerigo, Johannes Canadagaye, Johannes Kryn Anequendahonji (or Unaguaandchonge, commonly known as White Hans or Hance Kryn), four other Bear chiefs, and two Wolf clan chiefs: Abraham Teyorhansere of the Lower Castle of Tiononderoge and Peter Serehowane of Canajoharie.[56]

A far more important conference convened in Easton, Pennsylvania, in November, 1758. The principal Mohawk sachém to attend this meeting was Nickus Karaghtadie. Abraham Peters Canostens had died in January, 1757, and Nickus was the last male Peters of his generation. Nickus' first wife Elizabeth (the leading woman of the Turtle clan) had died in May, 1757, but by late 1758 he had remarried to a woman who had two young sons. Possibly reinvigorated by his new marriage, Nickus blasted Teedyuscung in a speech so vitriolic that it was not put on the official record. Nickus's later speech that expressed the Six Nations' lack of support for the Delaware leader was seconded by the Seneca chief Tagashata (Kyashuta) and other Iroquois leaders. The conference ended with the Six Nations and their "Nephews" the Delawares proclaiming their hearty support for the English cause. Immediately afterward Croghan took a delegation of warriors to the aid of British General Forbes, who was able to capture a deserted Fort Duquesne in November, 1758—deserted by the French after they lost the support of the western Delawares. Nickus Karaghtadie's effort may have exhausted him, however, for he died in early 1759.[57]

After the Easton conference in October, 1758 and the subsequent capture of Fort Duquesne (renamed Fort Pitt), the way was prepared for even more Indian support in the following year. Because the French at Fort Niagara were stopping Indians from going eastward

---

[56] *JP* Volume 9, pp. 626, 655, 727-733; Nicholas Wainwright, *George Croghan, Wilderness Diplomat,* (Chapel Hill: University North Carolina Press, 1959), pp. 122-125; *Minutes of the Provincial Council of Pennsylvania from the Organization to the Termination of Proprietary Government* Volume 7 (Harrisburg: Thomas Fenn & Co., 1851), pp. 498-510.

[57] Wallace, pp. 520-552; Wainwright, pp. 143-151; *JP* Volume 2, pp. 873, 890-891, Volume 3, pp. 1-4, 162, Volume 9, pp. 621, 650, 767, Volume 10, pp. 44-48; *Minutes of the Provincial Council of Pennsylvania,* Volume 8, pp. 190-203.

to trade with the English but providing scarcely anything of value to exchange with the Indians for their furs, the Senecas of the Genessee broached the idea of an attack on the fort to Sir William Johnson at a conference at Canajoharie in April, 1759. Johnson forwarded the suggestion to the new British commander-in-chief, Sir Jeffery Amherst. Amherst decided to send an army of British and colonial troops under Brigadier General Prideaux from Oswego to attack Niagara. Prideaux and his force departed from there on July 1 and arrived near Niagara five days later. With him were a contingent of 945 Iroquois warriors, nearly the whole fighting force of Iroquoia. This massive commitment of the League's manpower was an indication of how important the elimination of the French from the Great Lakes region was to the Six Nations. Once the French were gone, the Iroquois intended to regain the power they once had had over the western tribes south of the lakes.[58]

Upon landing on July 6 Sir William sent out a party of Canajoharie Mohawks, who surprised a working party from the fort and captured a Frenchman. Alerted to the presence of the British and Indian army, the fort's commander, Captain Pierre Pouchot, sent for the substantial French and Indian force that had been assembled at Fort Machault (Venango). He also sent the Seneca chief Kaendae out to talk with the Iroquois now besieging the fort. After several days of negotiations both groups of Iroquois—those inside and those outside the fort—retired up the Niagara River. While the British forces proceeded with the siege, the French relief force coming up from Lake Erie was defeated by colonial and regular troops and about one hundred Iroquois warriors, including the future Mohawk war chief, Joseph Brant Thayendanegea. With no remaining hope of relief, the fort surrendered on July 25. As he had promised, Johnson let the Iroquois plunder the fort. With the loss of this key western outpost, other French posts to the westward were rendered untenable or ineffective.[59]

Niagara's capitulation and the other great British success of that year, the defeat of the French forces at Quebec, left unconquered only a small segment of New France, the area around Montreal. The British campaign of 1760 consisted of a three-pronged attack

---

[58] *DRCHNY* Volume 7, pp. 376, 391-392; Francis Jennings, *Empire of Fortune* (New York: Norton, 1988), pp. 414-416; Anderson, pp. 330-333, 787 n4.
[59] Hamilton, *Sir William Johnson*, pp. 246-247, 254-258; Anderson, pp. 335-338; Kelsay, *Joseph Brant*, pp. 64-65.

converging on this last French bastion. The first force headed southwest from British-held Quebec, the second proceeded north from Albany up Lake Champlain and the Richelieu River, and the last and largest started from Fort Oswego on the southern shore of Lake Ontario, across the lake to the head of the St. Lawrence River, and down the river to Montreal. With this last force, commanded by Sir Jeffrey Amherst, was Sir William Johnson and nearly seven hundred Indian warriors along with many of their women and children. This force included fifty-one Mohawks from the Lower Castle of Tiononderoge, twenty-two from the Mohawk settlements on Schoharie Creek, and eighty-five from the Upper Castle of Canajoharie.[60]

The most important contribution of these Indian auxiliaries was diplomatic: with their help Johnson was able to convince the Iroquois living along the banks of the St. Lawrence to assist the British forces with their passage through the dangerous rapids between the head of the river and the city, rather then to attack them along this vulnerable stretch. Assistance rendered by Caughnawaga Mohawks through the rapids upstream from Montreal greatly reduced the numbers of British troops lost along the British line of march. As the Mohawks from the Mohawk Valley passed down the valley of the St. Lawrence to Montreal, five hundred of their Caughnawaga relatives stood peacefully on the banks, watching. With the surrender of the city itself on September 9, the 152 years of intermittent warfare between the Mohawks of the Mohawk Valley and the French of New France ended, a warfare that included, for much of the second half of this period, war with their own Caughnawaga relatives. To symbolize the healing of this longstanding rift, Sir William Johnson had five Caughnawagas row his whaleboat to the island of Montreal.[61]

With the end of New France also came the end to the strategic role the Iroquois confederacy had played as power brokers between the empires of England and France in the interior of North America. For much of the seventeenth century the Mohawks had been one of the dominant members of the Five Nations, and Mohawk diplomatic and military policy had, for the most part, agreed with that of the

[60] Wilbur Jacobs, *Diplomacy and Indian Gifts* (Stanford: Stanford University Press, 1950), pp. 180-81; Anderson, p. 388.
[61] Flexner, pp. 217-219; George Stanley, *New France: The Last Phase, 1744-1760* (Toronto: McClelland and Stewart, 1968), pp. 256-257.

rest of the League. The policy of Iroquois neutrality that began in 1701 was frequently not followed by the Mohawks, however. In the eighteenth century they often pursued their own, pro-British policy even as they declined in numbers and influence within the League. Their pro-British policy was largely a consequence of their physical proximity to British settlements (and thus to British interests), but it was probably also in part because the Mohawks wished to use British influence, often in the form of Indian Superintendent William Johnson, as a means to recoup their influence in the Confederacy. This strategy was at least partly successful, but it carried its own price—the abandonment of independent decision-making and action, until the Mohawks became known, by the late 1750s, as "Johnson's Mohawks" to many of the western tribes.[62] Notwithstanding their motives, had the Mohawks not been so staunchly pro-British in the middle decades of the eighteenth century the history of the French and Indian War, while probably having the same eventual outcome, would certainly have played out differently.

Bibliography

Aquila, Richard. *The Iroquois Restoration: Iroquois Diplomacy on the Colonial Frontier 1701- 1754*. Detroit: Wayne State University Press, 1983.

Barclay, Henry. Register Book, Fort Hunter, 1734/5. New York Historical Society Collections (photocopy in the Montgomery County Archives, Fonda, New York).

Baxter, James. *The Pioneers of New France in New England*. Albany: Munsell, 1894.

Beyond the Covenant Chain. Eds. Daniel Richter and James Merrell, Syracuse: Syracuse University Press, 1987.

---

[62] Ian Steele, pp. 21, 23. James Smith, *An Account of the Remarkable Occurrences in the Life and Travels of Col. James Smith* (Cincinnati: Robert Clark & Co., 1870), p. 69.

Bond, Richmond. *Queen Anne's American Kings*. Oxford: Clarenden Press, 1952.

Chetwood, O. P. *A History of Colonial America*. New York: Harper & Row, 1961.

Colden, C. *History of the Five Indian Nations*. Volumes 1, 2. New York: A. S. Barnes, 1904.

Dictionary of Canadian Biography. Volume 3, 1741-1770. Genl. Ed. Francess G. Halpenny, Toronto: University of Toronto Press, 1974.

Documentary History of the State of New York. Volumes 1, 2. Ed. E. B. O'Callaghan, Albany: State of New York, 1849-1851.

Documents Relative to the Colonial History of New York. Volumes 3, 4, 5, 6, 7, 10. Eds. E. B. O'Callaghan and B. Fernow, Albany: State of New York, 1853-1887.

Donohue, Thomas. *The Iroquois and the Jesuits*. Buffalo: Catholic Publishing Co., 1895.

Fenton, William. "Problems Arising From the Historic Northeastern Position of the Iroquois." *Smithsonian Miscellaneous Collections*. Volume 100. Washington, D.C.: Smithsonian Institution, 1940.

First Church, Albany, New York. Records in the New York State Library, Albany: Church Records SC 17568, Box 1, Volume 2.

Flexner, James. *Lord of the Mohawks: A Biography of Sir William Johnson*. Boston: Little, Brown, 1979.

The Four Kings. Ed. John Garratt, Ottawa: Public Archives Canada, 1985.

Graymont, Barbara. *The Iroquois*. New York: Chelsea House, 1988.

Hamilton, M. *Sir William Johnson, Colonial American 1715-1763*. Port Washington: Kennekat Press, 1979.

Handbook of North American Indians: Volume XV, Northeast. Ed. Bruce G. Trigger, Washington, D.C.: Smithsonian Institution, 1978.

Hawke, David Hawke. *The Colonial Experience*. New York: Bobs-Merrill, 1966.

Holland Society. *Yearbook for 1904*. New York: Knickerbocker Press, 1904.

Jacobs, Wilbur. *Diplomacy and Indian Gifts*. Stanford: Stanford University Press, 1950.

Jennings, Francis. *Empire of Fortune*. New York: Norton, 1988.

The Jesuit Relations and Allied Documents, Travels and Explorations of the Jesuit Missionaries in New France, 1610-1791. Volumes 49, 51. Ed. Reuben Thwaites, Cleveland: Burrows, 1896-1901.

Kelsay, Isabel. *Joseph Brant 1743-1807: Man of Two Worlds*. Syracuse: Syracuse University Press, 1984.

The Leisler Papers 1689-1691. Ed. Peter Christoph, Syracuse: Syracuse University Press, 2002.

"Letters From and Concerning the Reverend John Ogilvie, M.A., D.D., Written to the Society for the Propagation of the Gospel in Foreign Parts, 1747-1774." Compiler A. H. Young. *Ontario Historical Society Papers and Records*. Volume 22. Toronto: Ontario Historical Society, 1925.

The Livingston Indian Records 1666-1723. Ed. Lawrence Leder, Gettysburg: Pennsylvania Historical Association, 1956.

Lydekker, J. *The Faithful Mohawks*. Cambridge: Cambridge University Press, 1938.

82

Minutes of the Provincial Council of Pennsylvania from the Organization to the Termination of Proprietary Government. Volumes 7, 8. Harrisburg: Thomas Fenn & Co., 1851.

Morrison, Samuel E. *Samuel de Champlain: Father of New France.* Boston: Little Brown, 1972.

Narratives of New Netherland, 1609-1664. Ed. R. J. Jameson, New York: Scribner's, 1909.

Public Archives of Canada, Ottawa
    Claus Papers, MG19, ser. F1, Volume 23.

Reich, Jerome. *Leisler's Rebellion: A Study of Democracy in New York 1664-1720.* Chicago: University of Chicago Press, 1953.

Richter, Daniel. *Ordeal of the Longhouse: The Peoples of the Iroquois League in the Era of European Colonization.* Chapel Hill: University of North Carolina Press, 1992.

Sheldon, George. *History of Deerfield, Massachusetts.* Volume 1. Deerfield: E. A. Hall & Co., 1895.

Smith, James. *An Account of the Remarkable Occurrences in the Life and Travels of Col. James Smith.* Cincinnati: Robert Clark & Co., 1870.

The Sir William Johnson Papers. Volumes 1, 2, 3, 9, 10, 13. Eds. J. Sullivan, A. C. Flick, and M. Hamilton, Albany: State University New York Press, 1929-1965.

Sivertsen, Barbara. *Turtles, Wolves, and Bears: A Mohawk Family History.* Bowie: Heritage Books, 1996.

Stanley, George. *New France: The Last Phase, 1744-1760.* Toronto: McClelland and Stewart, 1968.

Steele, Ian. *Betrayals: Fort William Henry and the "Massacre."* New York: Oxford University Press, 1990.

Stone, W. L. *Life and Times of Sir William Johnson, Bart.* Volume 1. Albany: Munsell, 1865.

Trigger, Bruce G. *The Children of Anahaentsic.* Volume 2. Montreal: McGill-Queen's University Press, 1976.

Trudel, Marcel. *Histoire de la Nouvelle-France II: Le Comptoir 1604-1627.* Montreal: Fides, 1963.

Trudel, Marcel. *Histoire de la Nouvelle-France III: La Seigneurie des Cent-Associés, 1627-1663. Part 1.* Montreal: Fides, 1979.

Wainwright, Nicholas. *George Croghan, Wilderness Diplomat.* Chapel Hill: University North Carolina Press, 1959.

Wallace, P. A. *Conrad Weiser 1696-1760, Friend of Colonist and Mohawk.* Philadelphia: University of Pennsylvania Press, 1945.

Wraxall, Peter. *An Abridgement of the Indian Affairs Transacted in the Colony of New York.* Cambridge: Harvard Historical Studies 21, 1915.

GOVERNOR WILLEM KIEFT'S WAR AGAINST THE WIECHQUAESKECK, 1643-1644

John Alexander Buckland

When the West India Company started to land colonists on Manhattan Island in 1610 to establish the trading area of New Netherland, the Wiechquaeskeck were friendly but wary. Some of them had shot arrows at Henry Hudson's ship when it had sailed into the river in 1609, but most of them had greeted the foreigners. Since European traders and fishermen had visited their country occasionally, for many years before, the arrival of another large ship with billowing sails was not a surprise. Earlier, European traders had arrived at their shores and met with them.

For two decades, the Wiechquaeskeck and other nearby Lenape, then traded peacefully and profitably with the Dutch. As the years passed, however, tensions developed. Many more settlers arrived.[1]

The Wiechquaeskeck were a tribe, or band, in the great group of Algonquian-speaking Native Americans that stretched across most of Canada and down the northeastern coast of the United States. They belonged to a kinship group of Native Americans called the Lenape, Lenni Lenape, or Delaware, and they spoke the Munsee dialect of the Algonquian language. The Wiechquaeskeck band occupied present-day The Bronx and Westchester County in New York, and southwestern Connecticut. They traded, intermarried, and cooperated with about sixteen of their neighboring Munsee-

---

[1] John Alexander Buckland, *The First Traders on Wall Street: The Wiechquaeskeck Indians of Southwestern Connecticut in the Seventeenth Century* (Bowie: Heritage Books, Inc., 2002).

speaking bands.[2] These included the Hackensack, Navasink, and Raritan in northern New Jersey; the Manhattan, Tappan, Sintsink, Rechgawanck, and Wapping of the Hudson Valley; and the Canarsee, Massapequa, Nayack, and Rockaway of Long Island. These tribes were closely related, and when the Dutch attacked one, they effectively attacked all of them.

During the twenty years that the Munsee-speakers traded with the Dutch, points of friction grew on both sides. A relatively peaceful trading relationship slowly disengaged. It finally fell apart when the situation in New Netherland changed markedly in 1638. This change was to have a devastating effect on the Native Americans in the whole Hudson River estuary area. First, a weak and irresolute Dutch governor, Wouter van Twiller, was removed, and a tough former trader, Willem Kieft, was sent from The Hague to be Director, or Governor, of New Amsterdam. Second, the business climate was shifting. It was the final year of the West India Company's monopoly on the fur trade in the Hudson Valley, and the Dutch began to send in more settlers, who took over prime land. Third, because there were few fur-bearing animals left to catch in the area, the remnant Wiechquaeskeck had little to trade to get the pots, tools, and woolen cloth, that had become a necessity for them to have, so the Dutch did little trading with them anymore.

To increase their profits from fur trading, the West India Company had started with a policy of keeping friendly relations with the Indians, and of discouraging colonists from moving in and taking land. In 1638, the Company decided that it was necessary to increase New Netherland's population, however, and they encouraged more Dutch, Swedes and Germans to emigrate.[3] After Kieft's arrival, everyone could trade with the Indians and the rules for settlers moving onto Indian fields were eased. Many more settlers established farms in Indian territories and most became traders, too. Contacts with the Native Americans increased.[4] The newcomers scattered all around the New Amsterdam area and up the Hudson River Valley. The settler population soon doubled and had

---

[2] Otto, Paul Andrew, *New Netherland Frontier: Europeans and Native Americans Along the Lower Hudson River, 1524-1664* (Bloomington: Ph.D. diss., Indiana University, June 1955), p. 17.

[3] *Narratives of New Netherland, 1609-1664*, ed. J. Franklin Jameson (New York: Charles Scribner's Sons, 1909), p. 273.

[4] Otto, p. 135

reached 2,500 by 1645. Ships of eighteen countries were coming to New Amsterdam to trade.

There was also an influx of English settlers coming overland to the area from nearby New England colonies. Some arrived from Massachusetts. Some English farmers arrived from the Connecticut River Valley. They moved closer to New Netherland and bought Wiechquaeskeck lands. English farmers mingled with the few Dutch settlers around Stamford and Greenwich.

The Native Americans had increasing problems related to the presence of their European neighbors. The number of Native Americans remaining in the area had shrunk to only a fraction of what it had been before 1600. Over eighty percent of the natives had been devastated by new, imported diseases that had been unwittingly introduced by earlier traders.[5] The new Dutch farmers were taking over the best land, some in large estates headed by "patroons."[6]

There were frequent clashes throughout the countryside and the Wiechquaeskeck were in the middle of this maelstrom. There were many arguments with the land-hungry new farmers. Indians began to enter Dutch farms and take goods. Several remote settlers' homes were attacked and burned. The young Indian men were alarmed, and seethed with animosity.

Paul Otto, in his thesis about the relations between the Dutch and the Indians, describes how the Dutch had become dependent on the Native Americans, not only for the furs to trade, but also for much of their food.[7] The Dutch employed natives for labor and domestic help. Natives were both guides away from Fort Amsterdam and translators since many of them had learned the Dutch language. Some Indian women intermarried with the Dutch. Otto notes that the relationship between the Dutch settlers of New Netherland and the Munsee-speaking inhabitants of the land deteriorated sharply in the 1630s.

As the population grew and trade increased, Dutch farms scattered even farther, and tensions between the Dutch and the Native inhabitants multiplied. There was conflict over the use of the land. The Indians depended on their unfenced gardens of corn,

---

[5] Dean R. Snow, *The Archeology of New England* (New York: Academic Press, 1980), pp. 32-42.

[6] Proprietors of manorial estates.

[7] Otto, p. 124ff.

beans, and squash. The Dutch let their livestock forage freely in the woods and they often ruined Indian gardens.[8] The Indians sometimes killed the intruding livestock. The Dutch shot at the Indians near their farms.

Dutch sailors, soldiers, and others, stole furs and wampum from individual natives who had come to New Amsterdam to trade. Indians stole goods and livestock from Dutch farms. The Dutch were quick on the trigger. The Lenape were quick with arrows and knives. There was complete misunderstanding between them.

The Indians have been criticized for believing that revenge served as justice in the tradition of an "eye for an eye." But when the Indians killed a few people, the Dutch moved in massively for revenge and would destroy a whole village. The Dutch ideas of ownership differed with the Indian concept of property in which anything of your friend's that you wanted, you used. The cultural patterns had no mesh.

Most importantly, the Wiechquaeskeck and their neighbors had few furs left to trade with the Dutch. In the previous two decades, they had killed nearly all the beaver, marten, fox and other useful fur-bearers in their area for trade. By 1640, most of the native fur traders who paddled their canoes to New Amsterdam were no longer Munsee. Some were Mahican from several days' journey to the north. Many, coming even farther, were Mohawk from the Adirondacks. In 1628, the Mohawk had finally subdued the Mahican in the Albany area, and they had free passage on the Hudson River. Guns became a critical factor. The Dutch had previously given the Mohawk all the guns they wanted, in order to get their furs. The Mohawk were willing to shoot unruly Munsee, at Dutch request, or for their own purposes. The Dutch still would not officially sell guns to the Munsee, because they lived too close to the settlers. Other traders were selling inferior guns all through the Hudson Valley, however.[9]

Soon the Wiechquaeskeck had little to trade with the Dutch but vegetables, deer, and wampum, and they got very few trade goods in return. As the English settlers moved down from the east, the dwindling tribe steadily lost their corn fields and their access to the seafood along the shore. Their remnant was driven into an

---

[8] Otto, p. 167.
[9] Jameson, p. 274.

impoverished corner that they did not understand. They were being given and sold alcohol. The younger Native Americans became restless and angry. They struck back.

The Wiechquaeskeck Clash with the Dutch

Paul Otto writes that Dutch-Munsee relations took a decided turn for the worse beginning in late 1639.[10] Kieft made demands on the Indians and started to tax them because "we have protected *(them)* against their enemies." Dutch forces began fighting with the Hackensack, the Raritan, and other Lenape tribes on Long Island. To the Dutch, the Wiechquaeskeck were just one of five different tribes near New Amsterdam that Kieft tried to subdue.

It was a fearful time in New Netherland. In February, 1643, some Dutch farmers on Long Island wanted to kill nearby Indians, but were refused permission by Director Kieft. Despite that, the farmers took wagons, and stole corn from the Indians, killing three men in the process. The Natives retaliated by burning two houses near the fort. The Director sent men out to see what was happening. "The Indians showing themselves afar off, called out: "Be ye our friends? Ye are mere corn stealers."[11]

The Wiechquaeskeck had a dangerous incident with the Dutch in 1642.[12] A young man had waited twenty years to avenge the death of his uncle, who had been robbed of his furs, then killed as the boy watched. When he was grown, he used a hatchet to kill a man that he thought he recognized as the robber, an old wheelwright named Claes Swits. Kieft sent a message to the Wiechquaeskeck sakima (or sachem, chief of a group of Algonquian bands) demanding that the Indians surrender the murderer to the Dutch. The sakima refused, saying that it was legitimate revenge, and told Kieft of his frustration with the Dutch treatment of the natives. He said that he, "was sorry twenty Christians had not been murdered," and refused to hand anyone over to the Dutch.[13] In a few years, this unatoned murder would be made the Dutch excuse for a horrible mass killing of displaced Indians at Pavonia, New Jersey.

There were some nearby native tribes who were not in the same strained relationship with the Dutch. In that year, Pacham, a

---

[10] Otto, p. 213ff
[11] Brodhead, p. 184.
[12] Jameson, pp. 213, 273.
[13] Brodhead, p. 183.

Tankiteke sakima, was dealing on friendly terms with the English around Norwalk, Connecticut.[14] He was a Connecticut Paugussett rather than a Lenape. He cooperated with the Dutch when the Lenape Raritan tribe attacked Dutch farms on Staten Island. He joined some Long Island Indians to attack and kill a few troublesome Raritan. Pacham, who was said to be "great with the governor of the fort," (Fort Amsterdam) appeared in New Amsterdam. He displayed, "in great triumph a dead hand hanging on a stick, and saying that it was the hand of the chief who had killed or shot with arrows men [Dutch farmers] on Staten Island." He said that he "had taken revenge" for the sake of the colonists "because he loved the Swannekens (as they called the Dutch) who were his best friends." He also got along well with the English settlers around Norwalk.[15]

Thus, the natives of southwestern Connecticut were split between the Tankiteke (Paugussett) in Norwalk, who were more friendly with both the English and the Dutch, and some of the Wiechquaeskeck in Stamford and Greenwich, who had profited from land deals with the intruding colonists. There were men like Amogerone, Nawhorone, Ponus, Wesskum,[16] and others who are now remembered by place names because they were friendly. The angry, younger men lived further from the coast. The nearby Wiechquaeskeck elders could not stop the young men from swooping down to burn and pillage in the area, however. There were rampaging Indians from The Bronx to Stamford. There was an oral story in Greenwich that "even the stout-hearted lay down in fear and rose up in danger."[17] Not a European farmer felt safe. The men took their guns to work in the field. Many houses were attacked and burned. The Dutch in New Amsterdam watched the surrounding fighting. They felt helpless when their local troops were out attacking Lenape villages, while some of the Indians were walking freely on their streets.

---

[14] Jameson, p. 211.

[15] Ibid., p. 211.

[16] Greenwich Town Records, Land Records 1, 1640, Part 1.

[17] Elizabeth W. Clarke, ed., *The First Three Hundred Years. The History of the First Congregational Church, Greenwich, Connecticut* (Greenwich: The First Congregational Church of Greenwich, 1967), p. 25.

There is a popular oral story of that time about Cornelius Labden.[18] He was a Dutch farmer living in what would become the Greenwich area, with a wife and a sixteen-year-old daughter. One day, the story goes, some Indians pursued him to his house. He ran in the front door and had his wife and daughter hold the bar. He then ran out the back door, jumped on a horse, and fled. When he got to "Laddin's Rock," beside the Asamuck Brook, he rode right over the edge. The story is unclear as to whether he then died. What is often left out is that his wife and daughter were scalped, but Labden is the purported "hero" of the folk tale. It was part of the Dutch-Indian war.

The early English settlers who had come to southwestern Connecticut from New England, starting in 1639, found themselves in an unsettling situation. Some of the natives nearby were friendly and helpful. Others would emerge from the forest ready to kill and burn. No help was forthcoming from New England because support from them was too far away and they were too busy with their own restless natives. In desperation, two famous Greenwich settlers, Elizabeth Winthrop Feake, with her friend and neighbor, Captain Daniel Patrick, wrote to the Governor of New Amsterdam for protection. Their letter said:[19]

> Whereas, we, Capt. Daniel Patrick and Elizabeth Feake, duly authorized by her husband Robert Feake, now sick, have resided two years about five or six miles east of the New Netherlands, subject to the Lords State General, who have protested against us, declaring that the said land lay within their limits, and that they would not allow any person to usurp it against their lawful rights; and whereas, we have equally persisted in our course during these two years, having been well assured that his Majesty the King of England had pretended some to this soil; and whereas we know nothing thereof, and *cannot any longer presume to remain thus, on account both of this strife, the danger consequent thereon, and these treacherous and villainous Indians, of whom we have seen so many sorrowful examples enough.* We therefore betake ourselves under the protection

[18] Spencer P. Mead, *Ye Historie of ye Town of Greenwich* (New York: Knickerbocker Press, 1911), p. 14.

[19] Mead, p. 8.

of the Noble Lord States General, His Highness the Prince
of Orange, and the West India Company, or their Governor
General of New Netherlands, promising for the future to be
faithful to them, as all honest subjects are bound to be,
whereunto we bind ourselves by solemn oath and signature,
provided we be protected against our enemies as much as
possible, and enjoy henceforth the same privileges that all
Patroons of the New Netherlands have obtained agreeably
to the Freedoms.
      1642, IXth of April, in Fort Amsterdam
          DANIEL PATRICK
      Witnesses, - Evaradus Bogardus
          Johannes Winkleman
      [Italics added to show feeling.]

Thus, they agreed with Governor Kieft that Greenwich would
fall under Dutch jurisdiction, and that he would give them
protection from the Wiechquaeskeck uprising. They were the
principal landholders of Greenwich, and since Elizabeth was also
the niece of Governor Winthrop of Massachusetts, they were of
considerable local importance. The people of Stamford remained
under the English, however, but were cooperative with Greenwich,
because they, too, were fearful. They twice allowed Dutch troops,
who had landed on the Greenwich shore, to embark from their town
dock after attacks on nearby natives.
      The next winter, the situation in New Netherland took a turn for
the worse. In February, 1643, a group of Mahican had attacked the
Wiechquaeskeck on the Hudson River. Jameson wrote:

God wrecked vengence on the Witquescheck without our
knowledge through the Mahicanders [*Mahican*] dwelling
below Fort Orange, who slew seventeen men, and made
prisoners of many women and children. The remainder fled
through a deep snow to the Christian houses on and about
the island Manhatens. They were mostly humanely
received being half dead from cold and hunger, they
supported them for fourteen days, even corn was sent to
them by the Director. This opportunity to avenge the
innocent blood [of Claes Smits, killed by a
Wiechquaeskeck] induced some of the Twelve Men to

present to the Director that it was now time...to be allowed to attack those...on the Manhatens and on Pavonia...about eighty Indians were killed and thirty taken prisoners.[20]

This massacre by the Dutch at Pavonia (now Jersey City) has been described by numerous writers. It was a bloodthirsty killing of helpless people.

At about that time, Director Kieft was told that there was a Wiechquaeskeck "fort" in the general area of Stamford and Greenwich, so he sent a force to demolish it.[21] In March, 1643, he dispatched Ensign van Dyke and eighty soldiers on a nighttime expedition to destroy the rumored stronghold. They landed at Patomuck Brook (now Tomac Creek) in Old Greenwich and asked directions from Captain Daniel Patrick, who lived in the area, and spoke Dutch. Patrick was friendly with the local Indians, however, and may have been purposely misleading. He sent the Dutch force, in the middle of the night, across the Mianus River to the Wiechquaeskeck summer village complex of Petaquapen (now Cos Cob). They tore down and burned some Indian-built palisadoes, keeping two intact in case they were counterattacked. They then set upon the few longhouses and wigwams in Petaquapen. They killed about twenty old people, women, and young children who had been staying there for the winter. The rest of the natives had previously gone many miles back in the hills to Nanichiestawack (now Cross River, New York) for the winter hunting, wampum making, training, and festivities.

(The routes of this raid on Petaquapen, and of the larger attack the next year against Nanichiestawack, are shown in Figure 3.)

The Dutch were furious about being misled, and having killed only women and old people. They returned to Stamford, where they argued with Patrick about being fooled. The story is that Patrick spat in the face of one and turned away. He was promptly shot in the back of the head by a Dutch soldier with a pistol.

A day or two later, Mayn Mayanos, a sagamore of Petaquapen, rushed down to Stamford in a frenzied state. (See Figure 1.) He was

[20] Jameson, pp. 228, 275, 277.
[21] Ibid., p. 281.

enraged that the Dutch would kill old people, women, and children. Jameson wrote:[22]

> a bold Indian who alone dared to attack with bow and arrows three Christians armed with guns, one of whom he shot dead—whilst engaged with the other, was killed by the third Christian and his head brought hither. [Fort Amsterdam.]

Figure 1. Mayn Mayanos. Drawing by Bryan K. Buckland from Jameson, pp. 173, 300. Used with permission.

---

[22] Ibid., p. 281

The timing of this story varies. Franklin Jameson, the editor in 1909 of fresh translations of New Netherland documents, puts the date of the abortive raid and the killings by Dutch soldiers of both Daniel Patrick and Mayn Mayanos as 1644.[23] That is unlikely, and the confusion probably arose with the switch from the Julian to the Gregorian calendar. There appears to have been a full year between the Dutch foray at Petaquapen (Cos Cob) and the later. much larger attack at Nanichiestawack (Cross River), which clearly was in 1644.

Other attacks and murders followed, by both the Dutch and by all the tribes in the New Netherland area. Jameson says:

> In this confusion mingled with great terror passed the winter away, the season came for driving out the cattle, this obliged many to desire peace. On the other hand the Indians, seeing also that it was time to plant maize, were not less solicitous for peace, so that after some negotiation, peace was concluded in May Anno 1643…it was generally expected that it would be durable.[24]

But the peace was ephemeral. Soon both the Europeans and the natives were being killed at random, with "Terror increasing all over the land."[25]

The Wiechquaeskeck Go on a Rampage

More native tribes became involved because all the Munsee speakers were interrelated in some way. Eleven Munsee bands, including the Wiechquaeskeck, now fought an open war against the Dutch. Indian war parties attacked isolated colonists. Dutch settlers deplored that the Indians "killed all the men on the farm lands whom they could surprise…they burned all the houses, farms, barns, stacks of grain, and destroyed everything they could come at."[26]

Governor Willem Kieft tried to make peace on Long Island, but soon both the Dutch and the Indians were fighting there again. Kieft had no success in talking, or giving gifts, to the

[23] Ibid., p. 281.
[24] Ibid., p. 278.
[25] Ibid., p. 280.
[26] Otto, p. 186.

Wieschquaeskeck, or to the other Munsee bands. Since he was unsuccessful with this approach, Kieft made up his mind to crush the Native Americans, even though the settlers were helpless in the middle.

The English in New Haven Colony were aware of what was happening only fifty miles to the west. The leaders of New Netherland had asked them to send an auxiliary force of one hundred and fifty men to help in the fight. They turned the request down but they took the warning to heart. A General Court held at New Haven for the Plantations on the 6th of July, 1643 proclaimed:

> It is ordered that every male fro 16 yeares olde to sixty, within this jurisdiction, shall henceforth be furnished of a good gun or muskett, a pound of good pouder 4 fatham of match for a match-lock and 5 or 6 good flints for a fyre lock, and four pound of pistol bullets. Or 24 mullets [rowels, or star wheels] fitted to their guns and so continue furnished from time to time, under the penalty of 10s fine upon every defect in any of the afore-named particulars.[27]

In March, 1643, Roger Williams went to England to get a royal charter for his colony in Rhode Island. He sailed down the coast to take a ship for England out of New Amsterdam. (He had been banished from Boston because of his differences of opinion with the Puritan authorities.) He witnessed dramatic evidence of the warfare being waged between the Dutch and the Indians. He saw the fires of English houses burning near New Amsterdam, and "the Flights and Hurries of Men, Women, and Children."[28]

One of those fires was the house of his friend, Anne Hutchinson, in New Rochelle. She was a religious reformer and a "chirurgist" or surgeon. She had been banished from Boston for preaching unacceptable beliefs. She and her husband had settled on the island of Aquidneck (now Rhode Island), and sometimes worked with the Narrangansetts. When he died, she moved to a farm in New Rochelle in 1642, where she "planted" a substantial settlement, a

---

[27] J. Hammond Trumbull, ed., *The Public Records of the Colony of Connecticut, Prior to Union with New Haven Colony, May 1665* (Hartford: Connecticut Historical Society, 1850), p. 219.
[28] Edwin S. Gaustad, *Liberty of Conscience: Roger Williams in America,* (Grand Rapids: William B. Erdmans Publishing Co., 1991), p. 58.

"plantation." There, she became a traveling doctor and healed both European settlers and Native Americans from The Bronx to Stamford. She would ride with about eight other people and go to towns, farms, and Indian villages, helping everyone.[29]

On August 20, 1643, a party of revengeful young Wiechquaeskeck arrived at the Hutchinson plantation. They were led by a sagamore whose Indian name was Rampage (or Wampage). They killed everyone there except Anne's twelve-year-old granddaughter, whom they took captive. They burned the buildings. Rampage was so proud of this atrocity that he adopted the name "AnneHoeck" or Anne-killer. It is interesting to speculate whether the word "rampage," as in "to go on a rampage," came from this incident. The *Oxford English Dictionary* says that it was first used in 1715 and was of obscure origin. It was thought to be probably Scottish because of the word "ramp," but Rampage's actions were a definition of the word.

Governor Kieft's Military Forces

Willem Kieft had recruited an army of Dutch, English, and other European mercenaries and had them uniformed, armed, and drilled. The natives were unimpressed, since they used guerrilla tactics and refused to meet the Dutch in a pitched battle. While the Dutch preferred open confrontations, where they could deploy their force and use their massed guns, the Indians liked to strike at night in small groups, then melt into the forest. Thus, despite their strong central force, the Dutch colonists continued to suffer attacks that destroyed isolated houses and farms.[30] These occurred as far east as Stamford. The Dutch were hard-pressed to fight back against the widely dispersed Indians.

Kieft was the governor of a colony that was still run by the West India Company. For protection, they did not have regular Dutch army forces, but a militia that the Company had recruited and armed. Some of their soldiers had been regular Dutch army troops who had immigrated to New Netherland. The force was not solely Dutch men, however. There were Germans who were veterans of the Thirty Years' War in Europe. There were also professional soldiers from England, Sweden, Denmark, Scotland, Ireland, and

---

[29] The Hutchinson Parkway is named in her honor.
[30] Otto, p. 191.

Switzerland. The force was thus a motley group of nationalities, but their officers were all experienced and hardened professionals. Their leaders were tough, Dutch-trained officers, and they had Dutch arms. It was a formidable group. They were organized and potent.[31]

Most West India Company soldiers in New Netherland were equipped with matchlock muskets. (See Figure 2.) A few carried the arquebus, or heavy musket, which was awkward and needed a support stand. Other soldiers carried the formidable half-pike for close-in fighting. Officers wore swords, and most soldiers carried some bladed weapon, ranging from a saber to a short sword. They were thus very effective in hand-to-hand combat. Many wore the decorated high-crested steel helmets called "morions." (Those were not unlike nineteenth century European army helmets.)

At that time, the match-lock musket was relatively new. It was so-called because the firing mechanism required lighting a "match" that led to a primed charge in the gun. The match was a cord, or fuse, of gunpowder that was placed over a "pan" on the musket. The fire of the match would go down to the internal gunpowder charge and explode it, propelling out the musket ball. (If the internal charge did not explode, it was just a "flash in the pan.") These were heavy guns loaded with heavy pellets, which did great damage when they hit a target.

The Dutch had revolutionized European military tactics with this Donderbus, or "thunder gun." It was a shotgun with a flared top for pouring in the gunpowder and an iron pellet charge. It was thick and heavy for handling the explosive charge. It was short and not very accurate, but they learned to use it well. It was awkward to clean and re-load, however, so they trained their men in a precise maneuver. The soldiers lined up in three rows. After the first row discharged their deafening volley, they stepped to the rear to clean their musket barrels. The next row, which had been kneeling as they had been priming their muskets, cutting "matches" and putting powder in the flash pans, moved forward for the order to fire. The third row had been pouring a charge of gunpowder and iron pellets down the cleaned muzzle and tamping them into place. They were highly trained to work swiftly.[32]

---

[31] *Encyclopedia of the North American Colonies,* Volume I, ed. Jacob Ernest Cooke (New York: Charles Scribner's Sons, 1993), p. 496.
[32] Cooke, p. 497.

Figure 2. Dutch Foot Soldier. From Samuel Adams Drake, *The Making of New England, 1580-1643* (New York: Charles Scribner's Sons, 1895), p. 37.

The shock effect of the systematic, simultaneous, repeated fire was spectacular. The noise was truly thunder, and the volleys kept coming repeatedly. No one had heard the like of it in the New World. It was no wonder that both the Pequots at Fort Mystik and the Wiechquaeskecks at Nanichiestawack fled or cowered helplessly in their wigwams when the deafening roar came upon them.

In addition, a truly ferocious system had been adapted from European naval experience. Navies had learned that they could take miscellaneous metal pieces, heat them red hot, then tamp them down the barrels of their cannon. When these hot flying pieces hit the rigging of enemy ships, they would cut through ropes, wood, and canvas, and set the ships afire. The Dutch army copied this system, and heated the pellets as hot as they could on a camp fire, and then dropped them into the funnel-ended Donderbus. When these hot pieces embedded in the dry wood of wigwams, they set them afire. At both Mystic and Nanichiestawack, most of the hundreds of native deaths came from being burned alive as they shrank in fear and helplessness from the thundering volleys. In the seventeenth century, the Europeans always won pitched battles against the Indians. The Indians had their best chance in swamps and forests.

At about this time, the awkward matchlock musket was being replaced by the flintlock gun. In the flintlock, all the powder was inside, and the internal flint was hit by a mullet (a steel star-wheel), and the spark set off the charge within the gun. (Evidently the mullet often broke when the charge ignited, and had to be replaced, so many of them were issued to each soldier.) The flintlock needed fewer steps to reload than did the matchlock and, therefore, fewer men for the same firepower.

Kieft's military force was thus formidably armed as it marched against the Wiechquaeskeck. The Natives were overawed and stunned by thunder and iron in a way they could not have expected. The Pequot and Wiechquaeskeck were not proud as they lay helpless in their wigwams during the European attacks, they were shattered. Even today, soldiers throw plastic grenades into enclosed spaces, not to kill the people inside, but to stun them into submission. The effect of large, close, explosive noises is indescribable.

In the winter of 1644, some "veteran soldiers under Pieter Cock" and some "English under Sergeant Major Van der Hyl" (John

Underhill), together under the command of Councillor La Montagne, split and marched to Matsepe (now Newtown), and Heemstede (now Hempstead) on Long Island, "killing about one hundred and twenty men."[33] This was the force that was soon to cross Long Island Sound to attack Nanichiestawack.

The Attack on Nanichiestawack

Captain John Underhill, one of the officers in the Fort Mystik fight against the Pequot, had been called by the English settlers to be the military commander of Stamford, Connecticut, in the spring of 1642. He was living in Boston at that time, with little to do. Because of the Indian fighting in New Netherland, Stamford had been fearful of local native uprisings. The settlers from Wethersfield had just arrived in 1641, and about fifty-nine families had settled there. Some of them remembered the earlier Pequot attacks on their Connecticut River valley farms, so they persuaded Underhill to come to lead their defense. The Town of Stamford gave Underhill a house and a grant of eight acres in October, 1642.[34] He was made a freeman of the Colony, and was to act on the local court, which was auxiliary to the General Court of New Haven. Underhill was well-known, however, so the Dutch approached him. They knew he had been trained in Holland, and they soon persuaded him to work with their forces, instead.

On October 17, 1643, Kieft called a meeting of the Council of New Netherland,[35] which John Underhill attended. It was resolved "to make a hostile attack on Mamarunock, chief of the Wiquaskecks, and his tribe." They were not clear on the organization of the Wiechquaeskeck, but Mamarunock was well-known as a bothersome war-like sakima. (Actually, he was the sakima of a more westerly group of Wiechquaeskeck.)

Governor John Winthrop of Massachusetts heard about the request and wrote in his *Journal* that he regarded an appeal for help to New Haven as "a plot of the Dutch Governor to engage the English in a quarrel with the Indians, which we had wholly

---

[33] Jameson, p. 282.
[34] Stamford Town Records, Meeting Record, October 1642.
[35] Robert Webster Carder, "Captain John Underhill in Connecticut, 1642-1644," *Bulletin of the Underhill Society of America Education and Publishing Fund*, December 1967: 26.

declined, as doubting the justice of the cause."[36]   Winthrop little
realized how terrifying these times were for the Dutch settlers and
traders in New England. They had appealed for help time and time
again to Amsterdam, Holland. In one instance, a "Memorial of the
Eight Men at the Manhattans" was addressed in December, 1643, to
"Noble, High and Mighty Lords, the Noble Lords the States General
of the United Netherland Provinces:

> ...we poor inhabitants of New Netherland were...pursued
> by these wild Heathens and barbarous Savages with fire and
> sword; daily in our houses and fields have they cruelly
> murdered men and women; and with hatchets and
> tomahawks struck little children dead in their parents
> arms...or carried them away into bondage; the houses and
> grain-barracks are burnt with the produce; cattle of all
> descriptions are slain or destroyed...Almost every place is
> abandoned. We, wretched people, must skulk, with wives
> and little ones that still survive, in poverty together, in and
> around the fort at the Manhatas, where we are not safe....
>
> We are...powerless. The enemy meets with scarce any
> resistance. The garrison consists of but 50 @ 60 soldiers
> unprovided with ammunition. Fort Amsterdam, utterly
> defenceless....[37]

Kieft's force was nearly always out in the field. There was fierce
scattered fighting all that winter throughout New Netherland.
Shortly after the above "memorial" was written, a Dutch force
moved from Long Island to southwestern Connecticut:

> Our forces being returned from this expedition [to
> Hempstead, Long Island], Capt. Van de Hil was dispatched
> to Stanford [Capt. Underhill to Stamford], to get some
> information there of the Indians. He reported that the guide
> who had formerly served us, and was supposed to have
> gone astray in the night, [in the attack on Petaquapen] had
> now been in great danger of his life among the Indians, of

---

[36] Carder, p. 27.
[37] John Romeyn Brodhead, *Documents Relative to the Colonial History of the State
of New York, procured in Holland, England, and France*, Volume I, ed. E. B.
O'Callaghan (Albany: Weed, Parsons, and Company, 1856), p. 139.

whom there were about five hundred together. He offered
to lead us there, to shew that the former mischance was not
his fault. One hundred and thirty men were accordingly
despatched under the aforesaid Genl. Van der Hil and
Hendrick van Dyck, ensign. They embarked in three
yachts, and landed at Greenwich [in Tomac Cove] where
they were obliged to pass the night by reason of the great
snow and storm. In the morning they marched northwest up
over stony hills over which some must creep. In the
evening about eight o-clock they came within a league [3
miles] of the Indians, and inasmuch they should have
arrived too early and had to cross two rivers, one of two
hundred feet wide and three deep, and that the men could
not afterward rest in consequence of the cold, it was
determined to remain there until about ten o'clock. The
order was given as to the mode to be observed in attacking
the Indians - they marched forward towards the houses, the
latter being set up in three rows, street fashion, each row
eighty paces long, in a low recess protected by the hills,
affording much shelter from the northwest wind. The moon
was then at the full, and threw a strong light against the
hills. So that many winter days were not brighter than it
then was. On arriving there, the Indians were wide awake,
and on their guard, so that ours determined to charge and
surround the houses, sword in hand. They demeaned
themselves as soldiers and deployed in small bands, so that
we got in a short time one dead and twelve wounded. They
were also as hard pressed that it was impossible for one to
escape. In a brief space of time there were counted one
hundred and eighty dead outside the houses. Presently none
durst come forth, keeping within their houses, discharging
arrows through the holes. The general perceived that
nothing else was to be done, and resolved with Sergeant
Major Van der Hil, to set the huts on fire, whereupon the
Indians tried every means to escape, not succeeding which
they returned back to the flames preferring to perish by the
fire than to die by our hands. What was most wonderful is,
that among this vast collection of men, women and children
not one was heard to cry or scream. According to the report
of the Indians themselves the number then destroyed

exceeded five hundred. Some say, full seven hundred, among whom were also twenty five Wappingers, our God having collected together the greater number of our enemies, to celebrate one of their festivals in their manner, from which escaped no more than eight men in all, and three of them were severely wounded.

The fight ended, several fires were built in consequence of the great cold. The wounded, fifteen in number, among whom was the general, were dressed, and the sentinels being posted the troops bivouacked there for the remainder of the night. On the next day, the party set out very early in good order, so as to arrive in Stantford in the evening. They marched with great courage over that wearisome range of hills, God affording extraordinary strength to the wounded, some of whom were badly hurt, and came in the afternoon to Stantford after a march of two days and one night and little rest. The English received our people in a very friendly manner, affording them every comfort. In two days they reached here [Fort Amsterdam]. A thanksgiving was proclaimed on their arrival.[38]

The route of this attack in diagrammed in Figure 3.

The location of Nanichiestawack has been of interest, and several people have proposed different conclusions over the years. The best analysis and conclusion appears to be that of Colonel Thatcher T. P. Luquer in his article "The Indian Village of 1643."[39] Col. Luquer based his conclusions on his extensive knowledge of the Bedford-Cross River area and on his reading of the above report. He specifically noted the time that the expedition took in their march and the description of the two streams. The only possible river in northern Westchester County with a two-hundred-foot width and three-foot depth was the Croton River. It matched that description before 1906 when it was submerged in Croton Lake by the construction of the Cornell Dam. Luquer had considerable army marching experience and concluded that, at the time of the year when the expedition took place and the weather being unfavorable, an allowance of 1.5 miles per hour would be a reasonable marching

---

[38] Jameson, pp. 282-284.
[39] Col. Thatcher P. Luquer, "The Indian Village of 1643," *The Quarterly Bulletin of the Westchester County Historical Society* 21, no. 2, April-July 1945: 21-24.

rate. Since the march lasted about twelve hours, that would mean a distance of eighteen miles, which is the distance from the Greenwich shore to Cross River.

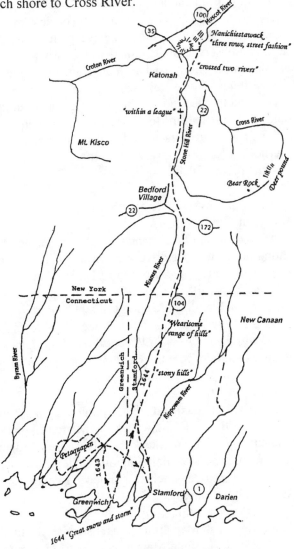

Figure 3. Dutch Attacks on the Wiechquaeskeck. Drawn by the author.
  1643 – van Dyke's attack on Petaquapen (Cos Cob)
  1644 – Underhill's attack on Nanichiestawack (Cross River)

I agree with Luquer that his interpretation of the Dutch report should be accepted as correct. However, Luquer had the line of march as starting from modern Greenwich Harbor. No landing existed there at that time. The landing at Tomac Cove was then called Greenwich. As did Luquer, I have gone along the route, measured it, and observed the landmarks. I went with Chitanikapai (Nicholas Shumatoff, Jr.) who has Indian ancestry, and had long worked in the Pound Ridge Reservation. He had traced the trails, campgrounds, and the deer pound there. He pointed out that if you drive Route 22 from Bedford to Cross River, you can see the two hills mentioned as you cross a bridge just before the Pepsi-Cola building turnoff. Nanichiestawack was on a site that is now under the water to the north of that bridge.

The Conclusion of Governor Kieft's War

Captain John Underhill had delivered what he called "an annihilating blow" to the Wiechquaeskeck. The league of Munsee tribes fighting the Dutch was effectively broken. The word got out to all the Hudson Valley, and a group of Native American leaders recognized that Underhill was the victor. In April, 1644, Indian leaders turned up in Stamford, "asking Captain Underhill to apply to the Governor of New Netherland for Peace."[40] *The Calendar of Historical Manuscripts in the Office of the Secretary of State, Albany*, includes an item from the Council Minutes, dated April 16, 1644:

> ...of the arrival at Stamford of Mamarunock, Wapgaurin, chiefs of the Kichtawanck, Mongochkonnome, Pappenoharrow, of Wiquaskeck and Nochpeem, together with the Wappings, to solicit Captain Underhill to sue in their names for peace, which is granted on condition that they keep quiet in future.

It is interesting that Mamarunock is listed as a chief of the Kitchawanck. He is the same Mamarunock (of Mamaroneck) that was called a Wiechquaeskeck sakima earlier in Kieft's War. Mongochkonnome was also a sakima of the Wiechquaeskeck at that time. He was to be followed in line by Sauwenarack, who signed a

---

[40] Carder, p. 32.

later treaty of peace with the Dutch in 1664. In turn, he was succeeded by Goharis, who signed numerous sales of land covering most of Westchester County from 1681 to 1684. These three sakimas sold much of the land in Westchester. In the 1644 document, the Wiechquaeskeck leaders promised, "now and forever to refrain form doing harm to either people, cattle or houses, or anything else within the territory of New Netherland."

John Underhill presented their appeal to the Dutch Director. Director Willem Kieft then sent emissaries to the key Native American leaders from New Jersey to the upper Hudson, and a treaty was drawn up at Fort Amsterdam. It was a formal treaty of peace, with a return of prisoners. It must have been an impressive sight to those who knew the Indian tribes in the Hudson River area. Several Mohawk ambassadors attended as mediators, including Sisiadego, Claes, Noorman, Oratonin, Auronge, and Sesekemas. The Mohawk were essentially the rulers of the Hudson Valley by that time. They preferred peace with the Dutch to make their fur trade operate smoothly. "John Onderhil" was also present. The signatures on the 1644 treaty document concluded with "Their Sackemakers or Indian Chiefs:"

Oratany, Chief of Achkinskeshaky (*Hackensack*)
Sesemus and William, Chiefs of Tappan and Rechgawanck
Pacham (*Tankiteke*), Rennekeck—left power with others
Those of Onany and their neighbors:
Mayauwetinnemin, for those of Marechkawaick
Nayeck (*Nyack*) and their neighbors; together with
Aepjen, in person, speaking for the
Wappinex, Wickquaeskeckxx, Sintsings, and Kitchawangs.

The signing included "the mark of Aepje," sachem of the Mahikanders (Mahican). Aside from the presence of the Mohawk leaders, Aepje (Aepjen) the Mahican, was the chief leader of all the River Indians in the Hudson Valley, which included all the Wieschquaeskeck.

Aepjen's Indian name was Skiwias (also spelled Eskuyias and Skiwiaen). "Aepjen," meaning "little ape" in Dutch, was a Dutch name of disrespect for him,[41] because he was short and hairy. He was the undisputed leader of the Mahican in what is now the Albany area. His wife's name was Kachkowa. Skiwias spoke for all the tribes of the lower Hudson River Valley.

Despite this important treaty, troubles with the Native Americans continued in New Netherland. There was a major Indian assault on New Amsterdam in September, 1655, called the Peach War. It started when a Dutch settler shot a River Indian woman who was picking peaches in his orchard. Also, from 1659 to 1664, the Esopus War raged further up the Hudson Valley around the present site of Kingston. This war probably drove the Rechgawanck south to The Bronx. One result of the 1645 treaty, however, was the release from captivity of Sauwenaro (Sauwenarack), a Wiechquaeskeck sakima in Westchester County. As noted, he later signed a number of land transfers in Westchester between 1660 and 1666, and the treaty in 1664.

Some Wiechquaeskeck continued to live in Westchester County in the late seventeenth century, but over the years, many transferred their land formally to the settlers. The few that were left in southwestern Connecticut slowly moved out. Their roots had been completely torn up at Nanichiestawack. Some Europeans then increased their sale of liquor to remnant natives in order to get them into debt and then seize their land. This led to many minor incidents, but there were no further serious complaints of fighting.

The big problem for the few remaining Wiechquaeskeck was the rush of new immigrant settlers from Europe looking for land. These land-hungry newcomers exerted great pressure. Finally, every plot of usable farming land in Connecticut was either acquired by a land transfer agreement or simply taken and used because there were no Indians camping on it. The destruction of Nanichiestawack was the beginning of the end for all the Connecticut Wiechquaeskeck.

In July, 1644, heavy Dutch reinforcements arrived at Fort Amsterdam from the West Indies. By then, the expense of the English soldiers was too much for Kieft, so he dismissed Underhill and his English company on July 22. He rewarded Captain Underhill with tracts of land on Manhattan Island, and near the present Bergen Beach and Oyster Bay on Long Island for his

---

[41] Shirley W. Dunn, *The Mohicans and Their Land, 1609-1730* (Fleischmanns: Purple Mountain Press, 1994), p. 311.

services in Kieft's war. Bergen Beach was then part of the town of Flushing. On Long Island, Underhill was an important figure, because he had successfully led the assaults on the Indian villages near Hempstead and at Cross River, New York, and had brought relative peace to the area. For a while he was Sheriff of Flushing, but he clashed with the Dutch when war threatened between them and the English to the north. He and his wife, Helena de Hooch, moved to Southold, Long Island, to get into English territory. He had married Helena years before when he had trained in the Dutch military service in Holland. After England and Holland signed a peace in 1654, and Helena died in 1658, Underhill moved back to Flushing. Elizabeth Winthrop Feake Hallett had moved there from Greenwich, and Elizabeth Hallett's daughter, also Elizabeth, married John Underhill.

Peter Stuyvesant became the Governor of New Netherland in May, 1647, replacing Willem Kieft. Relationships were still poor between the Dutch and the New Englanders, partly because of English settlers pressing closer and closer to New Netherland. Governor Stuyvesant and his counterpart, Governor Theophilus Eaton of Boston, exchanged letters accusing each other of giving liquor to the remnant Indians and of stirring up trouble. The Indians were still restless because they had suffered greatly in Kieft's War, and much hunting land had been taken from them. Stuyvesant had many problems in New Netherland dealing with fractious citizens and with the increasing sale of both liquor and firearms to the Native Americans. He strongly suppressed minor Indian uprisings in 1655, 1658, and 1663. The very few Wiechquaeskeck still left in southwestern Connecticut remained subdued. In the next few generations, most of them signed land transfer agreements, and moved out of their ancestral territory because of the great influx of Scottish and Irish sheep farmers who took over the land.

Willem Kieft sailed for Holland in 1647. His boat was wrecked in a storm off the southwestern coast of England on the way home. All were drowned.

Bibliography

Brodhead, John Romeyn. *Documents Relative to the Colonial History of the State of New York, procured in Holland, England,*

and France. Volume I. Ed. E. B. O'Callaghan, Albany: Weed, Parsons, and Company, 1856.

Buckland, John Alexander. *The First Traders on Wall Street: The Wiechquaeskeck Indians of Southwestern Connecticut in the Seventeenth Century.* Bowie: Heritage Books, Inc., 2002.

The Calendar of Historical Manuscripts in the Office of the Secretary of State, Albany. Council Minutes, April 16, 1644.

Carder, Robert Webster. "Captain John Underhill in Connecticut, 1642-1644." *Bulletin of the Underhill Society of America Education and Publishing Fund* (December 1967): 22-37.

Drake, Samuel Adams. *The Making of New England, 1580-1643.* New York: Charles Scribner's Sons, 1895.

Dunn, Shirley W. *The Mohicans and Their Land, 1609-1730.* Fleischmanns: Purple Mountain Press, 1994.

Encyclopedia of the North American Colonies. Volume I. Ed. Jacob Ernest Cooke, New York: Charles Scribner's Sons, 1993.

The First Three Hundred Years. The History of the First Congregational Church, Greenwich, Connecticut. Ed. Elizabeth W. Clarke, Greenwich: The First Congregational Church of Greenwich, 1967.

Gaustad, Edwin S. *Liberty of Conscience: Roger Williams in America.* Grand Rapids: Wm. B. Eerdmans Publishing Co., 1991.

Greenwich Town Records. Land Records 1, 1640, Part 1.

Luquer, Thatcher P. "The Indian Village of 1643." *The Quarterly Bulletin of the Westchester County Historical Society* 21, no. 2, (April-July, 1945): 21-24.

Mead, Spencer P. *Ye Historie of ye Towne of Greenwich.* New York: Knickerbocker Press, 1911.

Narratives of New Netherland 1609-1664. Ed. J. Franklin Jameson, New York: Charles Scribner's Sons, 1909.

Otto, Paul Andrew. *New Netherland Frontier: Europeans and Native Americans along the Lower Hudson River, 1524-1664.* Bloomington: Ph.D. diss., Indiana University, June 1955.

The Public Records of the Colony of Connecticut, Prior to Union with New Haven Colony, May 1665. Ed. J. Hammond Trumbull, Hartford: Connecticut Historical Society, 1850.

Snow, Dean R. *The Archeology of New England.* New York: Academic Press, 1980.

Stamford Town Records. Meeting Record, October 1642.

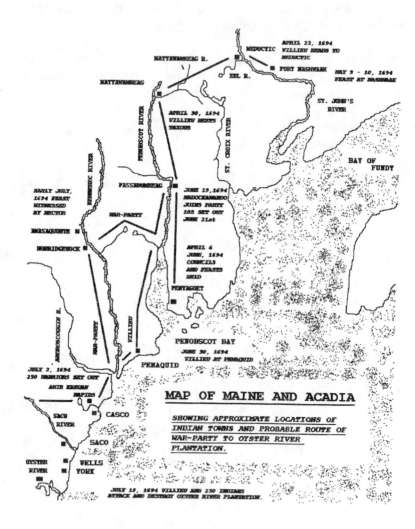

APRIL 23, 1694
VILLIEU HEADS TO
MEDUCTIC

MEDUCTIC

MATTAWAMKEAG R.

EEL R.

FORT NASHWAAK

MAY 9 - 10, 1694
FEAST AT NASHWAAK

MATTAWAMKEAG

ST. JOHN'S
RIVER

PENOBSCOT RIVER

APRIL 30, 1694
VILLIEU MEETS
TAXOUS

ST. CROIX RIVER

BAY OF
FUNDY

KENNEBEC RIVER

EARLY JULY,
1694 FEAST
WITNESSED
BY HECTOR

PASSADUMKEAG

WAR-PARTY

JUNE 19, 1694
MADOCKAWANDO
JOINS PARTY
105 SET OUT
JUNE 21st

AMASAQUANTE

APRIL &
JUNE, 1694
COUNCILS
AND FEASTS
HELD

NORRIDGEWOCK

PENTAGOET

ANDROSCOGGIN R.

WAR-PARTY

VILLIEU

PENOBSCOT BAY

JULY 2, 1694
230 WARRIORS SET OUT

JUNE 30, 1694
VILLIEU AT PEMAQUID

AMIR KEBORN
RAPIDS

PEMAQUID

SACO
RIVER

CASCO

MAP OF MAINE AND ACADIA

SHOWING APPROXIMATE LOCATIONS OF
INDIAN TOWNS AND PROBABLE ROUTE OF
WAR-PARTY TO OYSTER RIVER
PLANTATION.

SACO

OYSTER
RIVER

WELLS
YORK

JULY 18, 1694 VILLIEU AND 230 INDIANS
ATTACK AND DESTROY OYSTER RIVER PLANTATION.

THE GREAT MASSACRE OF 1694:
UNDERSTANDING THE DESTRUCTION OF
OYSTER RIVER PLANTATION[1]

CRAIG J. BROWN

"July 18. The Indians fell suddenly & unexpectedly upon
Oyster River about break of Day. Took 3 Garrisons (being
deserted or not defended) killed & Carried away 94 persons,
& burnt 13 houses- this was the f [i] r [st] act of hostility
Committed by [them] after ye peace Concluded at
Pemmaqd."[2]

Introduction

With these laconic words, the Reverend John Pike recorded in
his diary the devastating events of the morning of July 18, 1694,
when out of the darkness 250 Abenaki warriors descended upon the
sleepy little hamlet of Oyster River Plantation (now Durham and
vicinity).[3] They ravaged both sides of the river, cutting a swath of
destruction some six miles in length. In small detachments of eight
to ten warriors, they swept outward from the falls, killing and
capturing some ninety-four to one hundred people, fully one-third of

---

[1] The original version of this essay, entitled "The Great Massacre of 1694:
Understanding The Destruction of Oyster River Plantation," appeared in the
Fall/Winter 1998 edition of *Historical New Hampshire*, a quarterly publication of
the New Hampshire Historical Society.
[2] Rev. John Pike, *Journal of the Rev. John Pike, of Dover, New Hampshire*, ed.
Rev. A. H. Quint (Cambridge: Press of John Wilson and Son, 1876), p. 16.
[3] The French adopted the Gregorian calendar in 1582; England did not do so until
1752. In 1694, a nine-day difference existed between the French and English
calendars. I have used the English date throughout in keeping with the date
established by Pike.

the population. Half of the settlement was burned to the ground. The attackers destroyed countless crops and killed hundreds of head of livestock, bringing famine and financial ruin to the people who survived.

Tradition has long held that this raid was an accident, some macabre trick of fate. This war party was nothing more than a disgruntled band of outcasts collected from villages along the St. John's, Penobscot, and Kennebec rivers. Led by the French officer Villieu and attended by a Jesuit priest, the party set out intending to strike at or near Boston.[4] Through poor planning, the war party exhausted its supplies before reaching its target. Hunger and fatigue forced them to pitch into the settlement closest at hand. According to the usual story, that settlement just happened to be Oyster River Plantation.

The origin of this tradition can be found within the work of Francis Parkman. In his 1877 volume, *Count Frontenac and New France Under Louis XIV*, Parkman wrote of the decision to attack Oyster River: "Necessity decided them. Their provisions were gone, and Villieu says that he himself was dying from hunger. They therefore resolved to strike at the nearest settlement, that of Oyster River, now Durham, about twelve miles from Portsmouth."[5] In his otherwise meticulous work, Parkman appears to have consulted only a few sources when writing about the attack on Oyster River. Instead he relied heavily upon an account of the expedition written by the Sieur de Villieu, the French officer credited with leading the raid. Villieu, a sixty-year-old career army officer, was ambitious and not above bending the truth to cast himself in a favorable light. His inept participation actually threatened the success of the expedition on more than one occasion.

Before Parkman, historians Jeremy Belknap[6] and Thomas Hutchinson[7] had not viewed the attack as an accident. Both cited

---

[4] Jan K. Herman, a 1966 University of New Hampshire graduate student claimed, "And curiously, the death and destruction visited upon Oyster River had been meant for Boston." Jan K. Herman, "Massacre at Oyster River," *New Hampshire Profiles* October 1976: 50.

[5] Francis Parkman, *Count Frontenac And New France Under Louis XIV*, Volume 2 of *France and England in North America* (Boston: Little, Brown & Co., 1877; reprinted New York: The Library of America, 1983), p. 263.

[6] Jeremy Belknap, *The History Of New Hampshire*, Volume 1, ed. John Farmer (Dover: S. C. Stevens and Ela & Wadleigh, 1831), p. 138.

Cotton Mather who wrote, "the desolation of Oyster River was commonly talk'd in the streets of Quebec two months before it was effected."[8] Not all contemporary historians agreed with Parkman's view of the attack. Everett S. Stackpole[9] went back to Mather in his work. Samuel Adams Drake specifically stated that Oyster River was "singled out for fire and slaughter."[10] However, as Parkman gained in popularity, so too did his view of the attack.

In 1966, University of New Hampshire graduate student Jan K. Herman made news in the town of Durham with his work on the massacre. Quoting heavily from Parkman and Villieu, Herman concluded in his master's thesis: "The attack on Oyster River was an accident, initiated on the spur of the moment by a band of starving Indians with no effective leadership. Poorly planned from the beginning, the expedition never had a chance to reach the outskirts of Boston, throw that region into turmoil and therefore be of lasting strategic importance."[11] In 1976, Herman published an article based on his master's thesis in *New Hampshire Profiles*. Herman is the only modern scholar to have focused on the attack at Oyster River as his primary subject. Concluding as he did, Herman confirmed the theory originally advanced by Parkman, solidifying this as the popular view.

However, the attack on Oyster River was no accident. This raid was a joint military operation, conceived far in advance and launched in response to the Treaty of Pemaquid. Parkman and Herman failed to see the Abenaki as equals, and in doing so, portrayed them as tools or dupes of the French. Their work betrays a lack of understanding of the intricacies of Abenaki politics and the nature of their allegiance to the French. More recent historians have pointed out that, "although the tribes were quite willing to accept

[7] Thomas Hutchinson, *The History of The Colony And Province Of Massachusetts Bay* Volume 2 (Boston: Thomas and Andrews, 1795; reprinted Cambridge: Harvard University Press, 1936), p. 55.
[8] Cotton Mather, *Decennium Luctuosum* (Boston: n.p., 1699); reprinted in Cotton Mather, *Magnalia Christi Americana* (London: n.p., 1702), p. 86.
[9] Everett S. Stackpole, *History of New Hampshire* Volume 1 (New York: The American Historical Society, 1926), p. 182.
[10] Samuel Adams Drake, *The Border Wars of New England Commonly called King William's And Queen Anne's Wars* (----: Charles Scribner's Sons, 1897; reprinted Williamstown: Corner House, 1973), p. 96.
[11] Jan K. Herman, "Massacre On the Northern New England Frontier 1689-1694" (Master's thesis, University of New Hampshire, 1966), p. 43.

military assistance, they did not think of themselves as fighting a French war."[12] The Abenaki regarded themselves as a sovereign power on equal footing with the Europeans, and conducted themselves as such. The Indians were fighting primarily to recover kinsmen taken by the English and to push back English encroachment on their land. Parkman and Herman trusted Villieu and, in doing so, overemphasized French participation in the expedition. "The Abenaki considered the French ineffectual allies and few if any of the war parties were truly French led."[13] Because of the narrow range of sources available to them, Parkman and Herman relied heavily on the word of a single self-promoter. As a result, their view is incomplete and somewhat misleading. Only by examining the Abenaki role in the expedition can we gain a fuller understanding and ascertain the true nature of the Oyster River Massacre.

King William's War and the Treaty of Pemaquid

During 1687 and 1688, a series of seemingly disconnected events plunged the northern colonial frontier into a violent war. In New York, the Iroquois, instigated by the English, attacked French allies among the western Indians, disrupting the valuable fur trade in that region.[14] In response, then Canadian Governor, the Marquis de Denonville, led an expedition against the Senecas, the western most tribe of the Iroquois Confederacy. The invaders ravaged four Seneca towns, destroying a vast quantity of grain.[15]

In marching against the Seneca, Denonville violated the territorial boundaries of the Province of New York. Enraged, New York Governor, Colonel Thomas Dongan, fired off a series of hot-tempered letters to Denonville upbraiding him for his violation of English territory and unjust attack.[16] The English increased their material aid to the Iroquois. In November 1687, the Iroquois were formally adopted as English subjects and further hostilities against

---

[12] Kenneth M. Morrison, *The Embattled Northeast* (Berkeley: University of California Press, 1984), p. 128.
[13] Ibid.
[14] W. J. Eccles, *The Canadian Frontier, 1534-1760* (Toronto: University of Toronto, 1969), p. 117.
[15] William M. Beauchamp, *A History of the New York Iroquois*, Bulletin 78 (Albany: New York State Museum, 1905), p. 233.
[16] Parkman, p. 121.

them, by the French, were forbidden.[17] The Iroquois went on the warpath during the summer of 1688, launching several raids into French territory. In 1689, they sacked the town of La Chine, a mere six or seven miles outside Montreal, killing some two hundred inhabitants and carrying off 120 more.[18] For the French, the west would remain the main theater of operations throughout what became known as King William's War.

In western Maine, the years of 1687 and 1688 brought with them a heightening of tensions between the Abenaki and their English neighbors. Increased settlement, especially near the mouth of the Saco River, triggered a series of conflicts over fishing rights, livestock, and land ownership.[19] The English placed nets across the Saco River, blocking migrating fish, a major Abenaki food source in the spring. English cattle continually damaged the local tribe's unfenced cornfields.[20] The leaders of the Saco Indians approached the English complaining, "that the corn, [the English had] promised by the last treaty, had not been paid, and yet their own was destroyed by the cattle of the English; and that they, being deprived of their hunting and fishing b[e]rths, and their lands, were liable to perish of hunger."[21]

The Abenaki complaints fell on deaf ears. English failure to address these grievances violated a 1685 treaty that established mechanisms for resolving such difficulties.[22] Frustrated in their attempts at diplomacy, the Saco killed the offending cattle during the summer of 1688. In August, a dispute between settlers and Indians at North Yarmouth ended violently with casualties on both sides.[23] Prompted by this Indian uprising, Benjamin Blackman, justice of the peace at Saco, ordered the seizure of twenty Indians that he suspected of causing the unrest. The Abenaki responded in kind, seizing several settlers during a raid on New Dartmouth in September 1688.[24]

---

[17] New York State Museum, p. 233.

[18] Parkman, p. 135.

[19] Jere R. Daniel, *Colonial New Hampshire: A History* (New York: Kto Press, 1981), p. 106.

[20] Morrison, 113.

[21] William D. Williamson, *The History of the State of Maine*, Volume 1 (Hallowell: Glazier, Masters & Co., 1832; reprinted Freeport: Cumberland Press, 1966), p. 606.

[22] Morrison, p. 113.

[23] Williamson, p. 607.

[24] Hutchinson, Volume 1, p. 309.

While the events on the Saco were playing themselves out, Sir Edmund Andros, Governor of the Dominion of New England, sailed the *H.M.S. Rose* into the harbor at the mouth of the Penobscot River. Once anchored, Andros sent his lieutenant ashore at Pentagoet to summon the Baron de St. Castin, a French army officer.[25] He had established his trading post at Pentagoet near the mouth of the Penobscot. He married a daughter of Madockawando, the highly respected principal chief of the Indians living along the Penobscot River.[26] As the son-in-law of Madockawando, St. Castin enjoyed considerable influence among the Indians. The English, not wholly without merit, blamed the current Indian troubles on St. Castin.[27] When the lieutenant returned with word that St. Castin had fled, Andros promptly seized the trading post. All movable goods were conveyed to the *Rose*, leaving behind only the vestments in St. Castin's chapel.[28] Many historians point to this raid as the beginning of King William's War in the colonies.[29]

The Abenaki enjoyed considerable success at the start of the war. In June of 1689, several of the Eastern Indians joined with Kancamangus' Pennacooks in an attack on Cochecho (Dover).[30] That August, the English fort at Pemaquid (Maine), was destroyed.[31] Later that same month, a party of sixty Indians returned to New Hampshire, burning the Huckins garrison at Oyster River.[32]

During the fall of 1689, Louis de Buade, Comte de Frontenac succeeded Denonville as the governor general of New France (Canada). Frontenac, a member of the Court at Versailles and former governor general of New France, possessed experience with the peculiar military situation in the North American colonies.[33] He also brought with him news of the declaration of war in Europe between France and the League of Augsburg, which England

---

[25] Williamson, p. 597.

[26] Belknap, Volume 1, p. 124.

[27] Hutchinson, Volume 1, p. 309.

[28] Williamson, p. 587.

[29] Stackpole, *History Of New Hampshire*, Volume 1, p. 171.

[30] Pike, p. 12.

[31] Williamson, p. 612.

[32] Everett S. Stackpole, Lucien Thompson, and Winthrop S. Meserve, *History of the Town of Durham, New Hampshire* (Concord: Rumford Press, 1913; reprinted Portsmouth: Peter E. Randall Publisher, 1994), p. 87.

[33] W. J. Eccles, *Canada Under Louis XIV, 1663-1701* (London: Oxford University Press, 1964), pp. 77-78.

recently had joined.[34] With the French and English now in direct confrontation on both sides of the Atlantic, Frontenac sponsored joint parties of French and Indians sent against the English frontier settlements. In 1690, three of these war parties descended in spectacular fashion on the settlements of Schenectady (New York), Salmon Falls (Rollinsford, N.H.- South Berwick, Maine), and Casco (Maine).[35] After 1690, the war settled down into a pattern of retaliation and counter retaliation that inflicted much suffering on frontier communities but contributed little toward a meaningful victory for either side.[36]

In 1692, the fortunes of war began to turn against the Abenaki. A series of reverses undermined Abenaki confidence and heightened feelings of war-weariness. On the ninth of June, a combined force of five hundred French and Indians suffered a humiliating defeat at Wells (Maine), where English militia captain, James Converse, with only fifteen men in his immediate command, resisted every assault during a two-day siege.[37] There is little doubt that the Abenaki saw this defeat as a sign of misfortunes to come. The Chevalier de Villebon, who as governor of Acadia was subordinate to Frontenac, wrote of the Wells debacle as a "bad augury," explaining that, "it has, so far, been impossible to overcome the superstition that, if they receive such a reverse when they set out on the warpath, they must stop at once, no matter how large the party may be, or how insignificant the action."[38]

---

[34] The League of Augsburg consisted of Holland, Austria, Sweden, several German states, England, and Spain. England entered the league upon the ascension to the throne of William of Orange. King William's War is the name given to the North American portion of this conflict, known in Europe as the War of the League of Augsburg (1689-1697). King William's War was the first of the so-called French and Indian wars. Robert E. Lerner, Standish Meacham, and Edward McNull Burns, *Western Civilizations*, Volume 2, 12th ed. (New York: W. W. Norton, 1993), pp. 590, 591.

[35] Several accounts have been written about Frontenac's three war parties of 1690. See Parkman, pp. 154-172; Belknap, Volume 1, pp. 132, 133.

[36] Douglas E. Leach, *The Northern Colonial Frontier, 1607-1763* (New York: Holt, Rinehart & Winston, 1966), p. 112.

[37] Edward E. Bourne, *The History of Wells and Kennebunk* (Portland: B. Thurston & Co., 1875; reprinted Bowie: Heritage Books, n.d.), pp. 212-216.

[38] Joseph Robineau de Villebon, "Journal of Villebon," 3 October 1692 in *Acadia At The End Of The 17th Century, Letters, Journals And Memoirs Of Joseph Robineau de Villebon*, ed. John Clarence Webster (St. John: The New Brunswick Museum, 1934), p. 42.

To make matters worse, in August 1692, the English built a new fort at Pemaquid. Replacing the one destroyed in 1689, the new fort boasted stone walls rather than wooden palisades. Christened Fort William Henry, the new fort mounted fourteen to eighteen cannon, making it considerably stronger than its predecessor. A company of sixty men was detailed to permanently garrison the post.[39]

In order to divert the enemy's attention away from the construction of Fort William Henry, Massachusetts Major Benjamin Church led a military expedition up the Penobscot and Kennebec Rivers. At Penobscot, he encountered a large body of Indians, but failed to engage them in battle. While the main body eluded him, Church managed to take five prisoners and destroyed a quantity of corn and furs before returning to Pemaquid. After depositing his prisoners, Church proceeded up the Kennebec to the Abenaki fort at Teconnet. Forewarned of Church's approach, the Indians set fire to their fort and retreated into the woods. When the expedition arrived, they found only a couple of corn cribs that managed to avoid being consumed by the fire. Church set fire to the corn cribs and withdrew back down the Kennebec.[40] While this expedition failed to accomplish anything of real value, it served to demonstrate that the English were unafraid to conduct offensive operations into the Abenaki heartland.

The Abenaki soon discovered Fort William Henry despite the precautions taken to conceal its construction. With their French allies, they made plans for its immediate destruction. The ships of war, *Poli* and *Envieux*, were to besiege the fort from the sea, while Villebon and a large body of Indians attacked from land.[41] As the warriors positioned themselves for an attack, the French ships entered the harbor opposite the fort. However, upon seeing the fort, and the English warship at anchor nearby, they promptly withdrew without firing a shot.[42] For the Abenaki, this withdrawal was clear proof of French cowardice. The tribes disbursed for their fall hunting, disgusted with the refusal to attack.[43]

---

[39] Williamson, p. 636.
[40] Ibid.
[41] "Journal of Villebon," 21 Sept. 1692, in Webster, p. 43; Hutchinson, Volume 2, p. 52.
[42] Williamson, p. 688.
[43] Morrison, p. 127.

The spring of 1693 brought more unwelcome news. Captain James Converse, made legendary by his defense of Wells, was promoted to major. Given command of a strong militia force, he patrolled the coast from the Piscataqua to Pemaquid. Converse detached a portion of his men to construct another stone fort at Saco. Perched on the west bank of the river, the fort occupied prime hunting ground and blocked Abenaki access to the sea.[44]

The reverses of 1692 and 1693 eroded the Abenaki willingness to continue the war. During the summer of 1693, a group of ten to thirteen sachems, led by Madockawando, began to explore the possibility of peace. The humiliating failures at Wells and Pemaquid exposed the ineffectiveness of the French military alliance.[45] The Abenaki "found themselves deceived [in the] expectation of receiving assistance from the French."[46] The cost of the war and lack of French support crippled the Abenaki economy. Continual activities of the war parties interrupted traditional patterns of food gathering and fur production.

Late in July, Madockawando and his peace envoy approached the commander at Fort William Henry. Lamenting, "the distress they have been reduced unto," they expressed "their desires to be at peace with the English."[47] The chiefs sought to reopen trade with the English, Boston being their nearest and best market. The English traded at rates that were much more advantageous than what the French would agree to. The sachems hoped that with improved relations they would be able to recover kinsmen captured by the English since the outbreak of King William's War. The two parties entered into council and, by August 11, reached an agreement. As proof of their fidelity, the sagamores gave four of their number into Governor Phips' custody to be used as hostages.[48]

The Treaty of Pemaquid was an incredibly one-sided document, reflecting English pretensions of innocence. The English either ignored or failed to see how their own actions contributed to the

---

[44] Hutchinson, Volume 2, p. 51.

[45] Morrison, p. 127.

[46] Gov. Phips to Gov. Fletcher, 24 August 1693, Massachusetts Historical Society, File XXX, p. 342, Boston.

[47] Ibid.

[48] "The Submission and Agreement of the Eastern Indians, 11 August 1693," in *Documents and Records Relating to the Province of New Hampshire*, Volume 2, ed. Nathaniel Bouton (Manchester: John B. Clarke, 1868), p. 112.

opening hostilities at Saco in 1687 and 1688. The treaty made the Abenaki the sole aggressors stating, "whereas a bloody war has for some years now past been made and carried on by the Indians."[49] The English wrongly attributed the war to the "instigation and influences of the French."[50]

The English assumed that the thirteen signers of the treaty represented all the Indians "from the Merrimack River unto the most easterly bounds of said Province [Maine which was then part of Massachusetts]."[51] This belief reflected a profound lack of understanding of Indian politics and social structure. While each tribe had a principal chief, there were several minor chiefs at the head of each village group. Abenaki politics relied on the "vagaries of social consensus."[52] Those chiefs who had not signed the treaty would not necessarily feel themselves bound by it. Not understanding this subtlety, the English assumed that the Indian peace envoy's promises to "forbear all acts of hostility" and to "abandon the French interest," applied to all the Indians.[53]

The treaty imposed humiliating conditions on the Abenaki, who conceded perhaps more than they realized. The very trade they were so desirous of now came under the strict control of the Governor and General Assembly of Massachusetts. They gave up their very freedom, "herby submitting ourselves to be ruled and governed by their Majesties' laws."[54] In doing so, their only recourse in the event of a dispute lay in the English courts, which allowed the Indians no representation. In all likelihood, the Abenaki resented the treaty's terms. Even the notoriously pro-French historian, Charleviox concluded that, "these Indians often beheld themselves abandoned by the French, who counted a little too much on their attachment, and the influence of those who had gained their confidence."[55] Yet the Abenaki could not bear the cost of fighting the war alone.

For the English, the Treaty of Pemaquid was a masterstroke. The frontier settlements had suffered severely since the commencement

---

[49] Ibid.
[50] Ibid.
[51] Ibid.
[52] Morrison, p. 130.
[53] Bouton, p. 111.
[54] Ibid, pp. 111-112.
[55] Rev. P. F. X. de Charlevoix, *History And General Description Of New France*, Volume 4, trans. John Gilmary Shea, (New York: Francis P. Harper, 1900), p. 255.

of the war. Settlers confined to garrisons could not harvest crops. Food shortages were common. Commerce and trade were at a standstill. But now, with the eastern tribes under control, New England was free to garner all her forces for a second attempt on Quebec.[56] Flushed with success, Phips sent runners to the frontier settlements to proclaim the peace. To a war-weary region this was welcome news indeed. As fall gave way to winter, and no new outbreaks occurred, the settlers began to leave the garrisons, returning to their homes.

News of the treaty stunned the French command. From his base of operations at Fort Nashwaak on the St. John's River, Villebon understood full well the implications of this treaty.[57] Except for a few regulars and Canadian militia, the Abenaki warriors constituted his entire military force. Their neutrality, or worse yet, their allegiance to the English, put all of Acadia in a very vulnerable position. Villebon moved immediately to counter the effects of the treaty. On September 6, 1693, he dispatched Manidoubtik, a St. John's sachem, to see the Penobscot sachem, Taxous, on his behalf. As Madockawando's principal rival, Taxous refused to take part in the peace talks and opposed any accommodation with the English. Manidoubtik was to implore Taxous to raise a faction to end the peace pact.[58]

On September 11, Father Louis-Pierre Thury, Jesuit missionary and the orchestrator of a 1692 raid on York (Maine), arrived at Fort Nashwaak. In this man of God, the English encountered their most dangerous enemy. Thury had established himself at Pentagoet in 1687 at the invitation of St. Castin. Thury regarded the English as heretics and accompanied the Indians on many of their raids. He had lately been at Quebec, but left for the St. John's River as soon as news of the treaty became known. Thury reported to Villebon and the two agreed on a plan of action. Two days later, Thury departed for Pentagoet with the intention of fostering disapproval of Madockawando's treaty.[59]

---

[56] The first attempt in 1690 had failed miserably. In 1694, Phips was set for another attempt, but failed when sickness decimated the fleet sent to take part in the attack.

[57] Fort Nashwaak was on the St. John's River in what is now New Brunswick, Canada. At that time, it was the principal base of operations for the Governor of Acadia, Joseph Robineau de Villebon. Also referred to as St. John's and Naxoat.

[58] "Journal of Villebon," 15 September 1693, in Webster, p. 53.

[59] "Journal of Villebon," 20 September 1693, in Webster, p. 53.

A few days after Thury's departure, Villebon received a welcome guest. Madockawando's son arrived from Quebec on his way back from France where he had been a guest at the court of King Louis XIV. Villebon wrote of the meeting, "I made known to him his father's behaviour, and said that, having been made so welcome in France, it was his duty to induce his father to change his mind and that as soon as he arrived at his village, he should gather together a force of his own."[60] This the son promised to do, but concern for his hostage kinsmen would override his word.

News of the treaty came as a blow to Governor Frontenac. His entire eastern flank had evaporated. He had concentrated his efforts against the Iroquois in the west, relying on the Abenaki to hold Acadia. Without their presence on the frontier, Quebec was vulnerable to invasion from New England. Frontenac knew that it was the Abenaki raids that prevented Massachusetts from organizing a second major assault on Quebec. With no Indians to contend with, Acadia was likely to fall, paving the way for a thrust at Quebec.

Frontenac realized that the only way to regain his lost allies was to strengthen French influence in Acadia. He also knew that the best way to accomplish this was to strike a decisive blow against a good-sized target in the heart of the English frontier settlements. The raid needed to be well planned, well led, and sure of success. Frontenac set his plan in motion in October of 1693. On orders from the King, he removed Rene Robineau de Portneuf, Villebon's brother and French leader in the failed attack on Wells in 1692, on charges of illegal fur trading and debauchery. In his place, Frontenac installed the Sieur de Villieu, giving him orders to raise a war party and attack the English settlements.

Sebastian de Villieu was a career soldier, having entered the French army in 1648 at the age of fifteen. Villieu fought well against the Iroquois in 1666 and was granted a tract of land on the St. Lawrence River. Despite having done little to develop his grant, Villieu sought loftier appointments. In 1690, he had command of a company of volunteers and acquitted himself favorably during Phips' siege of Quebec. However, Villieu possessed little real experience in dealing with the problems of a frontier command. He

---

[60] "Journal of Villebon," 26 September 1693, in Webster, p. 53.

was used to the harsh discipline and regimentation of the regular army. Except for the 1666 campaign, Villieu spent little time away from the European settlements. At the age of sixty, he was completely unprepared for the undisciplined rigors of frontier life.[61]

Then again, Villieu was something of an opportunist. Once out of Frontenac's sight, Villieu sought to better his position in life. Neglecting his duties to Fort Nashwaak, he began a profitable business at the expense of the soldiers he was supposed to be commanding. He began appropriating supplies intended for his men to use in illegal trade with the Indians.[62] Frontenac later commended Villieu for his efforts; at the same time, however, he summoned him to answer charges related to this trading.[63]

Desiring nothing less than the governorship of Acadia,[64] Villieu took advantage of every opportunity to discredit his commanding officer, Villebon. Villieu detested having to answer to a man twenty-two years his junior. He acted with insubordination and disregard for Villebon's authority. It was clear upon Villieu's arrival at Fort Nashwaak in November 1693 that he had no intention of carrying out his orders with regard to the treaty.[65] Villieu's arrival on the fifteenth coincided with the loss of a shipment of provisions intended for Villebon's winter use.[66] This contributed to the overall supply shortage, rendering many of the troops at the fort unfit for duty. This shortage of supplies remained a source of contention between the two men.

Villebon, for his part, did little to ease tensions. Angered over his brother's dismissal, he was largely unimpressed with his new captain's credentials. With regard to illegal fur trading, Villebon was as guilty as Villieu. Several complaints filed with the Colonial Minister accused Villebon of using his position as governor in order to monopolize the Acadian fur trade.[67] Villieu's activities were a threat to this monopoly, contributing to the continual friction between the two men. However, the real threat to Villebon's fur

[61] Webster, pp. 200-202.
[62] "Journal of Villebon," 19 May 1694, in Webster, p. 55.
[63] Webster, p. 201.
[64] Ibid, p. 202.
[65] Ibid, p. 201.
[66] "Journal of Villebon," 25 November 1693, in Webster, p. 54.
[67] Eccles, *Canada Under Louis XIV*, p. 194.

empire came from the treaty itself. In this instance, Villebon's and France's interests were one and the same.

As Villieu settled into his new quarters, two Indians arrived bearing a message from Madockawando's rival, Taxous, who was livid over the signing of the treaty. He accepted Villebon's invitation to a meeting at Nashwaak, adding that he was already making preparations for a war party of considerable size. However, with winter fast approaching, the Indians had already gone to their favorite hunting grounds. Any war party would have to wait until spring.[68] There was nothing left to do except pass an anxious winter.

Expedition to Oyster River

The spring of 1694 brought an urgent renewal of the French and Indian plan to organize a war party. By early April, in answer to Villebon's summons, Indians began to gather at Pentagoet.[69] From Fort Nashwaak, Villebon set his plan in motion. On the sixteenth, he dispatched a Recollect friar to Meductic, a village a short distance up the St. John's River from Nashwaak. Villebon instructed the priest to tell the Indians, "that they were all to hold themselves in readiness, one party to go with me to await the vessels at the mouth of the river, and the other to join the force which was being collected at Pentagoet."[70]

The next step for Villebon was to bring in Villieu and get him to carry out his orders. With Thury's arrival on April 20, he found a ready and able ally. Villieu, in his account of the expedition, makes no mention of a meeting with Villebon and Thury, preferring instead to highlight his own patriotic zeal.[71] In a marginal note next to Villieu's log entry, Villebon remembers the episode quite differently: "This has made it necessary to inform the Government that the Sr. de Villieu, from the time of his arrival at Fort Nashwaak, had so little idea of joining the Indians on the war-path that the Sr. de Villebon was obliged to send for him and say, in the presence of M. de Thury, missionary, to whom he should have referred, that, as the Indians were ready to form a large war party, he had summoned him to find out if he were willing to go with them. He replied, thereupon, that he would do whatever he desired, and made his

---

[68] "Journal of Villebon," 24 November 1693, in Webster, p. 54.

[69] Villieu Account, Villebon Margin Note, 25 May 1694, in Webster, p. 59.

[70] "Journal of Villebon," 25 April 1694, in Webster, p. 55.

[71] Villieu Account, Nov. 1693, in Webster, p. 57.

preparations for departure."[72] The presence of Thury appears to have shamed Villieu into the performance of his duty.

Villebon, intending for Villieu to act as France's representative, ordered him to Pentagoet. Villieu was to "assure the Indians of the King's protection and of the danger in which they placed themselves by negotiation with the English, who, under the guise of friendship and extensive trade, would not fail to betray them as they had done in the past."[73] On April 23, a canoe carrying Villieu, Thury, and their supplies departed Fort Nashwaak for Meductic.[74] This first leg of their journey took only a couple of days. Situated on the west bank of the St. John's River, Meductic marked the start of the main east-west portage. From there, it was a short march to the Eel River and eventually on to Pentagoet.

Villieu and Thury received a cordial welcome upon putting in to shore. The Recollet friar sent by Villebon the week before had done his job well. The Indians of the village were held in readiness just as Villebon requested. Villieu reported the circumstances of their arrival in a light that was a little more favorable to him. In his account, Villieu wrote that it was he who had asked the Meductic Indians, "to go on the war-path with the Pentagoet Indians, informing them that he had been sent from France to lead them against the English."[75] Villieu further reported that the Indians could not decide what to do, "deferring their answer until the following day."[76] During this second council, the Indians pledged themselves to him, saying, "that they were ready to join him and would not leave him until many heads were broken."[77] To reward the Indians' fidelity, Villieu gave them a feast.

In light of the fact that the Recollect friar sent by Villebon had been at Meductic for over a week, it can be said that Villieu's recollections were somewhat colored. Villebon enjoyed considerable influence among the St. John's River Indians and noted the regularity with which they responded to his requests. In a marginal note to Villieu's log entry, Villebon called Villieu's

---

[72] Villieu Account, Villebon Margin Note, Nov. 1693, in Webster, p. 57.

[73] "Journal of Villebon," 29 April-5 May 1694, in Webster, p. 55.

[74] Villieu Account, Nov. 1693, in Webster, p. 57; "Journal of Villebon," 29 April-5 May 1694, in Webster, p. 55.

[75] Villieu Account, 3 May 1694, in Webster, p. 59.

[76] Ibid.

[77] Villieu Account, 4 May 1694, in Webster, p. 58.

statement concerning the Indians' indecision an outright lie, saying that, "Nothing could be more false."[78] Villebon further states that Villieu's comments are, "imaginary, since they were already pledged to the Indians of Pentagoet."[79] Villebon later wrote that "where he erred was in telling the Indians, that they were to follow him."[80]

Villieu and Thury left Meductic on April 26, heading west toward Mattawamkeag.[81] Arriving at the village on the thirtieth, the pair was pleased to find that Taxous, in response to Villebon's invitation the previous fall, was heading east along the same route. Taxous had lately come from Pentagoet where a mighty gathering of Indians had already taken place. Father Bigot, a colleague of Thury's with a mission on the Kennebec River, had come hither with the leading sachems of the Kennebec tribe. Together with Taxous, they determined a plan of action and selected a target. Villebon wrote of this council: "The determination of the Indians to make war on the English was so strong that, before the arrival of the Srs. de Villieu and Thury, Father Bigot had been to Pentagoet with the leading chiefs of the Kennebecs, who had held council with the chiefs of Pentagoet and even considered the place to be attacked."[82]

Villebon's description of the council at Pentagoet reveals two important facts. First, from the start, the Indians were acting independently and not under the direction of Villieu. Although Villieu accompanied them and provided input, he did not lead them. Secondly, the Indians, themselves, discussed where exactly to attack. Villebon's account is consistent with, and helps explain, Cotton Mather's statement: "'Tis affirmed by English captives which were then at Canada that the desolation of Oyster River was commonly talk'd in the streets of Quebec two months before it was effected."[83] Since missionaries were in contact with their superiors in Quebec, it is likely that Bigot sent word of the council's decision to them. Taxous, when meeting Villieu, was on his way to report this progress to Villebon.

In his description of this council, Villebon exposes another Villieu half-truth. Villieu reports that he prevailed upon Taxous to

---

[78] Villieu Account, Villebon Margin Note, 3 May-4 May 1694, in Webster, p. 58.
[79] Ibid.
[80] Villieu Account, Villebon Margin Note, 11 May 1694, in Webster, p. 59.
[81] Villieu Account, 5 May 1694, in Webster, p. 58.
[82] Villieu Account, Villebon Margin Note, 5 May 1694, in Webster, p. 59.
[83] Mather, p. 86.

accompany him to Passadumkeag, the main village of the Penobscots. This Taxous agreed to do and together they arrived in the early morning hours of May 2. At a feast held that evening, Villieu addressed the warriors. He urged them to follow him, "assuring them they would not fail to strike an important blow and by it acquire reputation, as well as plunder."[84] The warriors indicated that they were ready, but needed to receive their presents before they could set out. Presents usually consisted of war material, such as powder, shot, and guns. Villieu agreed and invited them to return to Fort Nashwaak.

When the warriors arrived at Nashwaak on May 13, it was clear that Villebon was surprised to see them. Villebon assumed that Villieu had followed his orders by going to Pentagoet to join the Indians gathering there. It would have been more expedient to send a runner to Villebon requesting the shipment of supplies to Pentagoet. Villebon was unaware that Villieu had only traveled as far as Passadumkeag. Upon speaking with the Indians, Villebon learned that Villieu had spent much of his time trading for furs. It was evident to Villebon that "the pretext of accompanying the Indians [back to Nashwaak] was merely to safeguard the trading operations which he, in a manner unbecoming to an officer, carried on at Pentagoet."[85] Villebon recorded that Villieu "returned from Pentagoet to bring back five bales of beaver skins and other pelts which he had obtained by trading."[86] The Indians themselves stated that Villieu had more, but they, "abandoned some of his pelts beyond the portage."[87]

Nevertheless, a special feast was put on at Nashwaak to honor the chiefs of the war party. At some point, a second feast was given for the young men to incite them to war. During these feasts, Villebon ceremonially adopted Taxous as his brother. Villebon stated that, "This was done, partly to place him under the obligation to take special care of the Sr. de Villieu and not to abandon him during the campaign."[88] To honor Taxous further, Villebon presented him with the best lace suit he could find. Villebon knew that the Indians "hold a single officer of small account among a

---

[84] Villieu Account, 11 May 1694, in Webster, p. 59.
[85] Villieu Account, Villebon Margin Note, 16 May 1694, in Webster, p. 59.
[86] "Journal of Villebon," 26 May 1694, in Webster, p. 56.
[87] Villieu Account, Villebon Margin Note, 16 May 1694, in Webster, p. 59.
[88] Villieu Account, Villebon Margin Note, 22 May 1694, in Webster, p. 60.

large number of warriors, especially when he has no knowledge of the neighbourhood or of the enemy's country."[89] It would not do to have France's representative lost during the expedition. This point appears to have been wasted on Villieu. Villieu overestimated his importance to the expedition, believing himself to be in control.

As the feasting drew to a close, Villebon passed out the presents Villieu had promised. Upon taking his leave of Villebon, Taxous assured him that, "although he was going to gather together a large war-party, he would not stop there but would make up another immediately after the first and induce Madockawando to join him, or render him contemptible to all the young Indians."[90] With two targets in mind, the war party left Nashwaak on May 16. After a brief stopover at Meductic, they continued on to Pentagoet, arriving there on May 25. Here, the Indians divided their presents and discovered that they "had received only a portion" of what they had expected.[91] Villebon's breach of protocol proved a serious insult to the Indians. Villieu reported that "they murmured loudly," and that this "almost destroyed their goodwill."[92]

While Villieu did his best to mollify the unrest caused by Villebon's indiscretion, Madockawando arrived with news that threatened to put an end to the expedition. Instead of attending the Pentagoet council in April, Madockawando and Edgermett, a principal Kennebec chief, had traveled to Pemaquid for a meeting with Governor Phips. On May 27, they returned, bringing the news that the English would deliver up their prisoners in one month's time.[93] With a major objective of the war about to be achieved, enthusiasm for the expedition diminished. To further cement good relations, the English offered to send a priest to teach the Indian children to read and write. Until this point, Thury had remained relatively quiet. He may have even derived amusement from Villieu's vain and amateurish attempts at leading this Indian war party. Now, upon hearing of the English minister, Thury "took vigorous measures to assure the success of the Sr. de Villieu's plans."[94]

[89] Villieu Account, Villebon Margin Note, 11 May 1694, in Webster, p. 59.
[90] Journal of Villebon, 22 May 1694, in Webster, p. 55.
[91] Villieu Account, 25 May 1694, in Webster, p. 60.
[92] Ibid.
[93] Ibid, p. 61.
[94] Ibid.

The pair's urgent pleas failed to move the members of the war party. Things remained at a stalemate until the thirtieth of May. As Villieu prepared to return home, however, he came upon an Indian who had accompanied Madockawando to Pemaquid. In return for the tobacco and drink Villieu provided, this Indian disclosed certain aspects of the meeting not revealed earlier. It seems that the unidentified Indian had accompanied Madockawando and Edgermett aboard an English frigate at anchor in the harbor. On the ship, they were met by Sir William Phips with whom they dined. As the men feasted and drank, Madockawando agreed to sell large tracts of tribal land. Then, to seal the agreement, the two chiefs, together with Phips, threw a hatchet into the sea. In this manner, the hatchet was buried where no descendant could recover it.[95]

In this news lay the salvation of the expedition. Villieu went immediately to Thury and told him the Indian's story. As soon as a letter from Father Bigot had arrived confirming the land sale, Thury informed Taxous. Taxous had long been jealous of the prestige that Madockawando commanded. According to Villieu, Thury's attempt to capitalize on Taxous' jealousy "had a wonderful effect."[96] Selling tribal lands to the enemy without consulting the other chiefs was an unthinkable insult. Enraged, Taxous decried Madockawando and his treaty. The young warriors again caught the fire of war. Preparations began at once to return to Passadumkeag. From there the warriors would set out on the warpath.

On June 7, the party left Pentagoet and began traveling up the Penobscot. While shooting a rapid on the ninth, Villieu's canoe capsized. Villieu flayed about in the cold rushing water until he managed to reach the overturned canoe. Clinging desperately, he was able to hang on until he slammed his head against a rock. Dazed, Villieu let go and was dashed against rocks as he was swept downstream. Unconscious, Villieu was eventually fished out of the river and carried the rest of the way to Passadumkeag.

By the time they reached the Penobscot village, Villieu had been overcome by a fever, which incapacitated him until the fourteenth.[97] During this time, Thury continued to advocate the persecution of Madockawando. Since the incident at Pentagoet, Madockawando

[95] Villieu Account, 8 June 1694, in Webster, p. 62.
[96] Ibid.
[97] Villieu Account, 18 June 1694, in Webster, p. 63.

and his clan had been subjected to every manner of taunt and insult. Still, Madockawando stubbornly refused to break the peace. On June 18, the first of two councils was held to determine a target. Disregarding the decision made by the Indians at the Pentagoet council in April, Villieu promoted his own choice. When he did not receive the answer he sought, Villieu concluded the council in disagreement. The following day, a second council was held, which concluded in the same manner as the first.[98]

Following this second council, a grand feast was held. There was dancing and singing, with the Indians' favorite dish of roast dog as the main entree. It was during this celebration that Madockawando's resolve would waver and break. He and his family had become the target of cruel jeers and hurled meat bones. Added to this was the constant pressure exerted by Thury, reinforced by years of religious indoctrination.[99] Bowing to the pressure, Madockawando acquiesced and joined the war party. In deference to Madockawando's wishes, the departure of the war party was postponed for one day. On June 21, 1694, they set out on the last leg of the journey to Oyster River.[100]

The thirtieth of June found the war party approaching the area around Pemaquid. While the main body continued on toward the Kennebec River, Villieu and three Indians made their way to Fort William Henry. Villieu disguised himself as an Indian and procured a bundle of furs. The four then entered the fort presumably to trade. While his compatriots bartered with the officers, Villieu made a careful inspection of the works, and in his own words, "made a most satisfactory plan."[101] When finished, he quietly slipped back into the woods to await the others. After a time, Villieu began to get impatient. He fired a pistol in an attempt to recall the tardy trio. The English officers, suspecting treachery, seized the three Indians. Somehow, the captives managed to convince the fort's commandant of their innocence. "On leaving the fort they went to find the Sr. de

---

[98] Villieu Account, 27 June 1694, in Webster, p. 63.
[99] One of the standard stories used by the Jesuits, in teaching religion to the Indians, was that the Virgin Mary was a French lady. Her son, Jesus, was murdered by Englishmen. After his death, he ascended into heaven and all who wanted to earn his favor must avenge his murder. Howard H. Peckham, *The Colonial Wars, 1689-1762* (Chicago: The University of Chicago Press, 1964), p. 48.
[100] Villieu Account, 27 June-30 June 1694, in Webster, p. 63.
[101] Villieu Account, 9 July 1694, in Webster, p. 63.

Villieu, upon whom one of them fell, giving him a very severe beating."[102] While the information that Villieu obtained proved valuable in a later campaign, it is unclear whether or not he wished to attack the fort at this time. What is clear is that the Indians had no desire to do so and the beating administered to Villieu left little doubt as to who was leading the war party.

While Villieu scouted the fort at Pemaquid, the main body of Indians entered the Kennebec River and traveled downstream toward its mouth. At the Kennebec village of Amasaquonte, a short distance above Norridgewock, several of the Kennebec chiefs and warriors prepared to join the war party. Hezekiah Miles, known to the English as Hector, was a friendly Indian in the employ of the Massachusetts militia. Hector had been captured in the 1691 raid on Berwick (Maine) and was being held at Amasaquonte at the time of this gathering. In a 1695 deposition, Hector described what transpired: "two or three days before they intended to set out they kild and boyled several dogs and held a Feast, where was present Egermet, Bomaseen (Bomazeen), Warumbee, Ahasombomet, with divers other of the chief among them. They discoursed of falling upon Oyster River and Groton, and Bomaseen was to command one of the companies."[103]

Bomazeen, a young, minor chief of the Kennebecs, played a significant role in the formation of the war party and in the attack itself. Bomazeen had signed the Treaty of Pemaquid in 1693. Acting as an emissary of goodwill, he had traveled to Boston several times during the winter of 1693/1694. In late November, Bomazeen was thrown in prison by the order of the Lt. Governor of Massachusetts. He was eventually released in mid-December, but was committed twice more in January and March.[104] Angered by this treatment, Bomazeen became a major proponent of an attack on the English. During the feast at Amasaquonte, the young chief was honored by being given command of a contingent of warriors for the coming attack.

Understanding the importance of the dog feast in Abenaki preparations for war is critical in understanding how Oyster River

---

[102] Villieu Account, Villebon Margin Note, 9 July 1694, in Webster, p. 63.

[103] Deposition of Hezekiah Miles, 31 May 1695, Massachusetts Historical Society, file VIII, p. 39, Boston.

[104] Report of Caleb Ray, Keeper of his Majesty's Prison in Boston, 4 Aug. 1693-1 Mar. 1694/5, Massachusetts Historical Society, File XL, p. 313, Boston.

was selected to be the war party's initial target. John Gyles, a six-year-old English boy when captured by the Abenaki in the 1689 attack on Pemaquid, spent many years among the Indians of the St. John's River and was actually being held at Meductic in 1694. His memoir written in 1736 describes the dog feast in great detail:

"When the Indians determine for war or are entering upon a particular expedition, they kill a number of their dogs, burn off the hair, and cut them into pieces, leaving only the dog's head whole. The rest of the flesh they boil and make a fine feast of it, after which the dog's head that was left whole is scorched till the nose and lips have shrunk from the teeth and left them grinning. This done, they fasten it on a stick, and the Indian who is proposed to be chief in the expedition takes the head into his hand and sings a warlike song, in which he mentions the town they design to attack and the principal man in it, threatening that in a few days he will carry that man's scalp in his hand in the same manner. When the chief hath sung, he places the dog's head as to grin at him whom he supposeth will go his second, who, if he accepts, takes the head in his hand and sings, but if he refuse to go he turns the teeth to another, and thus from one to another till they have enlisted their company."[105]

The importance of this dog feast cannot be overstated. This is how the Abenaki prepared for war, gathered their warriors, and chose the target. It is clear from the testimony of Hector and Gyles that the target selected was Oyster River Plantation. Villieu and the older chiefs among the Penobscots may have not agreed with this choice, but as the Kennebecs provided the largest contingent of warriors, and were more familiar with the territory in question, custom dictated that the honor of leading the attack belonged to them.

A few days after the feast, Bomazeen and forty warriors set out from Amasaquonte to rendezvous with the main body of the war party. The remaining Kennebec warriors were to travel by different

---

[105] John Gyles, "Memoirs Of Odd Adventures, Strange Deliverances, Etc.." *Puritans Among The Indians: Accounts Of Captivity and Redemption, 1676-1724,* eds. Alden T. Vaughn and Edward W. Clark (Cambridge: Harvard University Press, 1981), p. 120.

routes and join them farther on.[106] On July 1, the Kennebecs connected with the war party at a village near the Amir Kangan Rapids, on the Presumpscot River. Villieu and his three companions, fresh from their scouting trip to Pemaquid, arrived at the same time as the Kennebecs.[107] The following morning, they were joined by thirty more warriors from Narakomigo, a village on the Androscoggin River. By early afternoon they were ready to set out. Over the next five days, the war party traveled in a general westerly direction, skirting the English fort on the Saco and avoiding Major Converse's militia force.

On July 7, the war party met the remaining forty Kennebecs while crossing a lake. That night, the chiefs held the first in a series of councils. Villieu misrepresents the content of these councils by repeatedly saying that nothing was decided. Actually a struggle over the leadership of the war party was underway. A faction of young warriors, Kennebecs under Bomazeen for the most part, were in favor of keeping with the targets already established. This younger faction had become frustrated with the older leaders. The young chiefs and warriors saw this attack as a means to garner war honors and take revenge upon the English. The older chiefs, Madockawando in particular, had lost much prestige in the eyes of this younger group. They had little or no use for Villieu, who was under the care of Taxous. In spite of the wishes of the elders, the march resumed. Three days later, a second council was convened with the same result. Villieu reported that, "some wanted to strike above Boston, others below it."[108] The matter was decided the following morning. Villieu wrote that, "the following day the elders gave way to the young men, and, their idea having prevailed, they took command of the expedition."[109] There would be no further debate; the fate of Oyster River was sealed.

On July 13, the war party crossed over into New Hampshire in the vicinity of Lake Winnipesaukee.[110] Some within the band began

---

[106] Villieu Account, 10 July 1694, in Webster, pp. 63, 64.
[107] Ibid.
[108] Villieu Account, 11 July 1694, in Webster, p. 64. This is in effect what happened. Oyster River, which is above Boston, was attacked on July 18th. Groton, which is very near Boston, was attacked on July 27th.
[109] Ibid.
[110] Lake Winnepesaukee was a point along the main east-west trail into the area of what is now Portland, Maine. The trail led to the Merrimack River, the main north-

to complain of a lack of food, threatening to turn back if the plans were not changed. These threats seem to have come primarily from the older members of the party, Villieu chief among them. Villieu blamed the lack of supplies on Villebon, saying, "he had no supplies, the Sr. de Villebon refusing to give him any."[111] Villebon had, in fact, given Villieu, "a canoe and such supplies as he required."[112] Villieu failed to procure his own supplies, as was the custom, preferring to take from supplies allotted to the garrison. Villebon, calling attention to a "special budget," showed where Villieu had been "granted extras."[113] Apparently, Villieu had used most of his supplies while conducting his illegal fur trading. To cover that fact, Villieu attempted to shift the blame to Villebon. That evening, another council was held, during which, in spite of the complaints, "it was resolved to advance."[114]

The following day, the war party made its way down the Winnipesaukee River, and into the Merrimack. Leaving their canoes at Pennacook,[115] the war party was joined by a few warriors from the tribes around Boston.[116] Now numbering between 230 and 250 warriors, they struck out on the trail heading east. On the morning of the fifteenth, a scouting party of ten warriors was dispatched in the direction of Oyster River. The war party followed along in their wake, covering a distance of twelve miles. They were now no more than fifteen miles from the outskirts of Oyster River Plantation.

After a nine-mile march during the morning of the sixteenth, the war party was met by two of the scouts. They reported that the way to the settlement was open. The inhabitants suspected nothing and had set no patrols or watches. The remaining scouts had pushed on, trying to infiltrate the settlement itself. These spies were ultimately successful, bringing back a very detailed layout of the town.

---

south route into the Massachusetts interior. This route had long been used by war parties raiding settlements in central Massachusetts. The war party used this route to avoid the militia under Major Converse and to utilize the water route into Groton, Massachusetts, via the Merrimack and Nashua Rivers. Ann Jenkins testified that the war party left their canoes at Pennacook.

[111] Villieu Account, 25 May 1694, in Webster, p. 60.

[112] Villieu Account, Villebon Margin Note, 3 May 1694, in Webster, p. 58.

[113] Villieu Account, Villebon Margin Note, 25 May 1694, in Webster, p. 60.

[114] Villieu Account, 22 July 1694, in Webster, p. 64.

[115] Deposition of Ann Jenkins, 11 June 1695, Massachusetts Historical Society, File VIII, p. 40, Boston.

[116] Thury to Villebon, 2 Aug. 1694, in Webster, pp. 56, 57.

Survivors later reported that on the night before the attack, "knocks were heard by night at certain doors, and stones were thrown at garrisons, to find out whether the houses and garrisons were defended and whether any watch were kept."[117]

On the seventeenth, the war party struck the upper portion of Oyster River. Moving downstream, they approached the outskirts of Oyster River Plantation from the west. When the party was within three miles of the falls, they halted to await the remaining scouts. By three o'clock in the afternoon, all the scouts had returned and a plan of attack was formed. As soon as it was nightfall, they would begin moving into position. Once they had reached the falls, the war party was to divide into two divisions. The first division, under Bomazeen, would cross the river to the south shore. Once there, they would separate into bands of eight to ten warriors and position themselves around each garrison. Paquaharet, another minor chief of the Kennebecs, was to take the second division and do the same on the north bank. Madockawando and Taxous, along with Villieu and their people, were to attack the outlying farms to the north of the main settlement (now in Madbury). At dawn, a single musket shot was to be the signal to begin the simultaneous attack. No one was to be spared; they were all to be killed without regard to age or gender. Every building was to be burned. No crops or livestock were to be left standing. After they finished, the war party would reunite at the falls and move together on the final garrison (Woodman). From there, they would head west back to their canoes.[118]

It was a solid plan, designed to achieve massive destruction by preventing a unified defense. The Indians knew from experience that, at the first shot, those in the unfortified homes would try to escape to the garrisons. Having already surrounded the garrisons, the Indians would be waiting to intercept the fleeing villagers. It would then be a simple matter to sweep through the settlement, burning the homes and destroying whatever was left.

As soon as the sun had set and the moon was up, the war party began moving into position. Reaching the falls, they broke up, using stonewalls, boulders, and outbuildings to conceal their movements. The English settlers went to bed, never suspecting that the enemy was in their midst.

---

[117] Stackpole, *History of New Hampshire*, Volume 1, p. 183.
[118] Villieu Account, 26 July 1694, in Webster, pp. 64, 65.

A little after two o'clock on the morning of Wednesday, July 18, 1694, John Dean, a mill worker in the employ of Nathaniel Hill, was preparing to leave his home near the falls. He was on his way to Portsmouth on an errand and wanted to get an early start. Dean kissed his wife and daughter goodbye and quietly slipped out the front door. As he walked down the path, thinking of the day's work, he failed to notice the dark forms huddled in the bushes. John Dean probably never heard the shot that killed him.[119]

The Attack on Oyster River

The sound of the shot echoed all along the river, prematurely signaling the start of the attack. The parties close to the falls were in position, but those whose targets were further down river had yet to reach them. This provided an opportunity for some settlers to escape or prepare for defense. The units not yet in position hastened toward their targets, pitching into whatever they came across. The carefully constructed plan quickly degenerated into wholesale slaughter.

The attack on the south bank of the Oyster River was pressed with brutal ferocity. The family of Stephen and Ann Jenkins tried to escape the carnage by fleeing into their cornfield. In a June 1695 deposition, Mrs. Jenkins described what happened: "In the morning about the dawning of the day my husband being up went out of the dore, and presently returning cried to me and our children to run for our lives, for the Indians had beset the town: whereupon my husband and myself fled with our children into our cornfield, & at our entrance into the field, Bomazeen, whome I have seen since I came out of captivity in the prison, came towards us and about ten Indians more: & the sd Bomazeen then shot at my husband and

Durham Town Landing (following page)
Situated just below the present Oyster River Falls, the Durham Town Landing marks the general vicinity of Nathaniel Hill's mill. The shooting of John Dean near this spot triggered fighting up and down both sides of Oyster River. The white house on the south bank once belonged to the Revolutionary War General, John Sullivan, who is buried in the family plot behind the home. Photo taken by the author.

---

[119] Belknap, Volume 1, p. 138.

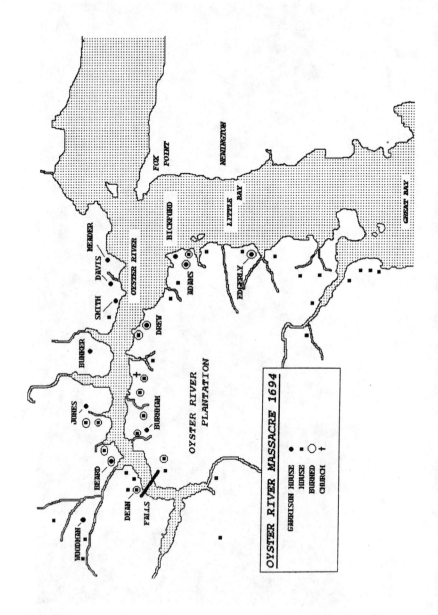

OYSTER RIVER MASSACRE 1694

GARRISON HOUSE ●
HOUSE ■
BURNED ○
CHURCH †

shote him down, ran to him & struck him three blows on the head with a hatchet, scalped him & run him three times with a bayonet. I also saw the said Bomazeen knock one of my children on the head & tooke of[f] her scalp & then put the child into her father's armes; and then stabbed the breast. And Bomazeen also then killed my husband's grandmother and scalped her."[120] Bomazeen took Ann and her remaining children captive. Binding them securely, he moved on to the next home.

The Drew garrison was the next to be struck. Francis Drew, the patriarch, made a dash for the Adams garrison to seek help, but was easily captured. He was bound and dragged back to within sight of his home, which he then surrendered on the promise of quarter. The promise of quarter was not upheld. Francis Drew was summarily tomahawked as his family was taken captive. Francis' wife was later abandoned by her captors and left to die in the woods. Nine-year-old Benjamin Drew was forced to run a gauntlet of Indians as a moving target for their tomahawks. Struck repeatedly, he could run no more.[121] Thomas Drew and his wife, Tamsen, were also taken prisoner. In 1698, Tamsen testified to her experience: "They heard a great Tumult and Noise of firing of Guns which awakened her out of her sleep, and she understanding that the Indians were in arms & had encompassed the House, willing to make her escape, she endeavored & att last got out the window and fled, but the Indians firing fast after her she returned to the House and her father in law [Francis Drew] took [her] by the hand and haled her into the House again, where upon she endeavored to get out at another window, but the Indians had besett that, so she returned to the other room where her friends were, and the window of that Room being open an Indian named Bombazine [Bomazeen] caught hold of her Arm and pulled her out att the Window & threw her violently upon the ground, she being then with child."[122] Tamsen's captors killed the child a short time after birth. However, after some four years of captivity, Tamsen was reunited with her husband.

Beyond the Drew garrison, near the mouth of the river, stood the garrison of Charles Adams. A party of warriors had just finished moving into position when they heard the shot that killed John

---

[120] Deposition of Ann Jenkins.
[121] Stackpole, Thompson, and Meserve, *Durham*, pp. 93, 94.
[122] Deposition of Damson (Tamsen) Drew, 23 May 1698, Massachusetts Historical Society, file VIII, p. 41, Boston.

Dean. They gained entry to the house undetected. In an instant, the warriors set upon the sleeping family. Within minutes, Charles Adams and fourteen members of his household had been tomahawked in their beds. The only survivor was a daughter named Mercy. Her captors carried her to Canada, where she remained for the rest of her life.[123]

Thomas Bickford's garrison was just a few hundred yards from the Adams home. Awakened by the sounds of battle, Bickford quickly saw what was happening to the Adams family. Gathering his family together, he led them down to the shoreline, where he saw them safely off by boat to join other refugees gathering across the bay at Fox Point. Determined not to let the Indians have their way, Bickford returned to his home and made preparations to defend it, alone. As daylight came, Thomas could see his attackers as they advanced. An English-speaking warrior, taking cover behind a stonewall, demanded that Thomas surrender. The Indian promised safety if Thomas accepted, or death by torture if he declined. In as many voices as he could fabricate, Bickford shouted insults back in defiance. As the shooting commenced, Thomas ran from window to window changing his clothes at each one. By appearing in different outfits, snapping off shots, and shouting orders to an invisible army, Bickford made the impression that a well armed garrison was held up in there with him. Losing heart, his attackers withdrew and left him in peace.[124]

The people living on the north side of the river fared a little better then their fellow settlers on the south bank. The Beard garrison, near where Beard's Creek empties into the Oyster River, was attacked at the opening shot. Indians had killed the original owner, William Beard, in 1676 during King Philip's War. His son-in-law, Edward Leathers, lived in the house, along with the rest of the family. At the first shot, Edward was able to barricade the front door. With the rest of the family in tow, he slipped out the back before the entire Indian squad could attack. In their attempt to reach the safety of the Jones garrison, the family members were pursued

---

[123] Stackpole, Thompson, and Meserve, *Durham*, p. 94.
[124] Mather, p. 86.

and cut down in flight. Edward and his son William were the only ones who made it into the garrison.[125]

Charles Adams Grave Marker

Grave marker placed by the Northam Colonists in 1971 to memorialize the burial place of the Adams family and others who died in and around the Adams' Garrison on that fateful morning of July 18, 1694. Photo taken by the author.

---

[125] Mary P. Thompson, *Landmarks In Ancient Dover, New Hampshire* (Dover: Dover Historical Society, 1892; reprinted Durham: Durham Historic Assoc., 1965), p. 178.

Bickford Garrison Marker
    Marker at the corner of Durham Point Road and Langley Road. Placed there by descendants of Thomas Bickford to commemorate Bickford's heroic, single-handed defense of his garrison during the attack on July 18, 1694. Photo taken by the author.

    The Jones garrison occupied a good defensive position along the west side of Jones Creek. Sometime after midnight, Jones was awakened by the sound of his dog barking. Believing wolves were after his hogs, he went out to secure them. Finding nothing amiss, he returned to the house, taking care to make sure that everything was locked up. During the whole time, Jones was under the watchful eyes of Indian warriors hiding in the bushes. The signal had not yet been given, so they left him unmolested. A little while later, still feeling that something was not right, Jones again got out of bed. He climbed up into the flankart and sat on the wall. After a few minutes, he heard the shot at the falls. Turning in that direction, he caught sight of the flash of a musket close at hand. Instinctively, Jones fell back into the flankart just as the musket ball struck the perch he had been sitting on. Since he had previously secured the house, the Indians were prevented from entering. Jones roused the rest of the household and mounted a desperate defense. After a few hours of hard fighting the Indians withdrew without inflicting any casualties on those in the garrison.[126]

Downriver from the Jones garrison stood the Bunker, Smith, and Davis garrisons. The distances between these garrisons were much greater than the distances between the homes on the south side. The warriors sent to attack these homes had much further to travel to get into position. The families inhabiting these garrisons were able to prepare and repelled several spirited assaults. All three garrisons were successfully defended with no loss of life.[127]

Bunker Garrison (following page)

In 1694, roads on the north side of the Oyster generally led away from the river and toward Cochecho (present day Dover, NH), leaving the down river garrisons fairly isolated. Abenaki war parties on the north bank had farther to travel and many were not in position at the time John Dean was killed. Even so, the Bunker Garrison came under attack several times throughout the day. It was successfully defended without loss of life. Although neglected, the garrison stood into the early 1900s when it finally collapsed and had to be dismantled. Many of the timbers still bore the scars of the July 18, 1694 attack. Photo from the author's collection.

---

[126] Belknap, Volume 1, p. 140.
[127] Stackpole, Thompson, and Meserve, *Durham*, p. 100.

On a neck of land on the shore of Little Bay, directly opposite Fox Point, stood the garrison house of John Meader. The Meader family could see the flames from the burning houses steadily advancing in their direction. Taking stock of the situation, they found that they did not posses enough powder or shot to mount a successful defense. Locking the house up as best they could, the Meader family boarded a boat and crossed over to Fox Point. Many accounts tell of them stepping out of the boat and turning around to see their home go up in flames.[128] This is doubtful because soldiers impressed at Hampton were quartered in Meader's garrison in the days following the attack.[129]

At the prearranged time, the smaller parties disengaged and reunited at the Falls. Once everyone was together, they proceeded to move en masse upon the Woodman garrison. The garrison stood in a truly formidable position, occupying a hill nearly surrounded by creeks and ravines. The warriors found Captain Woodman well prepared to meet them. To give the impression that a strong company of militia defended the garrison, Woodman set a bunch of hats on sticks. The sticks were then positioned in such a manner as to look like soldiers. The Indians fired on these fake soldiers doing little damage to the garrison.[130]

Seeing that any further attempts would be futile, the Indians decided that they were satisfied with the day's work. It seems that Villieu's only real contribution to the attack was to apprise his companions of the possible danger that they would be in if they stayed much longer. Villieu was leery of being surprised by a pursuing militia force bent on revenge. Thury conducted a brief mass, asking God to reward his charges for their valiant efforts. The war party then withdrew to a nearby hill where they could safely sleep until the next day.[131] The following morning, they departed for the return trip to Pennacook, leaving a ruined settlement in their wake.[132] The people of Oyster River Plantation were left to mourn their losses and bury their dead.

---

[128] Ibid.

[129] "Captain Woodman's Return for Subsistence of Soldiers at Oyster River, 1694," *Miscellaneous Provincial Papers From 1629 to 1725*, Volume 7, ed. Isaac Hammond (Manchester: John B. Clarke, 1889), p. 645.

[130] Belknap, Volume 1, p. 140.

[131] Villieu Account, 26 July 1694, in Webster, pp. 64, 65.

[132] Deposition of Ann Jenkins.

Woodman Garrison, *circa* 1890.

   Captain Jonathan Woodman was the commanding office of the Oyster River militia. A such, the Abenaki singled Woodman's Garrison out for a dramatic final assault by the entire war party.   As fighting raged throughout the settlement, Woodman prepared his defenses. he deceived his attackers with "dummy" defender, hats and coats mounted on sticks. Content with their plunder, and believing Woodman too strong to storm, the Abenaki withdrew after firing on the garrison. The garrison was lived in until 1896 when it was destroyed by fire. Afterwards, residents reported finding charred timbers with musket balls imbedded in them. Photo from the author's collection.

Aftermath and Conclusion

   Villieu, the man who complained that he was dying of hunger on the eve of the Oyster River raid, did not accompany the war party as it moved against Groton (Massachusetts).[133] Nor did he return to Fort Nashwaak. Upon questioning the captives taken at Oyster

---

[133] Villieu Account, 23 July 1694, in Webster, p. 64.

River, Villieu learned of a projected attack on Quebec. Using this as a pretext to report directly to Frontenac, Villieu bypassed Villebon and proceeded straight to Quebec. He arrived there on August 22 to find that Frontenac was in Montreal. Without delay, Villieu left Quebec, arriving at Montreal four days later.[134] Villieu told Frontenac his version of the raid, which was later to form the basis of his official report.

The Abenaki were greatly insulted by Villieu's behavior. As was their custom, they dispatched several messengers to Frontenac to "give utterance to the death cries of the enemy."[135] Although they left at about the same time, Villieu quickly out-distanced the messengers in his drive to reach Frontenac first. This was a major insult to the Abenaki, particularly the Kennebecs, who rightfully felt that the honor belonged to them.

When Frontenac questioned the Abenaki about Villieu's conduct while with the war party, they replied "that although they had been together in the enemy's country, they had never been united in action."[136] From the beginning, the Abenaki had a plan of action, a plan that Villieu did not agree with. Most likely, the numerous councils to which Villieu refers were his attempts at promoting a target of his choosing. Villieu may have favored an attack on Pemaquid, accounting for his scouting mission to that post. When the Indians failed to adopt his plan, Villieu reported that nothing had been decided. Eventually, Villieu gave up and the Indians' plan prevailed.

Despite the attack not being executed to perfection, the raid was considered a great success. In August, Villebon confided in his journal that "the blow struck was important, because it will put an end to the negotiations which have been going on, and leave no chance for their renewal."[137] The loss of Abenaki allegiance reflected by the Treaty of Pemaquid had placed the French in a very dire military position. The French knew that a successful attack was the best way to maintain their fragile alliance with the Abenaki. The success of the attack on Oyster River accomplished this very important strategic objective. Herman contradicted his own conclusion in this regard, "But looking at the events as the French

---

[134] Villieu Account, 30 July 1694, in Webster, pp. 65, 66.
[135] Villieu Account, Villebon Margin Note, 30 July 1694, in Webster, p. 66.
[136] Ibid.
[137] "Journal of Villebon," 9 Aug. 1694, in Webster, p. 56.

did from their vantage point, the operation at Oyster River was a success."[138]

For the Abenaki, the events surrounding the Oyster River Massacre brought a political crisis. The signing of the Treaty of Pemaquid had threatened traditional tribal methods of reaching consensus.[139] In signing the treaty, the thirteen sagamores, whether knowingly or not, appeared to speak for all of the Eastern Indians. This insulted the chiefs who had not signed the treaty, and in some cases provoked considerable ire. A successful raid was necessary in order to protect their sovereignty. Madockawando's self-interest, in his sale of tribal land, seriously undermined the prestige of the older sachems, particularly those among the Penobscot.[140] This allowed the younger chiefs among the Kennebecs, like Bomazeen, to come to power. Their plan, discussed in April at Pentagoet and finalized during the dog feast at Amasaquonte, was carried out at Oyster River in July.

For the English, the attack on Oyster River was devastating. Several letters written after the attack attest to the turmoil it created. Militia Captain Thomas Packer wrote from Portsmouth on the day of the attack: "Just now arrived a post from Oyster River. The Indians have destroyed the place killed & burned all they could. Nere [a one] have Escaped and are too badly wounded doe not know but they be all over our frontiers."[141] New Hampshire Lieutenant Governor John Usher wrote to Governor Phips: "we fear Severall other or Towns in the province are besett."[142] Writing directly of Oyster River, Usher reported, "judge the whole place is cutt off."[143] In Massachusetts, a delegation on its way to New York for a council with the Iroquois was called back. William Stoughton, of the Massachusetts Council, advised Governor Fletcher of New York: "the present circumstances of this Province by the fresh breaking out of the Indians & are such as cannot admit of any souldiers to be

---

[138] Herman, Master's thesis, p. 43.

[139] Morrison, p. 131.

[140] Ibid., pp. 131, 132.

[141] Capt. Thomas Packer to Lt. Gov. John Usher, 18 July 1694, in Bouton, p. 128.

[142] Usher to Phips, 18 July 1694, in Bouton, p. 128.

[143] Ibid.

lent from home, the Province of New Hampshire lying at this time bleeding."[144]

Nowhere was the turmoil greater than at Oyster River. The pre-dawn attack caught the settlers of the plantation unprepared. Just two days earlier, Captain John Woodman had assembled the people of the settlement, notifying them of the Treaty of Pemaquid.[145] As a result, the people had returned to their homes and disbanded the night watch. By the time the attackers withdrew, forty-five people lay dead with another forty-nine taken captive.[146] Half of the dwellings lay in charred ruins. The attackers butchered most of the livestock and burned many crops. Many of the wounded were evacuated to Portsmouth. Several of the survivors removed to Massachusetts.[147]

In 1982, historian Neal Salisbury wrote of Parkman's works, "aside from a romantic style which some readers still—a century later—find entertaining, their chief value is in orienting the beginner chronologically and geographically. As a colonial history and, particularly, as Indian ethnohistory, they are unreliable."[148] Parkman lived during the time before the discipline of modern Native American ethnohistory came into being. As a result, he fell prey to the common prejudice of the era and did not see the Abenaki as equals. Parkman wrote about the Oyster River Massacre as part of a much larger work. Consequently, he consulted a narrow range of sources, relying heavily on the word of Villieu. In doing so, Parkman may have discounted the numerous accounts that proved incompatible with Villieu's report. The actions of Villieu following the attack on Oyster River were not those of a man dying of hunger. Nor were the younger warriors and chiefs dissuaded from following through with their original plan by Villieu's hunger plea.

Native American ethnohistory had yet to become popular when Herman wrote his thesis. Although Herman had access to a much larger range of sources, he and Parkman labored under similar

---

[144] William Stoughton to Gov. Fletcher, 23 July 1694, Massachusetts Historical Society, file II, p. 221, Boston.

[145] Villieu Account, 30 July 1694, in Webster, p. 65.

[146] W. Sears Nickerson, "How The Smiths Came to Cape Cod," *Orleans, Massachusetts Cape Codder*, October 1960, unpaginated.

[147] Ibid.

[148] Neal Salisbury, *The Indians Of New England: A Critical Bibliography* (Bloomington: Indiana University Press, 1982), p. 16.

limitations. Herman also failed to see that the Abenaki operated on their own initiative. He overlooked the connection between Mather's statement concerning the attack being talked of in Quebec two months before it happened with the council held at Pentagoet in April. This attack was clearly not, "initiated on the spur of the moment."[149] Herman did not recognize Hector's deposition concerning the dog feast at Amasaquonte as confirmation of the Abenaki attack plan. Even when consulting the writings of Mather, Villebon, Thury, and Hector, Herman continually defers to Parkman and Villieu. He relied on Villieu's report without taking into account the record concerning his character. Villieu did not lead the war party, although he wanted Frontenac to believe so. Even today historians often point to Parkman as the definitive authority of the colonial time period. Herman may have been reluctant to reach a conclusion that ran contrary to Parkman's opinion.

The people of Oyster River Plantation were not sacrificed on the altar of fate. Their deaths reflected the accomplishment of a very real strategic objective. When the Abenaki are accepted as a sovereign people a more accurate picture of the Oyster River Massacre emerges. The Abenaki went to war in order to protect their land and their way of life. The signing of the Treaty of Pemaquid, by a small group of disaffected chiefs, demanded action from both the French and the Native Americans. The attack on Oyster River was the successful culmination of their joint action. By carefully analyzing the primary sources, within the framework established by modern ethnohistory, we gain a fuller understanding of the Oyster River Massacre. The true story is no less compelling than the legend.

Bibliography

Beauchamp, William M. *A History of The New York Iroquois.* Bulletin 78 (Albany: New York State Museum, 1905).

Belknap, Jeremy. *The History of New Hampshire.* Volume 1. Ed. John Farmer, Dover: S. C. Stevens and Ela & Wadleigh, 1831.

---

[149] Herman, Master's thesis, 43.

Bourne, Edward E. *The History of Wells and Kennebunk*. Portland: B. Thurston & Co., 1875; reprinted Bowie: Heritage Books, n.d.

Bouton, Nathaniel, ed. *Documents and Records Relating to the Province of New Hampshire*. Volume 2. Manchester: John B. Clarke, 1868.

Daniel, Jere R. *Colonial New Hampshire: A History*. New York: Kto Press, 1981.

de Charlevoix, P. F. X. *History And General Description Of New France*. Volume 4. Trans. John Gilmary Shea, New York: Francis P. Harper, 1900.

de Villebon, Joseph Robineau. *Acadia at the End of the 17th Century, Letters, Journals And Memoirs of Joseph Robineau de Villebon*. Ed. John Clarence Webster, St. John: The New Brunswick Museum, 1934.

Drake, Samuel Adams. *The Border Wars of New England Commonly called King William's And Queen Anne's Wars*. ----: Charles Scribner's Sons, 1897; reprinted Williamstown: Corner House, 1973.

Eccles, W. J. *Canada Under Louis XIV, 1663-1701*. London: Oxford University Press, 1964.

Eccles, W. J. *The Canadian Frontier, 1534-1760*. Toronto: University of Toronto, 1969.

Herman, Jan K. "Massacre at Oyster River." *New Hampshire Profiles* (October 1976): 50-52.

Herman, Jan K. "Massacre On the Northern New England Frontier 1689-1694." Master's thesis, University of New Hampshire, 1966.

Hutchinson, Thomas. *The History Of The Colony And Province Of Massachusetts Bay*. Volume 2. Boston: Thomas and Andrews, 1795; reprinted Cambridge: Harvard University Press, 1936.

144   The Great Massacre

Leach, Douglas E. *The Northern Colonial Frontier, 1607-1763.* New York: Holt, Rinehart & Winston, 1966.

Lerner, Robert E., Standish Meacham, and Edward McNull Burns. *Western Civilizations*, 12th ed. Volume 2. New York: W. W. Norton, 1993.

Massachusetts Historical Society
    File II
    File VIII
    File XXX
    File XL

Miscellaneous Provincial Papers From 1629 to 1725. Volume 7. Ed. Isaac Hammond, Manchester: John B. Clarke, 1889.

Morrison, Kenneth M. *The Embattled Northeast.* Berkeley: University of California Press, 1984.

Nickerson, W. Sears. "How The Smiths Came to Cape Cod." *Orleans, Massachusetts Cape Codder.* (October 1960): unpaginated.

Parkman, Francis. *Count Frontenac And New France Under Louis XIV,* Volume 2 of *France and England in North America.* Boston: Little, Brown & Co., 1877; reprinted New York: The Library of America, 1983.

Peckham, Howard H. *The Colonial Wars, 1689-1762.* Chicago: The University of Chicago Press, 1964.

Pike, John. *Journal of the Rev. John Pike, of Dover, New Hampshire.* Ed. A. H. Quint. Cambridge: Press of John Wilson and Son, 1876.

Salisbury, Neal. *The Indians Of New England: A Critical Bibliography.* Bloomington: Indiana University Press, 1982.

Stackpole, Everett S. *History Of New Hampshire.* Volume 1. New York: The American Historical Society, 1926.

Stackpole, Everett S., Lucien Thompson, and Winthrop S. Meserve. *History of the Town of Durham, New Hampshire.* Concord: Rumford Press, 1913; reprinted Portsmouth: Peter E. Randall Publisher, 1994.

Thompson, Mary P. *Landmarks in Ancient Dover, New Hampshire.* Dover: Dover Historical Society, 1892; reprinted Durham: Durham Historic Assoc., 1965.

Vaughan, Alden T. and Edward W. Clark, eds. *Puritans Among The Indians: Accounts Of Captivity and Redemption, 1676-1724.* Cambridge: Harvard University Press, 1981.

Williamson, William D. *The History of the State of Maine.* Volume 1. Hallowell: Glazier, Masters & Co., 1832; reprinted Freeport: Cumberland Press, 1966.

BATTLE OF CAPTINA CREEK

Harry G. Enoch

Introduction

In 1791 open war broke out on the western frontier, as Native Americans made one last attempt to rid the Ohio River Valley of white settlers. The previous October, Blue Jacket's Shawnee, Little Turtle's Miami, and their allies soundly defeated General Josiah Harmar's army near present-day Fort Wayne, Indiana.[1] Brimming with confidence following their success, the confederated nations of the Northwest Territory struck settlements all across the trans-Allegheny frontier. Families throughout the valley left their homes and retreated to nearby forts for safety. In western Virginia and Pennsylvania, new forts were thrown up, county militias were called out, and Ranger companies were sent to frontier outposts. By March, the war had expanded east and south of the Ohio River.

In May, a militia company set out in search of a small war party that had killed three daughters of Jacob Crow. They pursued them west to the Ohio River. At Baker's Fort in present-day Marshall County, West Virginia, the company crossed the river and met a party of Shawnee in battle near the banks of Captina Creek. The site is within the present town limits of Powhatan Point in Belmont County, Ohio. That day the Shawnee bested the whites in a hard-fought contest that left both sides bloodied. With the British fanning the flames and ineffectual support provided by Virginia, Pennsylvania, and the federal government, war ran on for three more years. It finally ended with General "Mad Anthony" Wayne's

---

[1] The military record of Harmar's campaign may be found in *American State Papers, Military Affairs, Volume 1* (Washington, DC: U.S. Congress, 1832), pp. 20-36.

victory at the Battle of Fallen Timbers in 1794 and was followed a year later by the treaty of Greenville.[2]

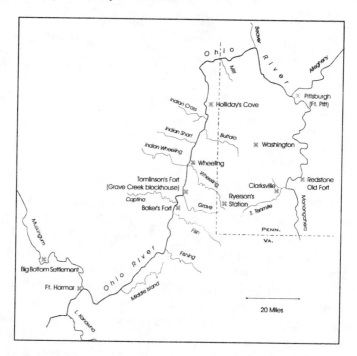

Captina Creek, a minor and today little-known military engagement, was nevertheless a signal battle in the border war.[3] Here the Shawnee, always fierce in battle, fought with a discipline and determination they had seldom displayed in previous encounters with whites. Here was a manifestation that their objective was not merely harassment, but rather the destruction and eradication of frontier settlements. Shawnee, Miami, Delaware, Mingo, and other

---

[2] There is no comprehensive history of the border war, but the western Pennsylvania–Virginia theater is documented in *American State Papers, Indian Affairs, Volume 1* (Washington, DC: U.S. Congress, 1833); Boyd Crumrine, *History of Washington County, Pennsylvania* (Philadelphia: H. L. Evarts and Co., 1882); I. D. Rupp, *Early History of Western Pennsylvania* (----: ----, 1847; reprinted Laughlintown: Southwest Pennsylvania Genealogical Services, 1989).

[3] A better-known incident was associated with Captina Creek at an earlier date. In 1774, Michael Cresap was falsely charged with the murder of Chief Logan's family and was blamed for bringing on Dunmore's War. For a discussion of this affair, see Reuben G. Thwaites and Louise P. Kellogg, *Documentary History of Dunmore's War, 1774* (Madison: Wisconsin Historical Society, 1905).

nations were allied in a mission to drive the whites out of the Ohio Valley and, if possible, back over the Alleghenies. The concern this incident generated at the time is indicated by the fact that following the battle, County Lieutenant David Shepherd sent a personal envoy to the capital to give U.S. Secretary of War Henry Knox an account of the action. The meeting was followed by Knox's acknowledgment of "the deplorable situation of the inhabitants" and his promise to send arms and ammunition to the frontier.[4]

This article describes and analyzes the battle of Captina Creek. A variety of sources are available: Several contemporary reports mention the incident, a number of the participants left their recollection of events, and a few authors have constructed accounts based partly upon personal knowledge and partly upon oral tradition. In trying to reconstruct the sequence of events at Captina and sort out the discrepancies in various accounts, one encounters several interesting historical problems: Who were the informants for the published reports on the battle? How reliable are they? Exactly when did the battle take place? What events immediately preceded the battle? What circumstances caused a militia company from Pennsylvania to cross the Ohio River? Who were the combatants? What were the consequences of the battle for each side? As it turns out, each of these questions may be answered with a reasonable degree of confidence. The following narrative examines these and other issues surrounding the battle of Captina Creek.

A diligent effort was made to recreate the battle from primary records. The use of secondary sources and the author's speculation have been clearly indicated. This narrative makes no attempt to provide a modern sociological perspective. My purpose was to piece together the story from available evidence in order to present a factual account—without bias to whites or Native Americans—of these nearly forgotten events.

Border War, Late 1790–Early 1791

In the Treaty of Paris, signed at the end of the Revolutionary War, England ceded to the United States her claims to the territory that now encompasses five states: Ohio, Indiana, Illinois, Michigan,

---

[4] Henry Knox to Beverly Randolph, May 31, 1791, *Calendar of Virginia State Papers* Volume 5, eds. W. P. Palmer and S. McRae (Richmond: n.p., 1885), p. 319.

and Wisconsin. The fate of the Native Americans inhabiting that region was not addressed. While the Iroquois League had been effectively destroyed by the war, the tribes of the Old Northwest did not consider themselves a conquered people.[5]

After the war, the Ohio River became a highway to the "promised land," as whites poured into newly opened country west of the continental divide, the towering Allegheny mountains. The Ohio nations and their Cherokee neighbors to the south joined in an effort to stem the tide of settlers. They waylaid flatboats coming down river, burned isolated cabins, and killed hunters, surveyors, and anyone else caught unprotected. Whites responded to these assaults with retaliatory raids against their Ohio towns.

Although the level of hostilities continued to escalate, the western settlements received little support from the eastern states. In response to the clamor, President George Washington finally ordered the governor of the Northwest Territory, Arthur St. Clair, to mount an expedition against the Ohio nations. In late September of 1790, General Josiah Harmar set out from Fort Washington (Cincinnati) with 1,453 men. His army consisted of 320 regulars bolstered by two battalions of militiamen from Kentucky and one from Pennsylvania. The Northwest tribes—led by Blue Jacket and Little Turtle—were well aware of Harmar's approach. After burning several deserted villages on the Maumee River near present-day Fort Wayne, Indiana, Harmar's troops were badly beaten in two separate engagements. In early November the army limped back into Fort Washington, having lost nearly two hundred men. The blow further angered and helped unite the tribes. Harmar had stirred the hornets' nest.

By February 1791, western Pennsylvania county leaders had begun to address the prospect of renewed border hostilities in which their militias would be called upon to play a critical role. In spite of the fact that these troops, with their limited arms, training, and discipline, were often less effective than regular army units, the militia had played an important role on the frontier during the Revolutionary War. By 1790 the population of southwest

---

[5] Tribes occupying the Northwest Territory in 1787 included the Delaware, Kickapoo, Mahican, Miami, Moravian, Munsee, Ojibwa (Chippewa), Ottawa, Potawatomi, Seneca, Shawnee, Wea, and Wyandot (Huron). Richard White, *Middle Ground; Indians, Empires, and Republics in the Great Lakes Region, 1650-1815* (Cambridge: Cambridge University Press, 1991), pp. 414-415.

Pennsylvania had swelled to over 35,000; Indian raids into the interior had nearly ceased; and steps had been taken to reduce, and eventually dissolve, the militia. General Presley Neville wrote from Pittsburgh recounting the sorry state of Allegheny County in 1791:

> The Militia are in great want of Arms. I do not believe that more than one-sixth are provided for. Five or Six years of continued Peace had destroyed all thoughts of Defence, and the game becoming scarce, the Arms have slipt off to Kentucky . . . where there appeared to be more use for them.[6]

County Lieutenant James Marshel of Washington County wrote to Governor Mifflin appraising the situation on the frontier in February:

> From the fullest evidence of the hostile intentions of the Indians, I have no doubt but that the service of our Militia will be necessary the ensuing Summer. Our situation on the frontier at this time is truly alarming. The late Expedition under the comand of General Harmar has had a very different effect from what was expected. The Indians appear elated with their success on that occasion and are roused by a Spirit of Resentment. It is evident that nothing prevents their crossing the Ohio River but the inclemency of the Season. . . .[7]

Marshel believed their adversaries would "not leave a Smoking Chimney on this side the Alliganey Mountains." Many westerners shared his sentiments. The military leaders portrayed Harmar's campaign as a great victory, and that notion inhibited the bold, decisive actions needed to stop the bloodshed brought on, ironically, by the "great victory." Westerners spoke their mind on this subject at every opportunity. With a touch of sarcasm, another Washington County official wrote to the governor in plainer tones of Harmar's defeat:

---

[6] Presley Neville to Richard Butler, March 25, 1791, *Pennsylvania Archives, Series 2*, Volume 4, eds. John B. Linn and William H. Egle (Harrisburg: C. M. Busch, State Printer, 1896), pp. 548-549.
[7] James Marshel to Thomas Mifflin, February 19, 1791. Ibid., pp. 538-539.

It must be the prevailing opinion, from the splendid accounts given by the governor of the Western territory and General Harmar of the success of our troops in the late expedition, that the hostile tribes have got at best a check and that the frontier people will be in safety. Nothing is further from the fact. With reluctance, indeed, do I dare to contradict the opinion founded on such respectable authority; but . . . the Indians boast of having obtained a victory, and this is further supported by the audacity and daily insolence which the frontiers have, ever since the return of the army, experienced at the hands of Indians.[8]

The governor forwarded these letters to Secretary Knox at the War Department. The county lieutenants of Pennsylvania and Virginia received a prompt response. On March 3, Knox wrote to inform them that the President had acted upon the requests for aid in the West—he ordered the frontier counties to defend themselves!

Gentlemen—The President of the United States has received your letter of the 19th of last month Stating certain depredations of the Indians. And he has commanded me to inform you that the Congress of the United States, having been deliberating for some time past upon the means which may efectually protect the frontiers, have just concluded thereon . . . It is to be hoped and expected, that as soon as the conditions shall be made known, that the hardy yeomanry of the frontier counties will engage readily and chearfully for a short period to act against the Indians and thereby prevent their depopulating the exposed parts of the [frontier].[9]

In his letter, Knox directed the militia to be filled by volunteers "or otherwise," but requested that the counties not burden the government with the expense of calling out "an unnecessary number

---

[8] David Redick to Thomas Mifflin, February 20, 1791. Ibid., p. 540.
[9] Henry Knox to the western county lieutenants, March 10, 1791, Draper MSS 3SS9-11.

of men." He outlined the strategy to be used by the militia (i.e., the Rangers):

> You will keep the said rangers in constant activity, in such directions as may best prove to secure the inhabitants, and to give information of the approach of the Indians.[10]

As a general rule, Rangers did not engage in offensive operations and rarely fought in pitched battles. Their primary mission was defensive. They were essentially scouting companies and were expected to stay on the go, patrolling a wide area for signs of Indians. When intrusions were detected, the Rangers would dispatch riders to the settlements warning residents to be prepared. They frequently used the forts and blockhouses along the Ohio River as a base of operations.[11]

In February, James Marshel called out the Washington County militia. In March, he wrote to Colonel Shepherd of Ohio County, Virginia, that he was sending a company to the frontier:

> It is with pleasure I Inform you that I am enabled to Join you in the Mutual Defence of the two Counties, for which purpose [I] have ordered out a Company of Militia, part of which I will send to fish Creek and a number to mill Creek, but will Consult you more particularly before I make any permanent arrangements.[12]

Mill Creek emptied into the Ohio River downstream from Pittsburgh near the Pennsylvania state line. Fish Creek and nearby Fort Baker lay at the southern extreme of Ohio County, twenty-four miles downstream from Wheeling. Marshel still held out hope that prompt decisive action would bring a quick end to the hostilities. His optimism would soon be dashed, however, as the war leapt across the Ohio River and spilled into Washington County.

---

[10] Ibid.
[11] For a good description of the frontier militia of western Pennsylvania, see Homer Clark, *Last of the Rangers* (Washington: n.p., 1906).
[12] James Marshel to David Shepherd, March 23, 1791, Draper MSS 3SS19.

"Crow Sisters' Massacre"

The Crow family lived on Dunkard Creek, about five miles downstream from Ryerson's Station. The patriarch, Jacob Crow, had settled on the creek in about 1775 with his growing family. On May 1, 1791, the Crows were the victims of a tragedy still remembered in southwest Pennsylvania.

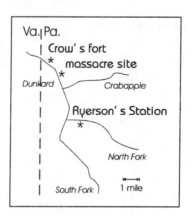

That Sunday morning, after visiting a sick neighbor, the four Crow sisters—Susan, Elizabeth, Catherine and Christina—were on their way home. The girls, who ranged in age from eight to sixteen, followed a path down Crabapple Creek, then turned down Dunkard. When they were about two miles from home, three Shawnee warriors rushed down the creek and surrounded the sisters. They carried their captives a little ways off into the woods and began questioning them. At the first opportunity, the girls made a run for it but were quickly caught. Elizabeth was tomahawked but managed to get away and hide. Christina was bludgeoned with a long rifle, but she got loose from her captor and ran for home. Catherine and Susan were not so fortunate. They were swiftly dispatched and scalped. The war had now come to Washington County, and the Rangers would soon be involved.

Battle of Captina Creek

Word of the attack no doubt reached Captain William Harrod that same day, May 1, at Ryerson's Station. Harrod's son, William Harrod Jr., recalled that after the attack on the Crow sisters, a Ranger detachment was sent out in pursuit. Although only three warriors had been involved, Harrod warned the Rangers to be cautious, especially if crossing the river into Indian country. The Rangers probably arrived at Baker's Fort in the evening on May 1.

Sometime that day, four scouts crossed the river near the fort to reconnoiter. About a mile north on the Ohio side, near the mouth of Captina Creek, the scouts were fired on. Two of the scouts were killed, one was captured, and one swam the river to safety. The Shawnee taunted the garrison from across the river, daring them to come over. Only a few of the Indians showed themselves at that time.

Early the next morning, May 2, a company of Rangers crossed the river in pursuit. They were led by Abraham Enoch and a party of between fifteen and twenty men. They picked up the trail and followed it north to Captina Creek. About a mile from the mouth of Captina, they came to a small meadow, later known as "the cove," where the creek makes a bend to the north. They crossed the creek, and just as they started down a narrow ravine, a Shawnee war party led by Charley Wilkey opened fire on the column from the high ground. The Rangers estimated their number between thirty to forty warriors.

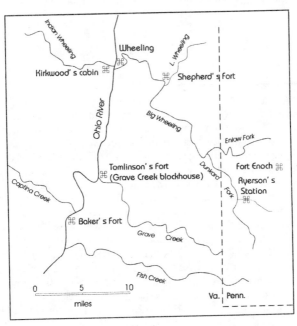

Miraculously, no one was killed in the first volley. The Rangers took cover and began to return fire, but the Shawnee had the advantage of number and position. After several rounds of fire were exchanged by both sides, Enoch was killed. The Rangers fell back to obtain better ground, but after suffering additional casualties from the withering fire, finally had to withdraw. The Shawnee pressed the attack long enough to block the Rangers' retreat down Captina, forcing them to take an overland route to Grave Creek.

Duncan McArthur, the youngest man in the company and later governor of Ohio, showed considerable presence.[13] After their commander was killed, McArthur collected what remained of the company and led the retreat back to Grave Creek. Along the way several men were seriously wounded and were left behind. After pursuing the fleeing Rangers a short distance, the Shawnee returned to the field to scalp the whites and bury their own dead. The Shawnee took their prisoner, John Daniels, and left the area.

The Rangers reportedly had seven killed. The next day a party went out from Baker's Fort to collect the dead. Some of the bodies had been mutilated. The dead were brought back and buried in a little graveyard near the fort.

*   *   *

---

[13] Duncan McArthur (1772-1840) was the son of a Scottish immigrant, who was born in Duchess County, New York, and grew up on the frontier of western Pennsylvania. The McArthurs were a poor family, and Duncan, the eldest, was hired out to work on the neighbors' farms and received minimal formal education. He was a volunteer in Harmar's campaign of 1790. McArthur was described as "tall in stature with a giant frame and possessed speed on foot which saved his life on several occasions." In the War of 1812, he served under General William Henry Harrison, whom he succeeded in command of the Northwest army. McArthur served a number of terms in the legislature, and became one of the most noted and popular figures in the Scioto valley. In 1830 he was elected governor of Ohio. After one term he retired to Ross County. McArthur married Nancy McDonald, and they had eleven children. Nancy was the sister of John McDonald, McArthur's biographer. The McArthur residence near Chillicothe was known as "Fruit Hill" and was a gathering place of the political figures and celebrities of his day. His wife died in 1836, and McArthur died on his farm a few years later. C. H. Cramer, "Duncan McArthur, First Phase, 1772-1812," *Ohio Archaeological and Historical Quarterly* 45, no. 1, 1936: 27-33; *Biographical Cyclopedia and Portrait Gallery of Ohio*, Volume 1 (Cincinnati: Western Biographical Publishing Company, 1894). p. 101.

Although the militia was an important part of the frontier defense during the border war, their peace-time role was vastly diminished. The function of the Rangers, however, ceased to exist altogether, as the frontier moved farther west. Later, as the last of the Rangers died off or moved away, their exploits became part of the region's folklore.

The Shawnee were unable to follow up on their success at Captina Creek. Though they could not drive the whites back across the Alleghenies, the Shawnee and other Northwest tribes continued to vigorously defend their Ohio homelands. A succession of brilliant chiefs, from Blue Jacket to Tecumseh, led a tenacious and courageous twenty-year resistance to further encroachment of their territory. Their determination was no match, however, for the endless numbers of whites who continued moving west in search of land. The tribes were pushed into a smaller and smaller area of Ohio and, finally, were forced to relocate out of the Ohio Valley forever.[14]

Baker's Fort and Captina Creek Today

After imagining one's self in the eighteenth century Ohio Valley, it is hard to adjust to the reality of the landscape near Baker's Fort today. North of the site, the highway presses close to the river in a "narrows" that opens into a two-mile-long bottom almost entirely filled with huge industrial plants. American Electric Power Company has two massive coal-fired electric-generating plants on the river, the Kammer Station and the Mitchell Station. Consolidated Coal Company operates a coal mine, a coal preparation plant and a barge-loading facility on the river. The fort site just south of Graveyard Run now lies under fill—boiler slag and clinkers—that also covers a pioneer graveyard.

A visitor who stopped at Fish Creek in 1803 saw this area as it was and as it might become. Thaddeus Harris's unsentimental vision of the future has now come true:

---

[14] John Sugden has produced two outstanding studies of this period: *Blue Jacket, Warrior of the Shawnees* (Lincoln: University of Nebraska Press, 2000) and *Tecumseh, A Life* (New York: Henry Holt and Co., 1998).

North bank (*on left*) of Captina Creek near the battle site. Cove Run
empties into Captina just beyond the utility poles.

View of the north end of the bottom near the site of Baker's Fort, looking
across the Ohio River, about one mile below Powhatan Point. Graveyard
Run drains the valley between the two hills, just to the left of the two coal
silos.

When we see the land cleared of those enormous trees with which it was overgrown, and the cliffs and quarries converted into materials for building, we cannot help dwelling upon the industry and art of man, which by dint of toil and perseverance can change the desert into a fruitful field, and shape the rough rock to use and elegance.[15]

The Captina battleground is across the Ohio River in Powhatan Point—about half a mile off Route 7 on Cove Road, where a gravel road intersects on the right. While this area is less developed than Fort Baker, a railroad and previous mining activity have altered the landscape significantly, and it is not possible to fix the precise location of the battle site today.

Analysis of the Captina Affair

Documentation for the battle of Captina includes newspaper articles, letters, interviews, depositions, a biography, pension applications and several published narratives. With the exception of the two contemporary reports, the earliest accounts of Captina were written more than forty years after the battle. In some instances the records present seemingly contradictory descriptions of the same events. At this time it is still not possible to reconcile all the different versions of Captina. In the analysis that follows, repeated footnotes to Captina accounts are omitted when the source is identified in the text. (See **Sources**.)

The first question that arises concerning the Captina affair is when did the battle occur? Accounts vary, placing the year from 1791 to 1794. When testimony about an event conflicts, resolution is best obtained from original documents prepared nearly contemporaneously with the event. Fortunately, two such documents exist—Colonel David Shepherd's letter to Secretary Knox and a newspaper article in the *York General-Advertiser*. Following the action, Shepherd sent the following message to Knox at the War Department, dated May 6, 1791:

---

[15]Thaddeus Harris, "Journal of a Tour into the Territory Northwest of the Alleghany Mountains," Reuben G. Thwaites, *Early Western Travels, Volume 3* (Cleveland: Arthur H. Clark Co., 1904), p. 353.

Within a few Days past the Indians have made a general attact on us and have killed Seven of our Scouts, Ensign Enox among the killed.

Shepherd's dispatch pinpoints the time, "within a few days past," and makes it unnecessary to choose between conflicting dates put forth decades after the event.

A second piece of evidence—a newspaper article on May 25, 1791—gives the date for the action at Captina: "On May 1st a party of Washington County Rangers stationed at the mouth of Fish Creek, discovered some Indians remote from the Ohio." The article provides the only contemporary account of the action that has surfaced to date:

> The party of rangers were waiting for information from Lieutenant Enix, who commanded the party on Dunkard Creek, being at the Fish Creek Station, where his brother commanded, called out fifteen volunteers and crossed the river. They soon came in sight of four Indians who fled, until they had completely drawn Mr. Enix into an ambuscade of forty or more, who then fired on them. Mr. Enix ordered his men to take shelter, he and his brave men lost their lives on the spot, with one missing. A party that crossed the river buried Lieutenant Enix and his men, confirmed eight Indians killed.

The article places the Crow family incident in the same timeframe, thus providing the incentive for the Rangers' mission.

> On that same day three Indians were about three miles from Mr. Ryerson's farm on the Dunkard Creek, took four young girls. They were taken some distance from their home, two were killed and scalped, the third was tomahawked and scalped (died a few days since) and the fourth was knocked down and afterwards made her escape.

The Crow sisters were killed on Dunkard Creek. Three miles up the creek from the site was a Ranger outpost, known as Ryerson's Station. Since this blockhouse was so near, word of that morning's attack certainly would have reached the company there by the afternoon of May 1. Assuming the Rangers left the same afternoon, they could have covered the seventeen miles to Baker's Fort in a few hours on horseback, or in five or six hours if on foot, getting there by Sunday night.

The Shawnee party and pursuing Rangers may have both traveled the Warrior Trail to the Ohio River. Native Americans had long used this east-west path to go to and from the Ohio country. Crossing the river just north of Fish Creek, the trail follows a series of ridges that ultimately stretch all the way to the Monongahela River, near Greensboro in Greene County. Striking the trail south of Ryerson's, the Rangers would have come to the river just south of Baker's Fort.[16]

There were two engagements with the Shawnee that occurred near Baker's Fort during the Captina affair. The first was an incident in which a party of scouts on the Ohio side of the river was fired on and had several casualties. The second was a battle in which a company sent over in pursuit was ambushed on Captina Creek and suffered additional casualties. Several accounts placed these events on the same day, but the weight of evidence indicates that they occurred on consecutive days. The scouting mission took place on the first day and the ambush on Captina on the second day. Given that the Crow sisters were killed the morning of May 1 and that the Rangers arrived at Baker's Fort that evening, it seems reasonable to assume that the events of the first day took place on May 1 as stated in the newspaper account.

Eleven-year-old Martin Baker was at the fort, and that day's events left a vivid impression. In later years he was fond of telling his version of Captina. One of his neighbors, Jeremiah Hollister, recalled, "I have often heard Martin Baker relate the account of the Battel." According to Baker, four scouts were sent over to the Ohio side to reconnoiter:

> They were Adam Miller, John Daniels, Isaac McCowan, and John Shoptaw. Miller and Daniels took up stream, and the other two down. The upper scouts were soon attacked by Indians, and Miller killed; Daniels ran up Captina about

---

[16] Phyllis Slater, "Warrior Path," *Tri-County Researcher*, 2, 1978: 134. Another ridge trail connects Ryerson's and Moundsville and could have brought the Rangers—or a portion of them—to the river near the mouth of Big Grave Creek.

three miles, but being weak from the loss of blood issuing from a wound in his arm, was taken prisoner [and] carried into captivity.

John Shoptaw stated in his pension application that he enlisted on March 1 and that the county lieutenant, James Marshel, appointed Shoptaw to lead a detachment of scouts composed of himself, Daniels, Miller and McCowan. Upon hearing the guns, McCowan and Shoptaw ran for their canoes, but before they made it, they were fired on too and so continued down river to a point nearly opposite the fort. Isaac McCowan was shot on the sandy river bank. John Shoptaw made it into the river and swam across.

One more noteworthy incident that day was reported. According to an account by Judge Jeremiah Hollister:

> The Indians made their appearance opesite the fort and, being able to speak some Englis, hallowed over to the fort, repeating several times, "Turn out, turn out."

Hollister, though not present at the Captina affair, was personally acquainted with men who were—Daniel and John Bain, Martin Baker and John Daniels. Several other accounts mention the fact that a few Indians showed themselves across the river on the first day. At this point the Rangers were not aware of the presence of a larger body of Shawnee.

Duncan McArthur, one of the key figures on the second day, did not mention the engagement on the first day, indicating that he was not present during the incident but, rather, was with the Rangers on their way from Ryerson's Station. This suggests that the scouts were at the fort and had already been fired upon and returned before the company arrived from Ryerson's. The Rangers got to the fort and made camp for the night. According to McArthur:

> Shortly after their encamping on the river, and at a late hour in the evening, a few Indians were discovered across the river from the fort, on the Ohio shore, carelessly walking about.

McArthur later expressed the opinion that the Indians purposely showed themselves to invite pursuit. It is not clear that he was aware of this fact at the time.

Several accounts suggest that after the scouts were fired on the Rangers went in pursuit almost at once. George McKiernan, for example, wrote that as soon as Shoptaw got back to the fort:

> All the able-bodied men at the post—sixteen in number—promptly volunteered for the service; and, without loss of time, marched up the bank, and crossed over opposite the mouth of Captina.

McKiernan, writing more than fifty years after the event, may have been filling in details that he lacked specific knowledge about. Samuel Tomlinson recalled that *"preparation* was immediately made to go in pursuit of the Indians" and that may be more accurate. Judge Hollister wrote that "the next morning the men, seventeen in number, left the station to fight the Indians." Lyman Draper, the noted collector of pioneer narratives, worried about this question in 1862 and wrote to Hollister that

> It would be difficult to judge from the several narratives, whether the four spies went over the same day of the fight, or the night before.[17]

I believe McArthur, who was the only participant to address the issue, should be taken as the authority on this point. He commented on the arrival of the company and the discovery of the Indians across the river, then stated that the men started out in pursuit "early the next morning."

In those days military commanders frequently called for a "council of war" after an engagement in order to plan the next movement. Such a council likely followed the arrival of the company from Ryerson's Station. We can imagine some of the issues that would have been raised. Those favoring immediate pursuit would have suggested that any hesitation might allow the small war party time to escape or to be reinforced. Those favoring delay would have pointed out that the Shawnee may have been

---

[17] Lyman Draper to Jeremiah Hollister, March 12, 1862, Draper MSS 7E31.

feigning small numbers and that it was too late in the day to execute an attack across the river.

We can now reconstruct the chain of events on the first day. On Sunday morning, May 1, Shawnee warriors happened on and killed the Crow sisters on Dunkard Creek, then the small party withdrew from the area, crossing the Ohio River in the neighborhood of Baker's Fort. Word reached Ryerson's Station that afternoon, and a detachment was sent in pursuit. While the Rangers were en route, the scouts were attacked near the river. By Sunday night, the Rangers reached Baker's Fort and a plan to be implemented the following morning was agreed upon.

*   *   *

According to Duncan McArthur, on the second day a party under Lieutenant Abraham Enoch crossed the river before daylight and proceeded to where the Shawnee had fired on the scouts from the bank. The names of those reported in the various accounts to have been out with the company on the second day include John Baker, Daniel Bain, John Bain, Alexander Boggs, John Line, Duncan McArthur, George McColloch, Abraham McCowan, John Sutherland, Ray Vennam, Dobbins, Hoffman and Downing. Most of these men were residents of Washington County at that time. This list of fourteen men may be a few short of the actual number. The number reported to have been in the company ranged from fourteen to twenty.

At first light on May 2, the Rangers started upstream and easily found the trail, which soon became distinct, if not obvious. Accounts vary to some degree regarding the route taken to Captina and the location of the battle site. McArthur is the only participant to describe the route, and his account is given preference below. Hollister later visited the battlefield with several participants, so he is accorded primacy on that point. (See the accompanying sketch maps.) According to McArthur:

> Early the next morning Lieutenant Enoch with fifteen men, amongst whom was McArthur, crossed the river before day. As soon as it was light enough to distinguish objects at a distance, Lieutenant Enoch and his party went to the place where the Indians had showed themselves the previous

evening, and found the trail of five or six Indians, and incautiously pursued them over the river hill to Captina creek.

"The river hill" refers to the bank of the Ohio River opposite Baker's Fort. The bank today rises thirty feet above the river level and would have been even higher prior to the Ohio River being raised behind a series of locks and dams. From the river the Rangers proceeded to the north, skirting a high hill on their left, until they struck Captina Creek. McArthur said they intercepted the creek "about one mile from the river, and not much further from the mouth of the creek."[18] The Rangers advanced along the creek bottom in single file. The creek at this point curves to the north and several small streams empty into Captina from the north side. Judge Hollister was shown the site by Daniel Bain in 1809. Hollister said the place was "known as the cove," and he made a drawing for Lyman Draper showing the location of the cove on Captina. The area still goes by that name, and the road paralleling the creek there is called Cove Road.[19]

The signs up to this time still indicated that they were following a small group of Shawnee. Whatever plan the Rangers had was foiled by a chief named Charley Wilkey. Wilkey and his band of Shawnee had the superior strategy and tactics that day, and they were executed most effectively. Showing only a few Indians the day before and leaving an obvious trail for the Rangers to follow was part of the trap set by Wilkey. The Shawnee set up the ambush very deliberately, by walking across the open area, then doubling back to hide overlooking the trail. Samuel Tomlinson's account described the tactic:

It was discovered that the Indians had passed through the field to the opposite side, where they had turned short around, and marched back and secreted themselves near the

---

[18] From the description, this point would be on the present site of the Clair Mar Golf Course on Route 148 in Powhatan Point, Ohio.
[19] One secondary account places the battle at the mouth of Cat's Run, which enters Captina Creek from the northwest, about two miles from the Ohio River. No source was given and none of the other accounts support this location. Scott Powell, *History of Marshall County from Forest to Field* (Moundsville: n.p., 1925), pp. 73-74.

edge of the woods, from whence the whites received the first fire.

Hollister stated that the Rangers followed the trail up Captina on the south side of the creek. Near the cove the trail crossed the creek and headed a little north, striking one of the small runs. Hollister described the setting:

> Two small runs or dreans come in to the creek [Captina] two or three hundred yards apart and between these runs there is a low ridge where our men were led into ambush.

The Rangers stayed on the trail, following the little stream. The tracks continued along the run through a low area flanked by rising ground. The Shawnee were strung out along a heavily-wooded hillside, concealed and waiting patiently. According to McKiernan, they hid behind "a bunch of dogwood trees covered with grape vines." Duncan McArthur recalled the scene:

> As the party of whites were pursuing the trail, they went down a small drain, with a narrow bottom. On the right of the drain was a steep, rocky bank, fifty or sixty feet high; on this bank thirty or forty Indians lay concealed.

The Shawnee had scouts out that morning and were well prepared for the Rangers' arrival. When the company entered the ambush zone in single file, the Shawnee sprang the trap, opening fire on the column from the ridge above. Amazingly, no one was killed in the first fire. The Rangers were outnumbered and had no good ground to fight from, however, they quickly found cover and returned fire. According to McArthur, the Rangers

> took shelter behind trees, logs, or rocks, and the battle was continued with animation on both sides for some time. Lieutenant Enoch and McArthur were treed near each other, and loaded and shot several times.

Since McArthur was the only combatant to leave a detailed account this action, it is appropriate to continue with his narrative:

The hills along Captina creek are steep, high, and craggy, the valleys narrow, so that the keen crack of the rifles, added to the deafening shouts of the combatants, causing the echo to vibrate from hill to hill, made it seem that those engaged in this strife of arms were fourfold the actual number. At length a ball from an Indian's rifle pierced the breast of the brave Lieutenant Enoch; he fell, and immediately expired.... Their commander being killed, and many of their gallant little band being slain or disabled, the remainder determined upon a retreat.

It is not clear that all of the Shawnee were armed with rifles. Among the artifacts left behind after the battle, according to Tomlinson, were "a sheaf of arrows, a bow, and a weasle skin full of red vermillion paint."

In his history of the border wars, Wills de Hass implied that McArthur attempted to lead a charge on the Shawnee. De Hass wrote that "young McArthur cried out, as they ascended the bank, to surround them." While this action is not corroborated, several accounts do credit McArthur with rising to the occasion and leading the company after their commander was killed. McArthur himself said so:

No officer was left to command, and although McArthur was the youngest man in the company, in this time of peril he was unanimously called to direct the retreat.

The Shawnee pressed their attack on the retreating Rangers and were able to inflict a few more casualties. John Baker was shot during the withdrawal. Downing stopped to assist, but Baker's wounds were too serious and he could not go on. Martin Baker described his brother's fate:

On [the] retreat my brother was shot in the hip. Determined to sell his life as dearly as possible, he drew off [to] one side and secreted himself in a hollow with a rock at his back, offering no chance for the enemy to approach but in front. Shortly after, two guns were heard in quick succession; doubtless one of them was fired by my brother, and from the signs afterwards, it was supposed he had killed an Indian.

George McColloch either got shot in the ankle (de Hass) or sprained his ankle (Tomlinson) and could not keep up with the company. De Hass said that one of the Rangers came to McColloch's aid:

> Ray Vennam . . . took him on his shoulder and carried him some distance, but McColloch, finding that they would be overtaken, entreated the other to take care of himself. Vennam concealed McColloch behind a log, and made his way to the fort.

Later, under the cover of darkness, McColloch was able to make his way back to the river. Accounts differ on how he got back to the fort. Tomlinson said McColloch arrived at the Grave Creek blockhouse "about ten o'clock the next day." De Hass described a daring rescue of McColloch during the night:

> That night a man's plaintive cry was heard from the opposite shore, and on Vennam saying it was George McColloch, those in the fort said no, it was an Indian. Vennam, however, was firm in his opinion that it was his friend, and accordingly went over in a canoe to get McColloch.

Most of the men made their way to Tomlinson's Fort rather than Baker's Fort. From the mouth of Captina on the Ohio River, it was one mile south to Baker's and seven miles north to Grave Creek. It is possible that the Rangers found the route along Captina blocked, requiring the men to head north over land. If their retreat took a northern route, they would have had to pass through some rugged terrain before striking the Ohio River about three miles west of Grave Creek.

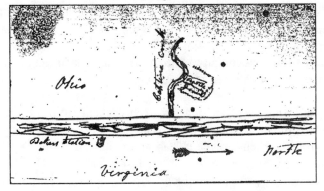

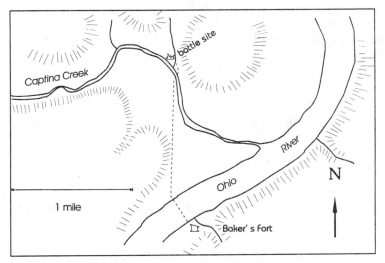

Battleground at Captina Creek
Top—Jeremiah Hollister's drawing of the battleground. (Draper MSS
7E30) **Bottom**—Scale drawing of the area made from a topographic map
showing the probable path of the Rangers on the morning of May 2.

* * *

While we have a number of accounts of Captina from the whites'
perspective, scant information is available on the battle from the
Shawnees' point of view. The captive, John Daniels, was with
Wilkey's band on the day of the battle. Hollister wrote that Daniels
returned to Baker's Fort after his release from captivity and "related
his story." Daniels confirmed that the Shawnee were expecting a
fight that morning and were prepared for the Rangers:

The spy John Daniels, who had been taken prisenor the day before, was tied to a dogwood saplin on top of the hill, and one indian left with him with orders, if the indians were whiped, for the indian to tomahawk Daniels and run. If not, to loose him and join the company.

After defeating the Rangers and driving them from the field, the Shawnee pursued for some distance before returning to the battleground to tend to their dead and wounded. They also killed the surviving whites and mutilated the bodies. The Shawnee suffered heavy losses themselves. Some years later, after peace was made, many of the whites got to know Charley Wilkey, who led the Shawnee at Captina. John McDonald talked to Wilkey about the battle and then included the following passage in his biography of Duncan McArthur:

> He [Charley Wilkey] told the author of this narrative that the battle of Captina was the most severe conflict he ever witnessed; that although he had the advantage of the ground and the first fire, he lost the most men, half of them having been either killed or wounded.

The prisoner John Daniels was the first white to view the field after the battle. He reported that the Shawnee had at least seven warriors killed in the action:

> Daniels was conducted down to the Battle ground where the indians buried or covered their dead with stone. There were seven indians killed and ware laid in a row and covered with a large pile of stone.

The Shawnee may not have had quite the degree of numerical superiority reported by the Rangers. Most accounts claimed at least a two-to-one advantage. McArthur put the Rangers at sixteen men and the Shawnee number from thirty to forty. However, Wilkey said half his men were killed or wounded. With 7 men killed, he must have had at least fourteen; assuming an equal number wounded would set a reasonable upper limit of Shawnee at twenty-eight.

After the Shawnee gathered their wounded, they left the area and proceeded west for at least thirty miles. At that point, they pitched one of the captured weapons into a creek, where it was later recovered. According to Daniel Wire's account, the gun had belonged to "Jack Bean" [Bain] and that John Baker had borrowed it from him. The Shawnee took the gun when they killed Baker and no doubt threw it away after discovering it was broken.

The entire action on the second day occurred in the period from before dawn until after dark. The company crossed the river before daylight, set out at first light and probably reached the cove in less than an hour—the distance being just over a mile. No one reported how long the battle lasted on the banks of Captina. McArthur provides a clue, but only in very general terms: "the battle was continued with animation on both sides for some time." He also mentions that they "loaded and shot several times" and that "at length" Enoch was killed. From that description one might estimate that the time could have been as short as ten to fifteen minutes or as long as an hour or so. The low end of that range would seem a little short for both sides to have had so many killed, but beyond that one cannot be more precise. Since the battle probably ended before midmorning, the retreat must have been lengthy if, as Tomlinson stated, the Rangers did not all get to Grave Creek until that evening.

Five of the Rangers killed on May 2 are identified. They include Abraham Enoch, John Baker, Abraham McCowan, John Line, and Hoffman (whom Tomlinson called "a Dutchman"). McArthur said that seven were killed, so two names may be missing from the list. McArthur added that "some [were] badly wounded," and McKiernan wrote that three were wounded in addition to Baker. McColloch may have been one of them; the other wounded were not named.

On Tuesday, May 3, the day after the engagement on Captina, the Rangers went back to retrieve their dead and wounded. McKiernan and de Hass stated that the company consisted of a strong party from Grave Creek[20] along with "most of the fugitives from the battle." Certainly, the "fugitives" needed reinforcement. They must have gone out in greater number than on May 2, since

---

[20] Joseph Tomlinson's settlement was at the mouth of Grave Creek, later the site of Moundsville, West Virginia. J. H. Brantner, *Historical Collections of Moundsville, West Virginia* (Moundsville: Marshall County Historical Society, 1947).

there was no way of knowing at that time whether or not the Shawnee were waiting to ambush the rescue party. Wilkey's band had left the area, however, and there were no wounded left to rescue. The Rangers would have been looking for John Baker, whom they discovered under a rock ledge where he had been killed. Many of the bodies had been "mutilated." Martin Baker's account gives the most graphic description:

> The next day the men turned out and visited the spot. Enochs, Hoffman and John Baker, were found dead and scalped. Enoch's bowels were torn out, his eyes and those of Hoffman screwed out with a wiping stick. The dead were wrapped in white hickory bark, and brought over to the Virginia side, and buried in their bark coffins.

A wiping stick is a rod fitted with a piece of cloth used for cleaning out the bore of a gun. The little cemetery where the Rangers buried their dead was located a short distance from Baker's Fort, on a stream aptly named Graveyard Run.

* * *

The description of the Captina affair presented in this work is entirely from the point of view of the whites, because theirs are the only available accounts. In the absence of written Native American records, we can only imagine how the events at Captina were perceived by the Shawnee. Charley Wilkey was the only Native American named in the Captina accounts. In his biography of Duncan McArthur, John McDonald indicated that after the peace he became acquainted with a Shawnee chief "known to the whites about Chillicothe by the name of Charley Wilkey." McDonald gave a brief description of Wilkey, who was described as being a "short, thick, strong, active man with a very agreeable and intelligent countenance." In the fall of 1792, the frontier scout Samuel Davis was captured on the Big Sandy River in Kentucky. McDonald said that "this body of Indians was commanded by a Shawnee chief, who called himself Captain Charles Wilky." Davis managed to escape from his captors and afterwards harbored no animosity to Wilkey.

"Davis always spoke of him as being kind and humane to him."[21] The Indians and whites in the vicinity of Ross County, Ohio, apparently thought highly of Wilkey also:

> He was communicative and sociable in his manners. The first three or four years after Chillicothe was settled, this Indian mixed freely with the whites and upon no occasion did he show a disposition to be troublesome. He was admitted by the other Indians, who spoke of him, to be a warrior of the first order—fertile in expedients and bold to carry his plans into execution.[22]

Wilkey's performance at the battle of Captina Creek in 1791 certainly bears out this description of him.

Conclusion

While accounts of the Captina affair may be considered somewhat fragmentary, careful study of available evidence allows us to add an interesting chapter to the ongoing investigation of border warfare. It has been possible to reconstruct the major events occurring between May 1 and May 6 with some degree of confidence; only a few of the details remain in question. At the end of our analysis we may conclude that the battle of Captina was an extraordinary engagement between the Shawnee and a company of frontier militia. The contest was unusually severe. Even more unusual, both parties maintained the contact despite heavy losses.

The battle at Captina Creek resulted in significant losses for the Rangers. In two engagements, they had at least nine killed, possibly an equal number wounded, and one captured. A cursory review of the affair suggests that the Rangers were ill-advised to pursue the Indians after the attack on the scouts; that they were foolhardy to have been caught in an ambush; and that they fought poorly, then fled from the battle in disorderly fashion leaving their dead and wounded behind. These conclusions are perhaps overly harsh and fail to reflect the circumstances of the time.

---

[21] John McDonald, "A Sketch of the Life and Character of Samuel Davis," *Western Christian Advocate*, November 2, 1835, a copy of which appears in Draper MSS 26CC45-48.

[22] Ibid.

During the panic of early 1791, the Rangers had to remobilize quickly after several years of relative calm. New units were recruited and new officers were put into the field. While the county lieutenants would have preferred to take time to train and equip the new units, the Rangers had to be rushed into service to deal with the emergency at hand. When the Shawnee struck twenty miles beyond the Ohio River, killing the Crow sisters in Washington County, every instinct of the frontier people called for immediate pursuit. A company from Ryerson's Station set out on this quest. While the decision to pursue across the river on the second day may have been made "incautiously," as McArthur with the advantage of hindsight later suggested, it was a decision that most Ranger commanders would likely have made in similar circumstances. Other commanders may have been more experienced, but on the frontier lack of seasoning was not sufficient excuse for timidity or inaction. It is one of the fortunes of war that men are sometimes pressed into situations for which they have not been adequately prepared. On the other hand, one should not fail to consider that the Rangers' defeat may have simply been due to the superior prowess of their Native American opponents.

From the point of view of the Shawnee, one might tell the tale of a war party that meticulously designed and methodically carried out a plan to draw the hated white enemy into a death trap. And though the plan was flawlessly executed, their adversaries fought back so fiercely that the outcome for a time hung in the balance. In similar instances in the past, after losing the advantage they would have broken contact. On this day, however, the Shawnee did not disappear into the forest. They fought, they maneuvered and they persevered until they drove their white enemy from the field.

Seen through the eyes of the Rangers, one finds the parallel tale of an unseasoned militia company that found itself in a desperate situation—out in the open, outnumbered, and facing an enemy located on the high ground. Through combined actions of personal courage these men fought until the unit sustained so many casualties that it became impossible to hold their ground. The Rangers returned to the battleground the next day, without knowing for certain whether the Shawnee had left or were waiting for them again, perhaps with reinforcements adding to their number. The Rangers brought their dead back home and buried them, and that was the end of the Captina affair.

Sources

The following documents were used to reconstruct and analyze the battle of Captina. The first name listed is the source of the account, followed (after the colon) by the reference to the document where the account appears. Accounts are listed in chronological order.

David Shepherd: letter to Henry Knox, May 6, 1791, Draper MSS 3SS37.

York [Pa.] *General-Advertiser*: Diana Bowman, *Pennsylvania Herald and York General Advertiser, Book 1, 1789-1793* (Apollo: Closson Press, 1993), pp. 99-100.

John Dailey: Draper MSS 6ZZ99 and a deposition in Daniel Bean's Revolutionary War pension application, Pennsylvania, Revolutionary War W. 8124.

John Shoptaw: John Shoptaw's Revolutionary War pension application, Pennsylvania, O.W. Inv. Rej. 21684.

John Yoho: deposition in John Bain's Revolutionary War pension application, Draper MSS 6ZZ100.

John Bain: deposition in Daniel Bean's Revolutionary War pension application, Pennsylvania, W. 8124.

Daniel Bain: Daniel Bean's Revolutionary War pension application, Pennsylvania, W. 8124.

Duncan McArthur: John McDonald, *Biographical Sketches of General Nathaniel Massie, General Duncan McArthur, Captain William Wells and General Simon Kenton* (Cincinnati: D. Osborn and Son, 1838), pp. 77-80.

George S. McKiernan: George S. McKiernan, "Battle of Captina. A Scrap of Border History," *American Pioneer*, 2, no. 4, 1843: 176-179.

Samuel Tomlinson: A. B. Tomlinson, "First Settlement of Grave Creek," *American Pioneer,* 1, 1843: 353-354.

William Harrod, Jr.: interview by Lyman Draper, November 1845, Draper MSS 37J171-172.

Martin Baker: Henry Howe, *Historical Collections of Ohio* (Cincinnati: State of Ohio, 1847), pp. 55-56.

Daniel Wire: Henry Howe, *Historical Collections of Ohio* (Cincinnati: State of Ohio, 1847), p. 367.

Wills de Hass: Wills de Hass, "1791, Affair at Captina, A Skirmish," in *History of the Early Settlement and Indian Wars of Western Virginia* (Wheeling: H. Hoblitzell, 1851; reprinted Parsons: McClain Printing Co., 1989), pp. 413-415.

Ezekiel Boggs: Roeliff Brinkerhoff, *A Pioneer History of Richland County, Ohio*, ed. Mary Jane Henney (Mansfield: Richland County Chapter Ohio Genealogical Society, 1993), pp. 338-339.

Jeremiah Hollister: letters to Lyman Draper, March 1 and May 20, 1862, Draper MSS 7E30, 33, 34, 40.

Samuel Hedges: interview by Lyman Draper, October 7-8, 1863, Draper MSS 19S220-221.

Bibliography

American State Papers, Indian Affairs. Volume 1. Washington, DC: U.S. Congress, 1833.

American State Papers, Military Affairs. Volume 1. Washington, DC: U.S. Congress, 1832.

Biographical Cyclopedia and Portrait Gallery of Ohio. Volume 1. Cincinnati: Western Biographical Publishing Company, 1894.

Bowman, Diana. *Pennsylvania Herald and York General Advertiser, Book 1, 1789-1793*. Apollo: Closson Press, 1993.

Brantner, J. H. *Historical Collections of Moundsville, West Virginia*. Moundsville: Marshall County Historical Society, 1947.

Brinkerhoff, Roeliff. *A Pioneer History of Richland County, Ohio*. Ed. Mary Jane Henney. Mansfield: Richland County Chapter, OGS, 1993.
Calendar of Virginia State Papers. Volume 5. Eds. W. P. Palmer and S. McRae. Richmond: n.p., 1885.

Clark, Homer. *Last of the Rangers*. Washington: n.p., 1906.

Cramer, C. H. "Duncan McArthur, First Phase, 1772-1812." *Ohio Archaeological and Historical Quarterly* 45, no. 1 (1936): 27-33.

Crumrine, Boyd. *History of Washington County, Pennsylvania*. Philadelphia: H. L. Evarts and Co., 1882.

de Hass, Wills. *History of the Early Settlement and Indian Wars of Western Virginia*. Wheeling: H. Hoblitzell, 1851; reprinted Parsons: McClain Printing Co., 1989.

Draper Manuscripts.
   3SS37.
   6ZZ99.
   6ZZ100.
   7E30, 33, 34, 40.
   19S220-221.
   26CC45-48.
   37J171-172.

Howe, Henry. *Historical Collections of Ohio*. Cincinnati: State of Ohio, 1847.

McDonald, John. *Biographical Sketches of General Nathaniel Massie, General Duncan McArthur, Captain William Wells and General Simon Kenton*. Cincinnati: D. Osborn and Son, 1838.

McKiernan, George S. "Battle of Captina. A Scrap of Border History." *American Pioneer* 2, no. 4 (1843): 176-179.

Pennsylvania Archives, Series 2. Volume 4. Eds. John B. Linn and William H. Egle. Harrisburg: C. M. Busch, State Printer, 1896.

Powell, Scott. *History of Marshall County from Forest to Field*. Moundsville: n.p., 1925.

Revolutionary War pension applications.
    John Bain
    Daniel Bean
    John Shoptaw

Rupp, I. D. *Early History of Western Pennsylvania*. ----: ----, 1847; reprinted Laughlintown: Southwest Pennsylvania Genealogical Services, 1989.

Slater, Phyllis. "Warrior Path." *Tri-County Researcher* 2 (1978): 134.

Sugden, John. *Blue Jacket, Warrior of the Shawnees*. Lincoln: University of Nebraska Press, 2000.

Sugden, John. *Tecumseh, A Life*. New York: Henry Holt and Co., 1998.

Thwaites, Reuben G. *Early Western Travels, Volume 3*. Cleveland: Arthur H. Clark Co., 1904.

Thwaites, Reuben G. and Louise P. Kellogg. *Documentary History of Dunmore's War, 1774*. Madison: Wisconsin Historical Society, 1905.

Tomlinson, A. B. "First Settlement of Grave Creek." *American Pioneer* 1 (1843): 347-358.

White, Richard. *Middle Ground; Indians, Empires, and Republics in the Great Lakes Region, 1650-1815*. Cambridge: Cambridge University Press, 1991.

ANDREW JACKSON'S INDIAN CAMPAIGNS: DISPOSSESSION AND REMOVAL, 1813-1837

Rogan H. Moore

Andrew Jackson was inaugurated as the seventh President of the United States on March 4, 1829. Throngs of Jacksonian supporters massed in the nation's capital throughout that day hoping to glimpse their beloved hero. After a brief inaugural address, "Old Hickory" retired to the White House, pursued by a jubilant crowd of well-wishers eager to shake his hand. Converging on the presidential mansion, this crowd of raucous frontiersmen transformed an East Room gathering of the "officially and socially eligible," into a drunken Saturnalia, in which expensive china was smashed, curtains were torn down and then shredded, and valuable furnishings were "stained by the feet of clodhoppers."[1] The gathering reached a feverish crescendo when tubs of punch were placed upon the White House lawn, sending many partygoers crashing through the glass windows of the East Room to get at the free liquor. On that memorable winter day in 1829, the Jacksonian administration truly arrived.

What Jackson's arrival meant to nearly sixty thousand Cherokees, Chickasaws, Choctaws, Creeks, and Seminoles, residing on over twenty-five million acres of land in Alabama, Florida, Georgia, Kentucky, Mississippi, North Carolina, South Carolina, and Tennessee, would soon be made manifest.[2] Federal Indian policy during the Jacksonian presidential years (1829-1837) centered on a program of Indian removal. This program became

---

[1] Larry Gragg, "The Reign of King Mob, 1829," *History Today* 28, no. 4, April 1978: 240.

[2] Gragg, p. 241.

embodied in the Federal Indian Removal Act of 1830. The Act provided the administration with the official authority needed to enforce the removal of the southeastern tribes from their ancestral homelands to lands west of the Mississippi River.[3] The roots of Jackson's policies regarding the Native Americans can be traced back to the President's days as a Major General in the Tennessee militia and the bloody Creek War of 1813-1814.

In 1813, the Shawnee chieftain, Tecumseh, planned to unleash a massive confederation of southern and northern tribes against the settlers, pushing his enemy over the Appalachian Mountains and into the sea. Tecumseh's charisma, superb oratorical skills, and powerful religious belief that European Americans were "white devils," convinced many Creeks, dubbed "Red Sticks," because of their brightly painted war clubs, to take to the warpath under his leadership. On August 30, the Red Sticks besieged Fort Mims in southern Alabama, killing 107 soldiers, 160 civilians, and 100 slaves.[4]

The Red Sticks found themselves facing a three-pronged retaliatory assault that winter. The Georgia militia, with a contingent of friendly Creeks, marched towards the hostiles from the east. A Federal Army with a contingent of Choctaws pushed up the Alabama River from the south. The Tennessee forces constituted the third prong and were divided into two parts, led by Jackson and Brigadier General John Coffee. The contingent commanded by Major-General Andrew Jackson, included six hundred Cherokee auxiliaries. Jackson approached the Red Sticks from the north. Finally engaging his foe on November 3, near the Creek village of Tallushatchee, in central Alabama, Jackson and General John Coffee's brigade of Tennesseans, systematically slaughtered 186 braves.[5] Jackson's casualties included five dead and forty-one wounded. Davy Crockett, one of Jackson's volunteers during the Creek War, later stated, "We shot them like dogs."[6] Many Creeks

---

[3] Anthony F. C. Wallace, *The Long, Bitter Trail: Andrew Jackson and the Indians,* ed. Eric Foner (New York: Hill and Wang, 1993), pp. 73-101.

[4] Edward Pessen, *Jacksonian America: Society, Personality, and Politics* (New York: Dorsey Press, 1978), p. 296.

[5] Ronald N. Satz, *Federal Indian Policy: 1829-1849* (Ann Arbor: University of Michigan, 1972), p. 74.

[6] Angie Debo, *A History of the Indians of the United States* (Oklahoma City: University of Oklahoma, 1984), p. 95.

decided to pursue peace after the battle. This brought on the fury of Red Stick Chief Red Eagle (also known as William Weatherford), who threatened to retaliate against anyone leaving the warpath. Red Eagle's threats convinced Jackson that Red Stick resistance, though weakened, had not been fully eliminated. He continued to wage war.

At Talladega, about thirty-five miles southwest of Tallushatchee, Jackson met and destroyed a Creek encampment, killing over three hundred Red Sticks. Jackson's force suffered 15 losses.[7] After a brief stop at his Alabama base of Fort Strother, freshly equipped with men and material, Jackson headed south, making camp along the Emuckfaw Creek on January 21, 1814. The Creeks made an initial stab at Jackson's encampment, but were quickly driven back. The Indians attacked again at Enotachopco Creek, with a similar lack of success. Jackson simply had more firepower at his disposal than the Creeks could effectively respond to.

At Horseshoe Bend on March 27, Jackson's force was aligned along the Tallapoosa River. Before them lay an imposing Creek fortress consisting of an outer perimeter made of hewn trees, with several huts within. Sending his cavalry commander, John Coffee, downriver to cut off any Creek flanking movements or possible line of retreat, Jackson began to cannonade the position. The fortifications managed to endure the initial bombardment. Relieved that their fortress held, the Creeks taunted their attackers with derisive laughter. His blood up, Jackson drew his sword and gave the order for his men to attack. Charging forward with fixed bayonets, Jackson's men broke through the Creek perimeter and entered the fortress. When the smoke cleared, 557 Creeks lay dead. The carnage was indiscriminate. Women and children lay in droves among the dead. Jackson's force suffered twenty-six losses. Another 107 were wounded.[8]

Red Eagle was not at the Battle of Horseshoe Bend. After it was over, he showed incredible courage by riding alone into Jackson's camp and offering his life in return for mercy towards Creek woman and children taken prisoner. Seemingly mesmerized by Red Eagle's bravery, Jackson agreed to provide adequate care for his prisoners. The chieftain pledged that the Creek Nation would leave the

---

[7] Robert V. Remini, *Andrew Jackson: Volume I, The Course of American Empire, 1767-1821* (New York: Harper, 1977), p. 193.

[8] Robert V. Remini, *Andrew Jackson And His Indian Wars* (New York, 2001), p. 79.

warpath and return to peace. "I am in your power. Do with me as you please. I am a soldier still. ... I have done the white people all the harm I could. ... I have fought them, and fought them bravely. If I had an army, I would fight them still. But I have none! My people are no more!! Nothing is left me but to weep over the misfortunes of my country."[9]

Old Hickory arrived at Fort Jackson on July 10 in preparation for demanding official peace from Red Eagle and other Creek leaders. The fort was positioned near where the Coosa River joins the Alabama River on a scenic path to the Gulf of Mexico. After calling for a general meeting of all Creek chiefs to be held on August 1, Jackson, acting on behalf of President Madison, readied his peace terms.

The Red Sticks came as directed. The chieftains of non-hostile Creek tribes, the latter having played a considerable role in Jackson's victory at Horseshoe Bend, also arrived as directed. The friendly Creeks were unsure why they needed to attend. Some supposed they would be honored, possibly rewarded for their loyal service to the United States government. They were wrong. Jackson was determined to inflict a terrible toll on the entire Creek Nation, regardless of its loyalties, by dispossessing them of most of their tribal lands. The General calculated that the cost to the United States government of the recent Creek War equaled the value of twenty-three million acres of Creek land, or more than one-half of their total acreage. The Creeks would retain only a fragment of their original lands. No differentiation was made between the Red Sticks and the Creeks that had aided Jackson in his victorious campaign. All Creeks shared in and suffered from the same harsh fate. Jackson's peace treaty was an outrage, but few Creeks left alive were willing to publicly say so.

The Treaty of Fort Jackson was signed on August 9, 1814. It made precautionary provisions for the Creeks to cease any contact with the British and Spanish, thus negating the possibility of a Creek alliance with these colonial powers. Additionally, the Creeks were to allow the United States free access over the open trails in their remaining territory. They were to permit the United States to establish forts and trading posts wherever needed, and to also hand

---

[9] Red Eagle quoted in Remini, *Indian Wars*, p. 82.

over to military authorities for trial all persons responsible for instigating the Creek War.

Ironically, most of the Red Sticks had managed to make their way to safety in Spanish Florida. There, they made connections with the Seminoles and plotted revenge. It was left to Jackson's old comrades-in-arms, the friendly Creek chiefs, to sign the treaty. They did so under duress and under protest. To cede the amount of land to the United States government called for in the treaty meant sure ruin for the Creek Nation. They saw this clearly. So did Jackson. The General dealt a fatal blow to the prowess of the Creek tribes, both ally and renegade, but he remained positive over both his victory and the terms of the peace treaty. Jackson's victory in the Creek War of 1813-1814, was used to break the power of that Native American people through the forcible annexation of the bulk of their ancestral lands to the United States.

The Treaty of Fort Jackson was an omen of things to come. The Creek tribes, as well as other Indian nations in the southeast, would be subjected to regulations of the United States federal government. Within twenty-five years of the treaty, the vast majority of the Cherokee, Chickasaw, Choctaw, Creek, and Seminole peoples, were either dead or transported to lands west of the Mississippi River.

The Creek War of 1813-1814 can be viewed within the greater context of the War of 1812. As a military commander, Jackson needed to be both ruthless and victorious. His greatest fear during the war was that the Red Sticks would ignite a larger Indian uprising throughout the south, and perhaps beyond, possibly turning the tide of the War of 1812 in Great Britain's favor. Despite these legitimate concerns, a deeply disturbing precedent had been established at Fort Jackson. Native Americans would be forcibly dispossessed of their tribal lands with the backing of presidential authority.[10]

Whether Andrew Jackson desired the physical removal of all Indian tribes from lands east of the Mississippi River by the time of the Treaty of Fort Jackson is unclear. What is clearer is that his subsequent negotiations for further Indian land cessions, commencing with the Cherokee cessions of 1816, and culminating with the Treaty of Doak's Stand, which brought about the Choctaw land cessions of 1820, leave little doubt that Indian removal became his ultimate goal. By 1816, Jackson, with his Creek victory of 1814,

---

[10] Remini, *Volume I*, p. 218.

and his crushing defeat of the British at the Battle of New Orleans in 1815 now behind him, began a policy of negotiating with the Indians for their lands situated east of the Mississippi River. He became determined that the people of the East would never suffer any Indian to inhabit this territory again.

Not everyone in the U.S. government supported Jackson's policies. Secretary of War, William H. Crawford, later agreed to return four million acres of land to the Cherokees that the Treaty of Fort Jackson had taken from them. The sum of $35,000.00 for war damages inflicted upon the Cherokees by the Tennessee militia was also to be paid.[11] Jackson was furious. He threatened political retaliation against Crawford if the Secretary did not make quick and effective amends. Bullied and cajoled, Crawford called for the appointment of a commission consisting of Jackson, General David Meriweather of Georgia, and Jesse Franklin of North Carolina, to look into the validity of Indian territorial claims. Crawford was obliged to include Jackson on the committee as a matter of political expediency.

Old Hickory, enraged over Crawford's liberal Indian policies, ran roughshod over the commission and totally dominated its affairs. Jackson firmly believed that the Indians had too much land. He wished to negotiate to reduce land owned by the Indian tribes of the south to the bare minimum necessary to feed, clothe, and house each tribe. Jackson had little faith in the integrity of the Native Americans and tended to view them as fickle, wandering savages, with little understanding of decency or morality. His views were typical of the time. Jackson felt that the Indian tribes had no legitimate right to the vast tracts of land they inhabited. They were, he believed, an impediment to further white settlement and a potential threat to civilization. He once remarked that, "An Indian is fickle, and you will have to take the same firm stand and support it, and you are sure of success." [12] The troika of Jackson, Meriweather, and Franklin, would push for Cherokee dispossession and removal.

The commission of Jackson, Meriweather, and Franklin, met on September 16, 1816, with the leading chieftains of the Cherokee Nation. Jackson demanded that the Cherokees relinquish their lands to the north and south of the Tennessee River. They refused.

---

[11] Debo, p. 96.
[12] Remini, *Volume I*, p. 326.

Realizing that he had pushed too far too soon, Jackson backtracked and mapped a long, twisting line from the south side of the Tennessee River, stretching south to the Coosa River. The Cherokees had to surrender all lands to the west and south of that line, in return for a lump sum of $5,000.00 and a further grant of $6,000.00 to be paid per annum over the following decade.[13] Completely dissatisfied with the commission's terms, the Cherokees implored them to reduce the land grant. Jackson would have no part of this and finally resorted to bribery to get the Cherokees to accept a treaty that was eventually signed in 1816.

The Chickasaws were next on the commission's agenda. The Indians were coerced into giving up large land holdings in Alabama, Kentucky, Mississippi, and Tennessee, for the modest sum of $4,500.00 with an additional $12,000.00 to be paid on an annual basis over the succeeding decade.[14] Bribery was utilized to win reluctant Chickasaw chieftains over. A treaty was signed on September 20, 1816.

After the Chickasaws came the Choctaws. This time Old Hickory did not stand before the chiefs in a full dress uniform glaring impressively at them. John Coffee, Jackson's trusted Tennessee cavalry commander, headed a three-man commission that hammered home a treaty with the Choctaws on October 24, 1816. The treaty forced the Choctaws to cede all of their lands east of the Tombigbee River for $10,000.00 in merchandise. Another $16,000.00 was to be paid them over the following twenty years.[15]

With the opening up of lands once controlled by Native Americans, the homesteaders, land speculators, and squatters poured in. No longer would these lands belong to the Indians. A people had been effectively removed; another people had begun to move in. By 1817, the Cherokees, already reduced to a fragment of their former glory, braced themselves and hoped that the worst was over.[16] Sadly, this too proved to be futile. On July 8, 1817, the Cherokees ceded a further two million acres of land lying east of the Mississippi River to the federal government. They were under the clear understanding that they would receive one acre of land west of

---

[13] Ibid., 329.

[14] Ibid., 330.

[15] Ibid.

[16] Francis P. Prucha, *American Indian Policy: The Formative Years, 1770-1834* (Cambridge: Harvard University, 1962), p. 174.

the "great river" for each acre they ceded to the east of it. In the coming two years, over 60,000 Cherokees left the lands of their forbears, equipped with the handouts of their "benevolent" Great White Father, usually a beaver trap, blanket, or rifle.[17]

It was this massive Cherokee land cession that brought Indian Removal from mere concept to stark reality. The treaty of 1817 set an historic precedent. While the earlier Treaty of Fort Jackson had pioneered the notion of large Indian land cessions in the Southeast, subsequent treaties ultimately paved the way for Indian removal.

Andrew Jackson had risen to fame as an Indian fighter. His prowess as a land negotiator added to his reputation. Old Hickory forced his will upon the Native Americans of the Southeast. In so doing, he had the unbridled support of the majority of settlers on the frontier. For Jackson, it was brilliant politics. With every stroke of his diplomatic pen, his popularity soared. Jackson was riding a seemingly endless crest of popularity, particularly with those Americans who shared with him the dream of territorial expansionism, or, what eventually came to be termed "Manifest Destiny."[18] The Native Americans became mere pawns to Jackson. He demonstrated little concern for their culture or their welfare. While there was no "trail of tears" in 1817, many Cherokees suffered from the terms of the treaty and lamented their fate. The trail of tears would become an apt description of the misery caused by the Federal Indian Removal Act of 1830.[19]

It is clear that Jackson employed tactics that devolved into a strategy that can now be termed "ethnic cleansing" in his dealings with the Native Americans of the Southeast. He used the Indians in much the same way that he utilized slaves on his Tennessee estate. Both simply furthered his interests. Despite the gusto with which he put renegades to the sword during the Creek War, and the ruthlessness he demonstrated in conducting Indian land treaties, Jackson never loathed the "Red Man" simply for his race. He merely detested the threat to centralized authority that the Native Americans appeared to pose. He was utterly convinced that the destiny of the United States lay in continued westward expansion, and that that expansion was threatened by the sheer physical

---

[17] Remini, *Volume I*, p. 335.

[18] Armin Rappaport, *A History of American Diplomacy* (New York: Macmillan, 1975), p. 97.

[19] Satz, p. 122.

presence of independent tribes existing within the borders of the republic. It was both consistent with his background as a westerner and a veteran of numerous Indian campaigns, not to mention politically expedient, for Jackson to eventually call "for the removal of the Indians and an end to the existence of an *imperium in imperio.*"[20]

The First Seminole War broke out in 1818 and interrupted Jackson's pursuit of further Indian land cessions. The Seminole people of Florida had refused to acknowledge federal claims to lands annexed after the Creek War of 1813-1814. They had pushed into southern Georgia, establishing a settlement at Fowltown. On November 12, 1817, Georgia militia under the command of General Edward P. Gaines burned the town to cinders. The Seminoles withdrew into Florida, and aided by the remaining Red Sticks, took their revenge nine days later when they ambushed an open-boat convoy, killing forty soldiers, seven women, and four children.[21] After the ambush, Jackson took personal command of the militia in Florida. He was determined to teach the Seminoles a hard lesson and also saw an opportunity to wrest from Spain their control over this highly prized territory. On January 22, 1818, marching out of Fort Scott, Major-General Jackson rode at the head of over a thousand men. This army was later reinforced with an additional one thousand troops. Jackson plunged deep into Spanish Florida in pursuit of hostile Seminoles.

The Seminoles had joined the warpath led by two Britons, both of them eager to establish a British foothold in Spanish Florida. Alexander Arbuthnott, a Scot who hailed from the Bahamas, had been in Florida trading with the Seminoles. The other Briton, Robert Armbrister, was a former Lieutenant in the Royal Marines. Armbrister urged the Seminoles to war with the United States. Jackson captured the septuagenarian Arbuthnott at the town of St. Marks, holding him for trial. Armbrister was captured at a Seminole camp called Bowlegs Town. The hapless Armbrister was executed by firing squad and Arbuthnott suffered death by hanging. Seminole resistance was subdued. On June 18, 1818, Old Hickory declared that the Seminole War was over.

---

[20] Remini, *Volume I* (New York, 1966), p. 79.
[21] Ibid.

Jackson was not finished with his Floridian adventure, however. He felt it opportune to attack the Spanish and captured Pensacola. Jackson believed that with Spain eliminated as a power in Florida, he could resume his Indian campaigns, this time against the Seminoles. After Jackson made himself the real power in Florida, the Spanish had little recourse but to agree to a treaty with the United States. The Adams–de Onis Treaty of February 22, 1819, ceded Florida to the United States for five million dollars. The western boundary with the Louisiana Territory was set at the Sabine River. In Florida, Jackson used military strength and his superior negotiating skills to bring further lands to the United States. Spanish Florida was formally ceded to the United States on July 17, 1821.[22] With Spain removed from the equation, the General resumed his drive for further Indian land cessions.

In 1818, with the blessing of President James Monroe, Jackson negotiated another treaty with the Chickasaws. The Chickasaws lost all of their Kentucky and Tennessee lands. A treaty was hammered out on October 19, 1818. The Chickasaws were to be granted $300,000.00 in $20,000.00 increments over fifteen years.[23] Another treaty with the Choctaws was signed in 1820, which obliged them to leave all lands east of the Mississippi River. The Treaty of Doak's Stand completed a seven-year period of negotiations between Jackson and the Native American tribes of the southeast. Signed on October 18, 1820, the treaty gave the Choctaws food and ammunition valued at $4,600.00, schools for their children valued at over $50,000.00, and an annuity of $1,000.00, to be paid for sixteen years.[24]

By 1820, Jackson had established the precedent for Indian Removal that would be writ large ten years later with the Federal Indian Removal Act. The Cherokee, Chickasaw, and Creek peoples were now subsisting on meager land holdings east of the Mississippi River. The Choctaws had been driven west of the Mississippi River. In Florida, the Seminoles, badly bruised after the First Seminole War, had been driven into the everglades. President Monroe appointed Jackson Governor of Florida in March 1821. Resigning his army commission, on June 1, Jackson took up the reins of his

---

[22] Rappaport, p. 86.

[23] Remini, *Volume I*, p. 339.

[24] Ibid., 397.

new office. The Seminoles would suffer further during Jackson's tenure as governor.

As President of the United States, Jackson's harsh treatment of the Native Americans also fell within the context of his support for state's rights. His view was somewhat contradictory, given the fact that he, as largely an instrument of the federal government, had engaged in several Indian campaigns, but it made for good politics. Jackson's views helped him to sweep the south in the Presidential election of 1828. George Washington had once thought of transferring the Indians to lands beyond the parameters of the young republic.[25] Both Thomas Jefferson and James Madison thought of trading uninhabited land in the west to the Indians for their lands in the more settled parts of the country.[26]   Jackson's belief that national growth could be accomplished through Indian removal was shared by many. Another factor influencing President Jackson was his personal background as an Indian fighter and land negotiator. By 1829, he was determined to gain control of the remaining Native American lands east of the Mississippi River.

Jackson pushed for a comprehensive Indian Removal Act. The Act passed through Congress and became law on May 28, 1830.[27] Dispossession was not just a *de facto* reality. It was now *de jure*. The Federal Indian Removal Act of 1830 would forever stain the pages of American history. The alternative to removal for Native American peoples was either the abandonment of their traditional cultures (cultural genocide), or death itself. The stage had been set for the trail of tears.

The Cherokees had already sought to demonstrate their cultural prowess by developing a written language, wearing western clothing, and taking up agricultural patterns based upon established American methods, but Jackson and his commission failed to take any of this into consideration.

Responding to the Act in 1830, the state of Mississippi abolished the tribal government of the remaining Choctaws in the state. For the next three years, the Choctaws would be moved west to the Indian territory of Oklahoma. This was indeed a trail of tears. Many Choctaws died along the way. Disease and malnutrition felled

---

[25] Satz, p. 9.

[26] George Dangerfield, *The Era of Good Feelings* (New York: Harcourt Brace, 1952), pp. 26-27.

[27] Debo, p. 101.

many. Others were murdered, or died from the physical hardships of the migration. Still others died of a broken heart.[28] In 1832, the state of Alabama claimed all remaining Creek lands in the state. Made vagrants by the state, the wretched remnants of the Creek Nation migrated north and settled near the remaining Cherokees. Five years later, their inevitable trek to the west was delayed by a reputed "Indian uprising." Some of Chief Opothle Yahola's Creeks had killed some settlers after a fight over provisions. The Governor of Alabama called upon the chieftain to put down the renegades, or face possible annihilation. The Chief subdued his people, placing the hostiles in irons. He then moved the Creek Nation to Oklahoma. Other members of the Creek Nation remained with the Cherokees in the east, before being rooted out. Still others sought the protection of the Chickasaws. By 1839, it was estimated that forty-five percent of the Creek population had been eliminated.[29]

The State of Georgia had claimed all remaining Cherokee lands as early as 1828, but it was in 1830 that Cherokee laws were deemed null and void. The Cherokees pleaded their case to the federal government. Secretary of War, John H. Eaton, delivered President Jackson's response to them. It became something of a statement of Jacksonian Indian removal policies. "If, as is the case, you have been permitted to abide on your lands from that period to the present, enjoying the right of the soil, and privilege to hunt, it is not thence to be inferred, that this was anything more than a permission, growing out of compacts with your nation; nor is it a circumstance whence, now to deny to those states, the exercise of their original sovereignty."[30] Eaton then alluded to the 1785 Treaty of Hopewell, which had fixed the boundaries of Cherokee, Chickasaw, and Choctaw lands, by stating that this treaty and succeeding treaties with the United States government allowed for mere possessory rights to the Indians, while actual sovereignty resided with the states themselves. In the landmark case of the Cherokee Nation versus the State of Georgia, of March 5, 1831, the Cherokees were considered "a distinct political society," and a "domestic dependent nation."[31] The relationship between the

---

[28] Ibid., p. 104.

[29] Prucha, p. 236.

[30] Ibid.

[31] Debo, p. 106.

Cherokee Nation and the state of Georgia was essentially defined as that of ward to guardian.

When two Christian missionaries to the Cherokees refused to take an Oath of Allegiance to the state of Georgia, they were arrested, beaten, and sent to prison. They appealed to the U.S. Supreme Court. In the case of Worcester versus the State of Georgia in February 1832, the two gained a significant victory. Chief Justice John Marshall's court ruled that the Cherokees were indeed a sovereign nation under their own laws and therefore the two missionaries—Samuel Worcester and Elizur Butler—could go free. The Cherokees were elated by the decision, but their joy was soon tempered by the bitter realization that the state of Georgia was ignoring the court's ruling. Jackson is said to have remarked, "John Marshall has made his decision; now let him enforce it."[32]

In the summer of 1838, General Winfield Scott, in command of 7,000 men, was ordered to Georgia to forcibly remove the suffering Cherokees. Scott, despite being "sickened by his assignment," carried out his orders.[35] Rounding up the Cherokees, he placed many in hastily constructed stockades. The Cherokees were then transported to Oklahoma. About 4,000 died along the way. Several hundred bolted from Scott and made their way to the North Carolina backcountry. They remained there despite numerous attempts to expel them.

The Chickasaws were forcibly removed after a series of treaties signed between 1832 and 1837, stripped them of the last vestiges of their autonomy. They went to Oklahoma. By 1838, the remnants of this proud people had settled near the Choctaws.

The Seminoles offered stiff resistance in Florida. In 1835, after refusing to abide by the provisions of an Indian Removal Treaty issued to them by the Jacksonian administration, the tribe, led by Chief Osceola, plunged deeper into the Florida Everglades. Officials in Washington dispatched bloodhounds. Soldiers arrived to root out the Indians. The Seminoles proved to be expert guerilla fighters and eluded their pursuers. Osceola was captured under a flag of truce, but the Seminoles fought on. About 2,000 Seminoles were captured and transported to Oklahoma, but many remained in Florida. A total of four wars would be fought against them, but they were never fully removed to the West. After the Second Seminole War ended, it

---

[32] Ibid., p. 108.

was estimated that the conflict had cost the federal government approximately thirteen million dollars.[33]

By the end of the Jacksonian administration, the Chickasaws, Choctaws, and Creeks, had been fully transported west. The Seminoles, though partially transported, were still free in the Florida Everglades. Most of the Cherokees had also been removed west, but some had avoided capture, establishing a foothold in the North Carolina backcountry.[34]

In 1842, the War Department informed President John Tyler, "There is no more land east of the Mississippi, remaining unceded, to be desired by us."[35]

Bibliography

Dangerfield, George. *The Era of Good Feelings.* New York: Harcourt Brace, 1952.

Debo, Angie. *A History of the Indians of the United States.* Oklahoma City: University of Oklahoma Press, 1984.

Gragg, Larry. "The Reign of King Mob, 1829." *History Today* 28, no. 4 (April 1978): 240-242.

Pessen, Edward. *Jacksonian America: Society, Personality, and Politics.* New York: Dorsey Press, 1978.

Prucha, Francis P. *American Indian Policy: The Formative Years, 1770-1834.* Cambridge: Harvard University Press, 1962.

Rappaport, Armin. *A History of American Diplomacy.* New York: Macmillan Publishing Company, 1975.

Remini, Robert V. *Andrew Jackson: Volume I, The Course of American Empire, 1767-1821.* New York: Harper, 1977.

---

[33] Ibid., p. 109.

[34] Ibid.

[35] Satz, p. 131.

Remini, Robert V. *Andrew Jackson and His Indian Wars*. New York: Harper, 2001.

Satz, Ronald N. *Federal Indian Policy: 1829-1849*. Ann Arbor: University of Michigan Press, 1972.

Wallace, Anthony F. C. *The Long, Bitter Trail: Andrew Jackson and the Indians*. Ed. Eric Foner, New York: Hill and Wang, 1993.

THE ST. ALBERT MOUNTED RIFLES

Cynthia Dunnigan

This paper investigates the formation, purpose, and composition of the St. Albert Mounted Rifles, a corps of the Canadian Militia for a short time during 1885. This is a noteworthy year in western Canadian history for a number of reasons, one of which is that it was the year of the "Riel Rebellion" or as it is now more commonly accepted, the establishment of Riel's provisional government. Regardless of how one phrases it, it was "...the second Metis attempt to stem the inexorable tide of European civilization."[1] The Mounted Rifles are an example of an allied group with a shared cultural identity. The identity portrayed revealed by them is contrary to the typical view or stereotype that was widely held, and is still held by some, about Metis identity.[2]

The stereotype, which is described more fully later in this essay, can be summarized as a view of the Metis as nomadic or at least semi-nomadic buffalo hunters, who were multi-lingual in that they spoke the languages of their mothers and their fathers, and who

---

[1] George Stanley, *The Birth of Western Canada: A History of the Riel Rebellions* (Toronto: University of Toronto Press, 1961), p. 179.
[2] Defining "Metis" is somewhat complicated in that in Canada, there are various provincial definitions, government definitions, and academic definitions. Although a more thorough definition appears later in this paper, for brevity I am including one introductory definition here. It is the definition used by the Metis National Council of Canada, included in *The New Peoples Being and Becoming Metis in North America* as "a distinct indigenous nation with a history, culture, and homeland in western Canada." Jennifer Peterson and Jennifer Brown, *The New Peoples Being and Becoming Metis in North America* (Winnipeg: University of Manitoba Press, 1996), p. 6.

were essentially assimilated into either mainstream or Indian society after 1885.

The questions that have guided this exploration into the St. Albert Mounted Rifles are: Who were the Mounted Rifles? How did they relate to the Riel Uprising? What is the Metis stereotype? What was the identity of the St. Albert Metis in 1885? What were the kinship ties among these men? And, were they formed primarily for the purpose of protecting the economic interests of those few families?

These questions are addressed with information from archival materials, oral history and historical literature. The oral history was collected from the late Mrs. Delia Gray who was the niece of Captain Samuel Cunningham, a central figure in the St. Albert Mounted Rifles. Mrs. Gray took part in tape-recorded interviews in 1993. The interviews were conducted and transcribed by the author and resulted in a transcript of approximately 750 pages, only a portion of which dealt with the St. Albert Mounted Rifles and Captain Cunningham.

The following is the story of the St. Albert Mounted Rifles. More specifically, it is the story of the factors that precipitated their formation, and how and when they were brought together, as well as the men who comprised the Mounted Rifles, and their relations to one another. There are brief biographical sketches of selected members to demonstrate the kin relations that tied the Mounted Rifles together. In looking at the men who volunteered for service there is an emphasis on Samuel Cunningham because he was the captain of the Mounted Rifles and proved to be of such interesting history and character, especially as it relates to Metis identity, that information about him beyond his involvement with the Mounted Rifles is included.

Historical Background

Terminology such as Status-Indian, non-status Indian, Metis, and others are terms that have been widely used at different times and within a variety of contexts in Canada. Some of these terms have their background in a legal context. For example, in Canada, status Indians or registered Indians are considered to be the responsibility of the federal government by virtue of the Indian Act. For the purposes of this Act one is considered an Indian if one is "registered as an Indian, or is entitled to be registered as an Indian."[3]

Non-status Indians are people with Indian ancestry as demonstrated by social, cultural, and linguistic heritage but "they are not defined as Indians in the legal sense. Members of this group are not considered registered Indians because their ancestors refused—or were not allowed—to make agreements with the Crown. Included in this category are those Indians who have undergone "enfranchisement"; that is, who have lost their Indian status."[4]

The Metis National Council of Canada utilizes the following definition to identify Metis people:
1. An Aboriginal people distinct from Indian and Inuit;
2. Descendants of the historic Metis who evolved in what is now Western Canada as a people with a common political will;
3. Descendants of those Aboriginal people who have been absorbed by the historic Metis.[5]

Historical accounts paint a picture of the Metis in the St. Albert area between 1860 and 1870 as a majority population that were forming an economically thriving community. Although they faced crop failures, famine, fires, raids and armed conflicts they continued to erect permanent structures, cleared land for agriculture, maintained cultural continuity, and, in general, flourished.[6] The sometimes-adverse conditions lent to the desire of the Metis to establish a permanent community and obtain title to their riverlots. They were aware of the example of the Manitoba Metis who had acquired title to homesteads in the Red River Settlement and wanted

---

[3] James Frideres, *Aboriginal Peoples In Canada Contemporary Conflicts* (Scarborough: Prentice Hall Allyn and Bacon Canada 1998), p. 25. The matter of who may be entitled to registration under the Indian Act is a complicated and lengthy discussion that is not for inclusion here. However, the following web link will take the reader to Section Five of the Indian Act. Section Five deals with matters of registration. http://lois.justice.gc.ca/en/I-5/70676.html#rid-70717
[4] Frideres, p. 29.
[5] Ibid., p. 38. Although the above definition is the one put forward by the national body for Metis people in Canada, all Metis in Canada do not universally accept it. Several provinces have Metis socio-political organizations that use their own definitions.
[6] Arlene Borgstede, ed., *The Black Robe's Vision: A History of St. Albert and District* (St. Albert: St. Albert Historical Society, 1985), p. 25.

surveys to be carried out so they could be assured of their land rights.[7]

Two kinds of land surveys existed. Most of the land surveyed in Alberta was done so under the Third System of Township Surveys. Under this system the land was divided into townships measuring six miles square, thus containing thirty-six sections, each one square mile in area. Sections were further subdivided into four-quarter sections containing 160 acres. To provide legal access, road allowances, measuring sixty-six feet in width, were provided for every mile in a north-south direction and every two miles in an east-west direction within the township. This grid-like survey did not make any provision for existing occupation of the land or impediments resulting from natural geographic features, with the exception of rivers and lakes.

The one exception to the township system of surveys were settlement plans. These surveys covered smaller areas and were undertaken mostly around the turn of the twentieth century to deal with local settlements. They are characterized, in many cases, by long narrow lots fronting onto a river or lake. Drawing on the eastern terminology from the area around the St. Lawrence River, they are often referred to as "river lots." Thus, these surveys came to be called riverlot surveys. Settlement plans were generally identified by a local name, such as Edmonton Settlement, many of which originated as part of the fur trade. Unlike the township system, the river lot surveys addressed existing occupation of the land. In particular, the surveyor adjusted boundary lines to accommodate existing structures and improvements to the land.

The St. Albert Metis lands were under threat due to growing numbers of immigrants in the area. In 1878 St. Albert was the largest Metis settlement in the Northwest and it was one of several Metis communities to send petitions to the government calling for recognition of Metis title to the land.[8] In 1883 the Metis were finally granted a land survey of the river lots but a township survey was planned instead. The prospect of a township survey caused an uproar among the Metis because they feared that a township survey

---

[7] Alexis Tetreault, "Historic St. Albert (1883-1889)," *Alberta Historical Review* 3, no. 4, 1955: 17. (Hereafter, *AHR* 3.)

[8] George F. G. Stanley, *The Birth of Western Canada: A History of the Riel Rebellions* (Toronto: University of Toronto Press, 1961), p. 246.

would cause families to be pushed together onto the same piece of land and it was feared that homes would be destroyed.

Money was raised by the St. Albert residents to send a special delegation to Ottawa to obtain promises for a riverlot survey and scrip for the Metis holders of land. This was a very proactive stance; they did not idly wait for the Scrip Commission to arrive. In 1883 the Metis raised funds to send Daniel Maloney to Ottawa with Roman Catholic Missionary Father Leduc. Maloney and Leduc lobbied the government to get a riverlot survey in St. Albert. They were successful and obtained a written promise guaranteeing a survey that was to be carried out just over a year later. [9] The lobby was successful not only in obtaining a survey but also in getting promises of scrip and representation on the Northwest Territories Council. Representation on the council was significant because it essentially assured the large Metis majority at St. Albert official recognition. [10]

Metis in other locations shared the concerns of the St. Albert Metis surrounding the scrip. In late 1884 the concerns escalated into a political issue that gave rise to retrieving Louis Riel and the Metis taking up arms.

There are writings galore on the life, person, character, and activities of Louis Riel and the so-called Rebellion of 1885. Within these writings there is a wide spectrum of opinions as to the people and the events that took place in 1885. For example, the question of whether Riel was messianic or insane, and whether the events of 1885 were an uprising or a government conspiracy. What is true is that to date most of the written record has been produced by non-Aboriginal writers, be they academics, journalists, or historians. It is only recently that readers have begun to have access to the oral histories preserved by Aboriginal people. [11] What is also true is that "there is no absolute truth about Riel and the Metis, only a set of facts that can be interpreted in a variety of ways." [12] The facts are

---

[9] Borgstede, p. 69.

[10] Tetreault, *AHR* 3, p. 17. According to Tetreault there were one thousand people at St. Albert in 1888 and 860 of these people were Metis. Ibid., p. 20.

[11] For example, Blair Stonechild has published written accounts taken from oral histories that recount the Indian perspective on the Metis events.

[12] Paul Driben, "The Rise and Fall of Louis Riel and the Metis Nation: An Anthropological Account," *1885 and After: Native Society in Transition*, eds.

Figure 1
Property owned by enlisted men.

1. Albert Cunningham
2. Samuel Cunningham
3. Magloire Grey (Gray)
4. Jos. Chalifou (Chelifeur)
5. Narcisse Beaudry (Boudry)
6. Ed. Nault (Neault)
7. Elzear Page (Pagee)
8. Victor Laurence
9. Chas. Beauregard (Bourgard)
10. Norbert Bellerose
11. Octave Bellerose (Bellrose)

Laurie Barron and James Waldram (Regina: Canadian Plains Research Centre 1986), p. 68.

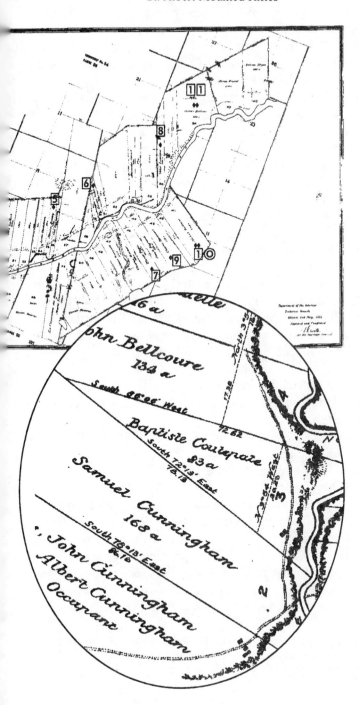

that there was a rapid increase in immigration with huge numbers of settlers taking up land and there were visions of extending the Canadian Pacific railway from coast to coast. In order to do that, it seemed necessary to fill western Canada with settlers to supply manpower and the products of agriculture to provision the builders of the railway. From the Metis perspective, they were already of the view that there was government inability to deal with Metis land claims and they had a desire to be able to continue traditional lifestyle pursuits like hunting, fishing and trapping.

Additionally, the disappearance of the buffalo, which had been a staple of the Metis life-way and subsistence, was causing the Metis to become more dependent on agriculture, a practice for which they required title to their land. When government surveyors went out in late 1884 to survey homesteads for European settlers "the land surveyed and allocated to them often cut across traditional Metis land."[13]   In late 1884, the Metis sent numerous and repeated petitions to Ottawa requesting resolutions to their land claims. Ottawa ignored the petitions. The Metis selected a few men to go into the United States and bring Riel back to take up their cause once again.   Riel returned to Canada and was welcomed as a returning hero. In December 1884, Riel sent his petition to Ottawa, which included the following:

1. Free title to the land presently held by people.
2. Provincial status for the Districts of Saskatchewan, Assiniboia, and Alberta.
3. The setting up of laws to encourage the agricultural settlement of the nomadic Indians and Metis.
4. And more liberal treatment to the Indians.[14]

There was a response from Ottawa in February 1885 saying that the petition had been received and that a commission would be established to investigate Metis claims, the first step was to be a census. The Metis response was disappointment and anger.[15]

At that point in the year, food supplies were running low and there was general hardship among the Indians and the Metis. In addition to this, the government was cutting back on expenditures

---

[13] D. Bruce Sealey and Antoine Lussier, *The Metis: Canada's Forgotten People* (Winnipeg: Pemmican Publications, 1975), p. 113.

[14] Sealey and Lussier, p. 118.

[15] Ibid., p. 120.

despite the knowledge that people were starving. Riel proceeded to establish a provisional government and in this endeavour he did not have the full support of all the Metis and First Nations but he had the support of some. All of these conditions and factions plus the attempts of the military and Mounted Police to arrest Riel led to armed conflict at a number of locations including Batoche, Duck Lake, Battleford, Fort Pitt, and Frog Lake.[16] All of this skirmishing led to rumours and media reports across the country.

As a Metis community one would expect that the St. Albert Metis would have sympathized with Riel, and it was reported in the March 21, 1885 edition of the *Edmonton Bulletin* that "[a] number of people here are in sympathy with Riel's movement, and there is great excitement over the news from the south branch," but in fact the St. Albert Metis did not support armed rebellion. They supported Riel's cause and a general quest for Metis land rights but according to some, they turned away from Riel after the death of two priests at Frog Lake.[17]

Another reason for the lack of rebellious behaviour from the St. Albert Metis is that they were more successful than Metis in other areas at getting the government to respond to some of their concerns. One source notes that it was the case that St. Albert was more successful than other settlements because "the concessions so readily granted to St. Albert were not extended to the settlements at St. Laurent, likely due to the fact that in the Edmonton district Metis settlement had preceded the survey."[18] Additionally, by the 1880s many of the St. Albert Metis had established a strong economic foundation for the community. Many of the Metis families were

---

[16] Ibid., pp. 122-123.

[17] Borgstede, p. 88. In Alberta, an event commonly called "The Frog Lake Massacre" occurred on April 17, 1885. In her book *Canada's First Nations*, Olive Dickason reports that the Frog Lake troubles occurred because there had been crop failures for two years so there was a shortage of food. As well, there was a general sense of uncertainty and unrest over lands, treaties, and settlers. First Nations suffered a long, hard winter with food shortages. On April 2, 1885, a group of First Nation men plundered the Frog Lake Hudson Bay Company stores. Nine people were killed in the skirmish. Two of these were the priests referred to by Bishop Grandin. Olive Dickason, *Canada's First Nations A History of Founding Peoples from Earliest Times* (Norman: University of Oklahoma Press, 1992), p. 310.

[18] Stanley, p. 258.

farming and opening businesses, as well as trapping, hunting, and guiding.[19]

One more piece of historical context relevant to 1885 is that it was just a few years before Treaty Eight was signed between the Canadian government and First Nations in northern Alberta in 1899. The entire province of Alberta was ceded to the government under the numbered treaties. Treaty Six was signed in 1876 and includes the central portion of the province. Treaty Seven was signed in 1877 and includes the southern part of Alberta. Treaties Six, Seven, and Eight were similar in nature in that they included an exchange of First Nation land for settlement in return for land set aside for reserves, hunting, fishing, trapping rights, farming assistance, annuity payments, and some provisions for education.

The treaties did not include the Metis. There were scrip commissions that accompanied the treaty commissions. The scrip commissions were purposed with extinguishing Metis claims to the land. They offered the Metis two types of scrip: money scrip, usually $240.00, or land scrip, which was usually 240 acres. The scrip commissions differed from the treaty commissions in that scrip was a unilateral and individual extinguishment of claims to land whereas the treaty commissioners conducted discussions which involved the collective and led to negotiated agreements.

The St. Albert Mounted Rifles

Three major precipitating factors led to the formation of the St. Albert Mounted Rifles.
1. The desire of the Roman Catholic Church to protect their priests.
2. The European settlers who lived in the area feared nearby First Nations and Metis communities joining in the rebellion.
3. The need to protect economic interests, both those of the well-established Metis community and those of the other settlers.

The role and reasons of the Roman Catholic Church are documented in the letters and writings of Bishop Grandin and other missionaries. The particular interest of Bishop Vital Grandin in protecting the St. Albert settlement may stem from the death of two missionaries. In a letter to the editor of the *Manitoba Free Press*, Grandin paints the two priests as martyrs when he writes of them:

---

[19] Borgstede, p. 59.

Rev. Pere Fafard O.M.I. ... has worked for the last ten years in these difficult arduous missions with zeal and heroic self-sacrifice. Rev. Pere Marchand O.M.I. was born at Château Geron, diocese of Renores France; he was yet in the beginning of his apostolic career and had all the qualities which constitute a perfect missionary. Both of these missioners commenced life with a bright worldly prospect before them but they gave up all its riches and renounced its honours-preferring a missionary's life of self abnegation and suffering-which life has at last been crowned by martyrdom.[20]

In fact, the commencement of the formation of the Mounted Rifles was not until Grandin himself was so motivated. This is attested to in writings of Kate Maloney, the daughter of Daniel Maloney, one of the Mounted Rifles; she noted that "[w]hen the first rumors of a rebellion reached here no heed was paid to such a thing. The first real stir was when the news came to Bishop Grandin of two missionary priests ... together with seven other white men being killed at Frog Lake on April 2nd."[21]

The general fear that people were experiencing is chronicled in articles in the *Edmonton Bulletin* and in some of the personal letters and diaries of people living in the Edmonton and St. Albert areas during the spring of 1885. For example, the diary entries of James Long, a settler at Namao, give an indication of the perspective of the average person during April and May 1885. Mr. Long's April 9, 1885 entry chronicles the growing fear:

I went to Edmonton today for mail, took Lissie and baby intending to visit Mrs. Sanderson till Sunday We found them terribly excited about hostile Indians- have formed a company of volunteers and are fixing up and fortifying the HB fort and fixing up all the arms that can be found- ...Mrs Sanderson and Mrs. Kellys are going to the RC mission for

---

[20] Provincial Archives of Alberta, O.M.I. Collection 84.400/33-927. (Hereafter, PAA.)
[21] Maloney (St. Albert Archives, St. Albert 1885 File).

safety they think Lissie and baby should go to I consent that
they should go as danger seems very certain.[22]

The diary entry indicates that people feared attacks from First
Nation people. Tetreault writes that news of the Duck Lake and
Frog Lake troubles arrived at St. Albert on March 28 and early April
1885, respectively.[23] He also indicates that many people were
gathering together and moving to places considered safe, such as
Bishop Grandin's new school, his warehouse, and his shops.[24]

  Mr. Long's entries can be taken as a typical view if the media
reports from the time are an indication of the mainstream
perspective. It was reported in the *Edmonton Bulletin* that,

> Fifteen scouts of the St. Albert volunteer company patrol in
> the settlement, with a view to keeping an eye on the
> somewhat mysterious doings of the Indians camped in the
> rear of the settlement. Reports from St. Albert in reference
> to the Indians were of such an alarming character that on
> Thursday night last guards at the Fort were doubled and the
> infantry company lying in camp was held ready to start for
> St. Albert at a minutes notice.[25]

Later in April, Mr. Long wrote the following in his diary, "am
alone all day thinking about the savages and the possibility of all
being killed immediately."[26] Mr. Long's writings indicate that there
was a high level of fear among the people and part of this was due
to the fact that it was felt that there was no protection.
  On April 20, 1885, Mr. Long wrote about an easing of the
apprehension: "Sutherland brought news that six hundred soldiers
are on road from Calgary for here expected in this week everyone's
countenance changes instantly now we feel safe which we have
done not for two weeks."[27]

[22] PAA 70.377/1SE Diary of James Long. Wherever I have quoted the diary of
James Long I have not changed the way he wrote in his diary. I have not made any
grammatical or vocabulary changes or additions.
[23] Tetreault, *AHR* 3, p. 18.
[24] Ibid., p. 199.
[25] *Edmonton Bulletin*, May 23, 1885, p.1
[26] PAA 70.377/1SE.
[27] PAA 377.70/1SE.

Although the Metis, in particular, were concerned with protecting their own economic interests, this was an overall concern through the area. The concerns about protecting farms, buildings, and livestock had been written about in the April 4, 1885 *Edmonton Bulletin*,

> The interests at stake here are surely as important as at Pitt, Battleford or Carlton, then why should this, the most remote settlement in the country, be the least protected. Indeed, as the road to the larger and perhaps richer part of the territories-the Peace, Athabasca and Mackenzie river districts lies through Edmonton, it is more important that order should be maintained here than at any other point in the North-West....[28]

At first, the non-Aboriginal settlers were not comfortable with the idea of arming the Metis. This was reported in the *Edmonton Bulletin*,

> There has been ample time since alarm was first taken to have sent in a supply of at least arms and ammunition, or if it was feared to trust the people here with arms, as some acts of these in authority would indicate, the necessity was all the greater to send in an armed force to protect life and property.[29]

It was only once the non-Native settlers viewed the St. Albert Mounted Rifles as an anti-Riel group that they received approval from the general population. The Mounted Rifles publicly asserted their position in a letter to the editor printed in the April 25, 1885 edition of the *Edmonton Bulletin*. The letter was signed by the following prominent Metis men: Samuel Cunningham, Octave Bellerose, John Cunningham, Baptiste Courtepatte, John Rowland, Adolphus Rowland, Louis Chastellaine, and Lawrence Gurneau, all of whom indicated their indignance over a statement that appeared in a Winnipeg newspaper. The statement read as follows:

---

[28] *Edmonton Bulletin*, April 4, 1885, p. 2.
[29] Ibid.

The Hudson's Bay Company received a telegram from their agent at Edmonton last night stating that the half-breeds there were holding secret meetings for some time, and are now organizing for action of some kind. Trouble is expected at once.[30]

In their response letter, the Metis men made several points:
1. They acknowledge that in the past they found fault with the government;
2. They point out that the Metis have as much right to the land as their First Nations relatives;
3. They address the fact that while treaties were made with First Nations none were made with the Metis and;
4. That they have long been cultivating their lands.

The message of the first half of their letter was that they were marginalized, treated neither as First Nations nor as Europeans, and yet not regarded as a distinct people. They were not accorded the same treatment that the government bestowed on European settlers and the writers challenged the readers to "[g]ive an instance of a land dispute between a half-breed and a foreigner where the half-breed was not sacrificed."[31]

The second part of the letter was a strongly worded and fair-minded response to the claim that the Metis were holding secret meetings for the purpose of making trouble. An excerpt from the second part of the letter indicates their outrage at the accusations and states their position as to the rebellion,

We have never thought of rebellion or inciting to rebellion. How under such circumstances have these strangers the assurance to ask us to take up arms in defense of them and theirs? Were we indeed what they think of us we would take arms in truth, but for the purpose of enforcing justice to ourselves...We wish to state that instead of siding with blood-thirsty Indians, we are ready to take arms against

---

[30] *Winnipeg Weekly Sun* in *Edmonton Bulletin*, April 25, 1885, p. 3
[31] *Edmonton Bulletin*, April 25, 1885, p. 3

those monsters who dare to spill the blood of defenseless people, not sparing even the lives of our priests.[32]

Reading between the lines of the above paragraph there is a message about identity. In proclaiming their anti-Rebellion stance they were telling the government and the white settlers that as Metis they have rights to the land, the same as the First Nations, and further, that true to their European ancestry they are among the first settled agriculturalists in Western Canada. By virtue of both their Aboriginal and non-Aboriginal ethnicity they deserved an assured claim to their land, because they are the relatives of the First Nations and because they had followed the Christian ethic of their European fathers, that land was to be cultivated and productive.

Following the publication of the letter, the St. Albert Mounted Rifles were formed and a few Metis men were selected to go and talk to the Cree in the area.[33] The May 23, 1885 *Edmonton Bulletin* reported on this meeting:

> On Tuesday last S. Cunningham and O. Bellerose went out to Riviere Qui Barre to interview the Indians assembled there to take part in the thirst dance. They found them very sullen and not inclined to talk. Nothing could be learned from them directly as to their intentions....[34]

The second decision was that Bishop Grandin would request permission from the Department of Militia and Defense to organize a company of men as a home guard.[35] The company was organized within a few days and recruiting carried on until Captain Desgeorges accepted the St. Albert Mounted Rifles into Active Service of the Militia of Canada on May 25, 1885.[36] Maloney describes the volunteers,

> ...two Oblate lay brothers, four trusty Irishmen, the remaining thirty-five all Halfbreeds. The Officers, excepting the first lieutenant, were also Halfbreeds, being

---

[32] *Edmonton Bulletin*, April 25, 1885, p. 3
[33] Borgstede, p. 90.
[34] *Edmonton Bulletin*, May 23, 1885, p. 1
[35] See Appendix 1 for a complete roster of the St. Albert Mounted Rifles.
[36] Tetreault, *AHR* 3, p. 19.

chosen according to their ability. The men were furnished with 40:70 repeating Winchester rifles. Each man furnished his own mount. There was no standard of height or measurement, thus they were tall and short, fat and lean. Most of them wore moccasins and moved silently. They were all fearless, keen eyed, unerring shot and expert horsemen, being able to lie flat on a horse and rise instantly.[37]

The Mounted Rifles spent a few weeks training and on June 7, they marched to Lac La Biche in response to a rumor that Big Bear's men had looted the Hudson's Bay Company stores.[38] A few of the Mounted Rifles stayed behind to serve as a home guard. The June 20, 1885 *Edmonton Bulletin* reported that the Mounted Rifles "…captured a band of Indians, some of them wounded, making their way from Big Bear's camp to Lac La Biche. The Rifles are patrolling in the vicinity of Saddle Lake."[39] According to Maloney, other than this incident, much of the time that the Mounted Rifles were assembled was spent doing regular military routines such as riflery, and drills; additionally, some of the men hunted or assisted trappers in the area.[40]

The Mounted Rifles existence was very short-lived; they returned to St. Albert in two detachments at the beginning of July 1885 and they were disbanded a few days after the arrest of Big Bear on July 2, 1885.[41] Although the Mounted Rifles as a corps of the Canadian Military were short-lived, they had a continuing impact on the Metis in St. Albert because they were "…a source of great pride and distinction as a whole. Long after the disbanding of

[37] Maloney (St. Albert Archives, St. Albert 1885 File).

[38] Borgstede, p. 91. Big Bear was a well-known Western Canadian Cree-Ojibwa leader. According to Dickason, Big Bear led a huge band of two thousand Crees around 1873. One thing he was known for was his resistance to signing Treaty Six. He saw unity among First Nations as a key to resisting European settlement. He eventually signed Treaty Six in 1882 to obtain rations for his starving followers who had been reduced in number to just over two hundred people. Dickason, pp. 29, 30.

[39] *Edmonton Bulletin*, June 20, 1885, p. 1

[40] Maloney (St. Albert Archives, St. Albert 1885 File).

[41] Borgstede, p. 92.

the unit, members of the Mounted Riflemen continued to foster a sense of local accomplishment and military tradition in St. Albert."[42]

Samuel Cunningham and The Enlisted Men

Sam Cunningham, captain of the Mounted Rifles, was a man who was involved in the pursuit of Metis rights for much of his life. The kin ties that existed among the St. Albert Mounted Rifles form a web of family, much of it centering on Sam Cunningham.[43] Through extended family and intermarriage he was surrounded with a network of political, cultural, and social support. Mr. Cunningham's life, family, and culture challenge conventional notions of Metis identity. He and the community of St. Albert Metis in 1885 do not fit the stereotype.

To appreciate this, one must begin with the conventional understanding of Metis culture and identity. In his book *The Government and Politics of The Alberta Metis Settlements*, T. C. Pocklington elaborates the following points as descriptors of the commonly held view or stereotype of Metis culture:[44]

1. Economically, the Metis are portrayed as dependant primarily on the buffalo hunt. The main basis of their economic life is taken to be provision of pemmican for fur traders.
2. This dependence on the buffalo is closely connected to a nomadism largely inconsistent with the economic activities, especially agriculture, which demand settled communities.
3. Culturally, the Metis are regarded as having much more in common with their maternal than their paternal ancestors.
4. Though nominally Christian, they are portrayed as fundamentally uncivilized, lacking in foresight, and living from day to day.
5. Politically, the Metis are regarded as extraordinarily naïve.

---

[42] Ibid.

[43] See Appendix 2 for a diagram highlighting the families each man was associated with and outlining the connections between the families. This diagram is not intended to be generationally organized, but rather, its primary purpose is to show interconnections.

[44] T. C. Pocklington, *The Government and Politics of the Alberta Metis Settlements* (Regina: Canadian Plains Research Centre, University of Regina, 1991), p. 1. I must note here that Pocklington does not ascribe to or promote this stereotype in his book. He uses it as a starting point in his book, which then explores the government and politics of the Alberta Metis settlements. I use it here because it is a concise description of the typical view that was held about Metis identity.

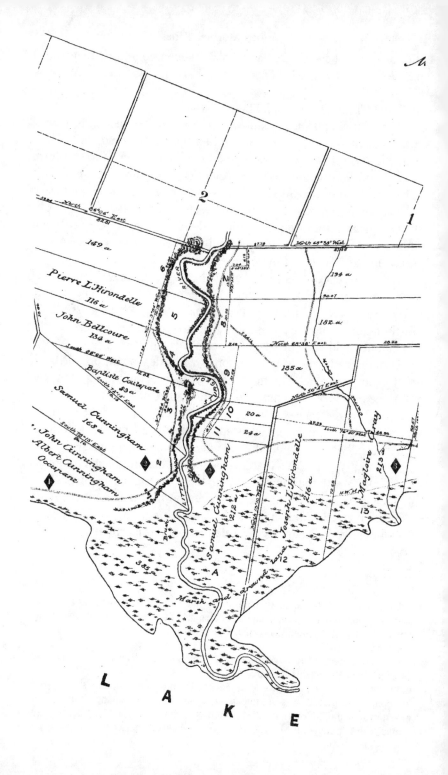

6. The conventional account of the Metis concentrates almost exclusively on the person of Louis Riel.
7. The final ingredient in this version of Metis history is that it ended, and had to end, soon after the rebellion of 1885.

With that in mind, one can explore how the men of the Mounted Rifles do not fit this stereotype. For many of the Metis men on the Mounted Rifles some reference to personal financial security or success can be found. One author summarizes this as: "To those Metis who had already established successful farms, the prospects of raids and pillaging by Riel's followers were particularly disturbing."[45]

There are various connections between the men who served on the St. Albert Mounted Rifles. Of the forty-two men who are listed by St. Albert historian, Arlene Borgstede, information about the families and professional lives of at least twenty of the men is available.[46] Of the men for whom information was available it was found that they were connected by political passions, and/or related to one another through marriage or other family connections and friendship.

Sam Cunningham was born to John Patrick Cunningham and Rosalie L'Hirondelle on April 8, 1849 at St. Albert, Alberta. He was the third of eleven children and was related to people all over the St. Albert, Lac Saint Anne, and Villeneuve areas. He traveled Alberta working to better conditions for the Metis and First Nations.[47] He was the first mayor of Grouard, a member of the Legislative Assembly, and an interpreter at the signing of Treaty Eight.[48] In terms of Mr. Cunningham's financial situation he is said to have had a well-equipped farm of 168 acres and to have owned one hundred fifty "fat" cattle.[49] Sam Cunningham's younger

---

[45] Borgstede, p. 89.

[46] Ibid., p. 90.

[47] Delia Gray, personal interview, 1993.

[48] Maloney (St. Albert Archives, St. Albert 1885 File); Canadian Parliamentary Company, Northwest Territories Assembly (Ottawa: J. Durie & Son, 1887), pp. 377-378; Richard Price, *Legacy: Indian Treaty Relationships* (Edmonton: Plains Publishing, 1991), p. 142.

[49] Borgstede, p. 71; Maloney (St. Albert Archives, St. Albert 1885 File).

brother, Alfred, born in 1868, was the 17-year-old staff sergeant of the Mounted Rifles.[50]

In November 1885 Sam Cunningham decided to run for the Northwest Territories Council. Three weeks prior to Sam's announcement of his intentions, Mr. Dan Maloney had put his own name forth but upon hearing of Sam's intention Maloney withdrew his own name and announced his support of Sam.[51] Sam's decision to run was supported by the Roman Catholic clergy; a letter from Bishop Grandin includes the following reference to Sam's campaign:

> You have read the letter of the governor. I am convinced and Father Lacombe is also convinced about having Sam Cunningham as Councilor of the North-West. As a Captain he showed a presence of mind that showed us we could rely on him.[52]

Members of the Mounted Rifles put Mr. Cunningham's nomination forward. He was representative for St. Albert on the Northwest Territories Council from 1885 to 1888.

Captain Cunningham was involved with the signing of Treaty Eight in a couple of ways. First, in June 1899 Sam Cunningham was the interpreter for the Cree during the negotiations of Treaty Eight.[53] Historian and author, David Leonard writes that Sam Cunningham was involved in the proceedings of Treaty Eight and he was part of a Metis delegation that approached the Lesser Slave Lake police in 1897. The delegation spoke out against the signing of Treaty Eight. According to Leonard the reason for their opposition was a fear that fishing and game laws might be enforced. Cunningham was concerned that the traditional way of life of the First Nations and Metis people would be disturbed.[54]

In a 1902 letter from surveyor A. W. Ponton to the Indian Commissioner, there was a story about the tenacity and negotiating skills of Samuel Cunningham. Ponton was surveying land in

[50] Borgstede, p. 90.
[51] Ibid., p. 155
[52] PAA O..M.I. Collection, 84.400/33-927.
[53] Price, p. 142
[54] David Leonard, *Delayed Frontier: The Peace River Country to 1909* (Calgary: Detselig Enterprises, Ltd., 1995), p. 18.

severalty at Swan River, Alberta, and he was aware that several
First Nation people wanted to accompany him to the sites of their
land selections. When Ponton was ready to do this, several young
men were away and the others refused to go without all being
present. An agreement was finally reached but when no one turned
up to take part in the survey Ponton discovered the following,

> I learned that the Indians were collected and camped on the
> River about six miles from my camp, and that Samuel
> Cunningham who had been engaged as Interpreter was with
> them, and that all were coming to talk with me next day. I
> was disappointed, however, on this occasion, as, instead of
> coming to talk with me, they broke up their camp, and
> returned, to the Lake, owing to some disagreement among
> themselves, and so opposed were they, at this meeting, to
> any settlement, that they took away Cunningham's canoe to
> prevent his reaching my camp, and also refused to tell him
> where it was, he was therefore compelled to return on foot
> to Drift Pile River to obtain a horse, and food, to enable him
> to seek my camp—Cunningham eventually persuaded the
> Indians at the "Narrows" to send word to Assineau River
> that they would give them one more chance to meet together
> and select their land, and if they refused to join in the
> selection, that they would select their own lands without
> further reference to them---I am pleased to be able to report
> that this meeting was agreed to, and on their arrival at my
> camp a better understanding was soon arrived at--[55]

Ponton closed his letter with the following praise of
Cunningham: "I would mention that I am greatly indebted to
Samuel Cunningham for the assistance he gave me in dealing with
these people."[56]

There were three members of the Gray family on the St. Albert
Mounted Rifles. They were Joseph Jr., Ambroise, and Magloire.
The Grays were descendants of Iroquois from Eastern Canada.
They came west and settled in Jasper House where Joseph Gray, Sr.
was born. Later, the Grays relocated to the Lac Sainte Anne-

---

[55] Public Archives of Canada, RG 10, Vol. 7777, File 27131-1. (Hereafter, PAC.)
[56] Ibid.

Onoway-St. Albert area because it seemed to be an area where they could prosper.[57] There were two Joe Grays in 1885: Joe, Sr. and his son. One can surmise that it was Joe Jr. who was the Mounted Rifle because, according to Metis historian Dr. Anne Anderson, he would have been 27 years old while Joe Sr. would have been 78 years old.[58] Joe Gray, Sr.'s daughter, Suzanne, married Captain Samuel Cunningham in 1869. Captain Cunningham served on the Rifles with three of his brothers-in-law. Magloire, who had 213 acres of cultivated land, was a sergeant, while Joe and Ambroise were privates.[59]

Daniel Maloney was the only non-Metis officer on the St. Albert Mounted Rifles; he was the First Lieutenant.[60] Dan Maloney and Sam Cunningham worked together on various community development projects and political initiatives. For example, in October 1884 Maloney petitioned Lieutenant Governor Dewdney to purchase the St. Albert Bridge, which was owned by the Mission, and to remove the toll charges. When the bridge was built in 1862, Father Lacombe said, "My friends, I am through crossing the river, walking in the mud on the bank, and pushing the scow. I'll build me a bridge. All those who help me will cross over it free. The others will not. I will have a man there to watch."[61] The government agreed to purchase the bridge if it was confirmed by three upstanding citizens that the bridge was in good shape. W. Cust, Maloney and Sam Cunningham were the three citizens who swore that the bridge was in good working order.[62]

Octave Bellerose was the Second Lieutenant of the St. Albert Mounted Rifles.[63] Octave was the son of Olivier and Suzette Bellerose. He was married to Lucie L'Hirondelle who was the

[57] Eddie Gray, "Ambrose and Mary Gray," in Elizabeth Turnbull and Jean Payne, eds., *The Pathfinders: A History of Onoway, Bilby, Brookdale, Glenford, Goldthorpe, Heatherdown, Hillcrest, Nakamun, Rich Valley, Speldhurst, Stettin, and Sturgeon River* (Winnipeg: Onoway Women's Institute, 1978), p. 351
[58] Anne Anderson, The First Metis: A New Nation (Edmonton: Uvisco Press, 1985), p. 237; *Edmonton Bulletin*, August 8, 1885 in Borgstede, p. 83.
[59] Maloney (St. Albert Archives, St. Albert 1885 File).
[60] Borgstede, p. 90
[61] Alexis Tetreault, "Historic St. Albert (1861-1868)," *Alberta Historical Review* 2 no. 2 (1954), p. 16. (Hereafter, *AHR* 2.)
[62] Borgstede, pp. 138-139.
[63] Emile Tardiff, *Saint Albert* (Edmonton: La Survivance, 1958), p. 32.

daughter of Jean Baptiste L'Hirondelle.[64] Octave served on the
Mounted Rifles with his father-in-law Jean Baptiste L'Hirondelle.
As to having economic interests, it was reported in the *Edmonton
Bulletin* on August 21, 1884 that "Octave Bellerose had finished a
new house on his farm at Big Lake Settlement. The event was
celebrated by a ball in the evening to which people traveled nine
miles on foot."[65] The house was a two-story log house built on
River Lot 38.

   That Octave held political clout among the Metis is evident from
an incident that took place after the disbanding of the St. Albert
Mounted Rifles. When Edgar Dewdney was approved as Federal
Minister of the Interior, many at St. Albert actively supported him
and they were trying to pass a resolution to formally congratulate
him but the Metis were hesitant to sign because Dewdney was
reputed to be one of the government officials who had refused to
deal with Metis grievances in 1885. Octave persuaded them to
sign.[66]

   Norbert Bellerose was a Mounted Rifle. Norbert was the son of
Olivier and Suzette Bellerose, which means that he was the brother
of Octave Bellerose. Norbert and Octave's sister Aloise, married
Adolphus Rowland in 1884 one year before Adolphus, Norbert, and
Octave served together on the Mounted Rifles.[67] Adolphus
Rowland was later linked by marriage to other members of St.
Albert Mounted Rifles as his two sisters: Mary and Amelia married
the Cunningham twins: Henry and Alfred, who were Sam
Cunningham's brothers.[68]

   Narcisse Beaudry was a sergeant on the Mounted Rifles and he
was a Metis businessman who opened the St. Albert Hotel in 1883;
it was one of the first commercial privately run businesses in St.
Albert.[69] In addition to the hotel, after 1870 Narcisse also built a

[64] Dorothy Chartrand, "The Octave Bellerose Family" in Arlene Borgstede, ed.,
The Black Robe's Vision: A History of St. Albert and District (St. Albert: St. Albert
Historical Society, 1985), p. 95.
[65] Ibid., p. 97.
[66] Borgstede, p. 157.
[67] Dorothy Chartrand, "The Olivier Bellerose Family" in Arlene Borgstede, ed.,
The Black Robe's Vision: A History of St. Albert and District (St. Albert: St. Albert
Historical Society, 1985), pp. 43-45.
[68] Gray interview, 1993.
[69] Borgstede, p. 133.

two-story building out of which he ran a trading post until 1887.[70] Between the hotel and two-story building with a trading post Narcisse had substantial investments in the community.

Narcisse had several family connections to other members of the Mounted Rifles. Narcisse was connected to the Cunningham family through marriage as Narcisse's daughter Maria married Daniel Cunningham, the brother of Captain Sam and Staff Sergeant Alfred.[71] Narcisse was also related to the Gray family as Joe Gray, Jr., a member of the Mounted Rifles was the son of Joe Gray, Sr. who was married to the mother of Narcisse Beaudry in August 1885.[72] Narcisse and Joe Gray, Jr. were stepbrothers.

J. B. Pepin had 138 acres of cultivated farmland in 1884.[73] Additionally, Pepin was a political ally of Sam Cunningham; he nominated Sam for the Northwest Territories Council in September 1885.[74] Pepin was active in Metis politics and he was the first vice-president of the St. Albert Metis Association.[75]

Another of Captain Cunningham's political allies was Jean Baptiste L'Hirondelle who was a corporal on the Mounted Rifles. In September 1885 Jean Baptiste was one of the men who nominated Sam for the Northwest Territories Council.[76] Jean Baptiste was also one of the committee members on the St. Albert Metis Association when it first formed.[77]

Xavier L'Hirondelle was a private on the Mounted Rifles.[78] Xavier was a son of Jean Baptiste L'Hirondelle Sr. and Catherine Loyer, and he was issued Metis scrip in 1885.[79] The Jean Baptiste L'Hirondelle who was a Mounted Rifle was probably the brother of Xavier L'Hirondelle since according to Anderson, Jean Baptiste, Sr.

---

[70] Dorothy Chartrand, "The Narcisse Beaudry Family," *The Black Robe's Vision: A History of St. Albert and District*, ed. Arlene Borgstede (St. Albert: St. Albert Historical Society, 1985), p. 98.

[71] Borgstede, p. 99.

[72] *Edmonton Bulletin*, August 8, 1885 in Borgstede, p. 83.

[73] Borgstede, p. 71.

[74] Ibid., p. 153.

[75] Ibid., p. 152.

[76] Ibid., p. 155.

[77] Ibid., p. 153.

[78] Tardiff, p. 32.

[79] Vitaline (L'Hirondelle) Rooke, "Xavier & Philomene L'Hirondelle," *The Black Robe's Vision: A History of St. Albert and District*, ed. Arlene Borgstede (St. Albert: St. Albert Historical Society, 1985), p. 127.

would have been 68 years old in 1885 while Jean Baptiste, Jr. would have been 29 years old.[80]

Victor Laurence was the son of Louis Laurence and Olive Bellerose. Louis died before Victor was born. Victor was raised primarily by his mother's parents, Olivier and Suzette Bellerose, the parents of two other Mounted Rifles: Octave and Norbert.[81] Victor was born March 8, 1862 and he grew up on River Lot 34. Later he was given River Lot 36 from his grandfather Olivier Bellerose who also owned River Lot 35. Victor's wedding was attended by three hundred guests at his mother's two-story house and it was said to be "one of the grander festivities ever held in St. Albert."[82] In addition to having substantial economic interests, Victor also had family connections with other Mounted Rifles as mentioned earlier: Octave and Norbert Bellerose were his uncles.

Chas Beauregard was born December 24, 1842 and he was married on October 18, 1865 to Marie Bellerose, daughter of Olivier and Suzette Bellerose. Marie was the sister of Octave Bellerose, also a Mounted Rifle.[83] Charles had business interests; he owned shares in the Sturgeon River Grist Mill, purchased in 1878. Also, he worked for the Hudson's Bay Company.[84]

John O'Donnell was a Mounted Rifle. William James John O'Donnell married Ellen Bellerose, another daughter of Olivier and Suzette Bellerose, in 1883.[85] O'Donnell was related through marriage to the Bellerose brothers who served on the Mounted Rifles and to Chas Beauregard, who was also married to a daughter of Olivier and Suzette Bellerose.

---

[80] Borgstede, p. 256.

[81] Anne (Laurence) Hogg, "The Laurence Family," *The Black Robe's Vision: A History of St. Albert and District*, ed. Arlene Borgstede (St. Albert: St. Albert Historical Society, 1985), pp. 50-52.

[82] Hogg, p. 50.

[83] Chartrand, "Olivier Bellerose," p. 43.

[84] Walter Vallette, "Charles Beauregard, Jr.," *The Black Robe's Vision: A History of St. Albert and District*, ed. Arlene Borgstede (St. Albert: St. Albert Historical Society, 1985), p. 95.

[85] Florence O'Donnell-Singer and Ellen O'Donnell, "Charles Beauregard, Jr." in Arlene Borgstede, ed., *The Black Robe's Vision: A History of St. Albert and District* (St. Albert: St. Albert Historical Society, 1985), p. 122.

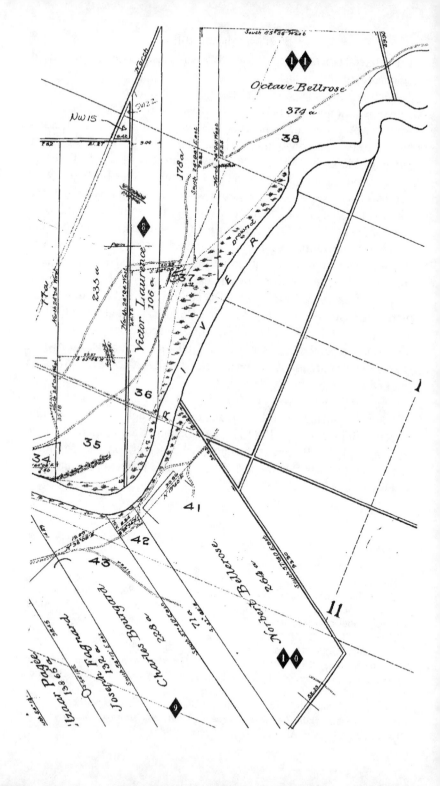

The main Metis families who were at the core of the Mounted Rifles were the Bellerose and Cunningham families. *The Gazette* reports that "[t]hose Metis who joined the volunteers owned their own land, were well off, and had no intention of seeing the fruits of their industry pillaged by Indians."[86] A map of the river lots, listing their owners during the late 1800s, shows that the men who volunteered for the Mounted Rifles owned a substantial amount of the land in St. Albert. (See Figure 1.)[87]

The connections between the men who were Mounted Rifles did not end in 1885. These men continued to act on their political agendas as they had before they worked together on the Mounted Rifles. For example, The St. Albert Metis Association was formed in October 1896 "...to take action on a single political issue—the attainment of scrip for those Metis born between 1870 and 1885."[88] The President was Octave Bellerose; the vice-presidents were Baptiste Pepin and Severe Villeneuve. The secretary was Adolphus Rowland; the committee members were John Rowland, Jean Baptiste L'Hirondelle, and John Cunningham.[89] All of the men listed above were enlisted as St. Albert Mounted Rifles except Severe Villeneuve. At least two of the families were connected through marriage because two of John Rowland's daughters were married to John Cunningham's twin sons. John's son Henry married John Rowland's daughter Mary in 1895, one year before the inception of the association.[90] Also, the secretary, Adolphus Rowland was the son of committee member John Rowland. The involvement of these men who were the St. Albert Mounted Rifles on the St. Albert Metis Association is significant here because the Metis Association was formed for the purpose of championing Metis rights, particularly land rights. These St. Albert Metis continued their political activism beyond 1885.[91]

---

[86] *The Gazette*, January 11, 1884 in St. Albert Archives, St. Albert 1885 Riel Rebellion.

[87] Figure 1 is a plan of St. Albert Settlement, approved and confirmed by E. Deville, Surveyor General 1884.

[88] Borgstede, p. 152.

[89] Ibid.

[90] Gray interview, 1993.

[91] Incidentally, the St. Albert Metis Association evolved into part of what is today the Metis Nation of Alberta Association. This association is the socio-political body that represents Metis people in Alberta. In 1996, approximately 53,000 Albertans identified themselves as being Metis.

The information included in this paper points to the St. Albert Metis as having a status rather more elite than some Metis in that they owned property, buildings, businesses, and farms.[92] Many of the Metis who volunteered for the Mounted Rifles and for whom written information could be found, had economic interests to protect. In particular, the Cunningham and Bellerose families had established solid economic bases because both families owned several settlement lots containing buildings, cultivated lands, and livestock.

It is apparent that the St. Albert Metis are in contrast to the stereotype discussed earlier in this paper. They were not primarily dependant on the buffalo hunt as demonstrated by the abundance of improvements to the land, cultivated farmland, permanent buildings, and established businesses. While they continued hunting and trapping, they were not mainly nomadic because they were tied to their agricultural investments. In terms of culture, the St. Albert Metis did continue the traditions of their Indian mothers but they also adopted the socio-economic practices of their European fathers.[93]

The support shown to the St. Albert Metis by the Roman Catholic Church in general and individual missionaries in particular speaks to more than a nominal Christianity. Politically, the St. Albert Metis were astute and proactive as demonstrated by their lobbying, fund-raising, letter-writing, and use of the media. While many think only of Louis Riel when they conjure an image of a Metis hero or leader, it is obvious from the long list of men who made up the Mounted Rifles that there were many praiseworthy Metis politicians and leaders working in their own communities to make a better life for Metis people in Alberta.

---

[92] While there were many Metis in Canada whose identity did fit the generally held stereotype, and while the St. Albert Metis were one of the exceptional Metis communities in terms of owning farms, livestock, and buildings while continuing their hunting and trapping activities, anecdotally speaking, it is unlikely that they were the only Metis who did not fit the stereotype. In Canada, there are many Metis political organizations that derive from this and other time periods.

[93] There were rare exceptions to the Indian Mother/White Father combination but it was almost universally true that the Metis of the late 1800s had First Nation or Metis mothers while their fathers were of European ancestry.

Appendix 1
Enlisted Men

(This list is reproduced from Borgstede, p. 90.)

Samuel Cunningham
Daniel Maloney
Octave Bellerose
Narcisse Beaudry
Magloire Grey
J.B. Pepin
Albert Cunningham
Elzear Page
J.B. L'Hirondelle
Dieudonne Courtepatte
Jos. Courtepatte
Adolphus Rowland
J.B. Belcourt
Ambroise Grey
Jos. Chalifou
Jos. Grey
John Bolduc
Wm. McKenna
Gabriel Belcourt
Norman Vandal
Daniel Loyer

Michel Callioux
Norbert Bellerose
Jules Savard
Jos. Page
Ed. Nault
Xavier L'Hirondelle
Fran. Boisgontier
Victor Laurence
Felix Dumont
James Laderoute
Patrick Kelly
Fran. Beaudreau
Jeremiah Auger
Chas. Beauregard
Ed Carly
John Laronde
Peter Donald
John O'Donnell
Bpt. Supernant
John Callioux
Bpt. Besson

Appendix 2 - Genealogy Table

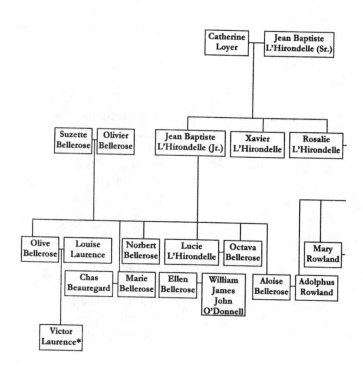

Legend:

═══ - First marriage for Joseph Gray (Senior)

*Victor Laurence's father, Louis Laurence, died at a young age and Victor was
subsequently raised by his mother's parents, Olivier and Suzette Bellerose.

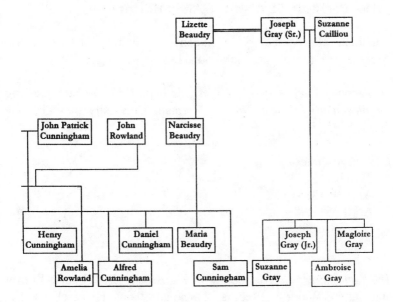

Bibliography

Anderson, Anne. T*he First Metis: A New Nation*. Edmonton, Uvisco Press, 1985.

The Black Robe's Vision: A History of St. Albert and District. Ed. Arlene Borgstede, St. Albert: St. Albert Historical Society, 1985.

Canadian Parliamentary Company. Northwest Territories Assembly. Ottawa: J. Durie & Son, 1887.

Dickason, Olive. *Canada's First Nations A History of Founding Peoples from Earliest Times*. Norman: University of Oklahoma Press, 1992.

Edmonton Bulletin.
   March 21, 1885
   April 4, 1885
   April 25, 1885
   May 23, 1885
   June 20, 1885

1885 and After: Native Society in Transition. Eds. Laurie Barron and James Waldron, Regina: Canadian Plains Research Centre, 1986.

Frideres, James. *Aboriginal Peoples In Canada Contemporary Conflicts*. Scarborough: Prentice Hall Allyn and Bacon Canada, 1998.

Gray, Delia. Interviewed by the author on May 21 and May 26, 1993. Edmonton.

Leonard, David. *Delayed Frontier: The Story of the Peace River Country to 1909*. Calgary: Detselig Enterprises, Ltd., 1995.

The Pathfinders: A History of Onoway, Bilby, Brookdale, Glenford, Goldthorpe, Heatherdown, Hillcrest, Nakamun, Rich Valley, Speldhurst, Stettin, and Sturgeon River. Eds. Elizabeth Turnbull and Jean Payne, Winnipeg: Onoway Women's Institute, 1978.

Peterson, Jennifer and Jennifer Brown. *The New Peoples Being and Becoming Metis in North America*. Winnipeg: University of Manitoba Press, 1996.

——. *The Government and Politics of The Alberta Metis Settlements*. Regina: Canadian Plains Research Centre, 1991.

Price, Richard. *Legacy: Indian Treaty Relationships*. Edmonton: Plains Publishing, 1991.

Provincial Archives of Alberta
    69.305 Item 218 Sam Cunningham Dockets 1884
    69.305 Box 2, Item 11A Sam Cunningham Dockets 1886
    69.305 Box 18, Item 1645 Albert Cunningham Dockets 1895
    70.377/1SE Diary of James Long
    O.M.I. Collection 84.400 Box 33 Item 927

Public Archives of Canada
    Letter from A.W. Ponton to the Indian Commissioner. RG 10, Volume 777. File 27131-1.

Sealey, D. Bruce and Antoine Lussier. *The Metis: Canada's Forgotten People*. Winnipeg: Pemmican Publications, 1975.

St. Albert Archives
    St. Albert 1885 Riel Rebellion File
    St. Albert 1885 File
    St. Albert Mounted Rifles File

Stanley, George F. G. *The Birth of Western Canada: A History of the Riel Rebellions*. Toronto: University of Toronto Press, 1961.

Stonechild, Blair and Bill Wasser. *Indians and the Northwest Rebellion: Loyal Till Death*. Calgary: Fifth House Publishers, 1997.

Tardiff, Emile. *Saint Albert*. Edmonton: La Survivance, 1958.

Tetreault, Alexis. "Historic St. Albert (1861-1868)." *Alberta Historical Review* 2, no. 2 (1954): 11-20.

——. "Historic St. Albert (1883-1889)." *Alberta Historical Review* 3, no. 4 (1955): 17-20.

INDEX

232

Index

DUTCH, Arrival in Lenapehoking 1
Colonial Expansion 23-26
Commercial Ventures 8 13
Commercial Ventures, Loss of 38-39 Conflict with Lenape 7 78
Encourage Dutch, Swedes, and Germans to Emigrate to New Netherland 76 First Contact with Lenape 4 Goods Reciprocity Concept 6 Land Ownership Expectations 22 Policy to Improve Relations with Lenape 19-22 Relations with Munsee-speakers Disentigrates, Reasons for 76 Trade with Mohawks 44-45
EASTERN INDIANS, 108 140
EASTON, Pennsylvania 66
EATON, John H 190 Theophilus 99
EDGERMETT, 120-121
EDMONTON, 205 207-208
EDMONTON SETTLEMENT, 198
EEL RIVER, 117
EGERMET, 123
ELIZABETH, 61 66
EMUCKFAW CREEK, 181
ENGLAND, 48 52 54 68 86-87 99 108
Cedes Territory to United States 149-150 King of 53 81 Recommences War with France 1702 53 Recommences War with France 1744 57
ENGLISH, Arrival in New Netherland 39 Migration from New England to New Netherland Area 77 Migration from New England to Southwestern Connecticut 81
ENIX, Lieutenant 160
ENOCH, Abraham 155-156 164 166-167 171-172
ENOCHS, 172
ENOTACHOPCO CREEK, 181
ENOX, Ensign 160
ERIE, Pennsylvania 59
ESANQUES, 9
ESKUYIAS, 97
ESOPUS, Native American Band 35-38 Wars 35-38 98
EZEARE, 56
FAFARD, Rev Pere 205

FALLEN TIMBERS, Battle of 148
FATHER RALE'S, War 55
FATHER RASLE'S WAR, 55-57
FEAKE, Elizabeth 81-82 Elizabeth Winthrop 81 Robert 81
FEDERAL INDIAN REMOVAL ACT OF 1830, 180 186 188-189
FINNS, Arrival in American Colonies 22
FISH CREEK, 153 157 160-161
FISH CREEK STATION, 160
FIVE NATIONS, 43 48 51-52 56 59 68
FIVE NATIONS NEUTRALITY, 52-54
FLETCHER, Governor 140
FLORIDA, 179 183 187-188 191 Everglades 191-192
FLUSHING, New York 99
FONDA, New York 46
FORBES, General 66
FORT, Amsterdam 77 80 82 84 92 94 97-98 Baker 153 159 Beversreede 24 Casimir 28 31 Christina 26 26 28 31 Dummer 56 Duquesne 60 66 Edward 62-63 65 Hunter 64 Jackson 182-183 Lebeuf 59 Machault 67 Mims 180 Mystik 90-91 Nashwaak 113 113 115-117 119 138 Necessity 60 Niagara 60 66 Orange 44-45 82 Oswego 58 61 68 Pitt 66 203 St Frederic 57 Strother 181 Washington 150 Wayne Indiana 147 William Henry 65 110-111 122
FOWLTOWN, 187
FOX POINT, 132 137
FRANCE, 48 52 65 68 108 114 117 120
FRANKLIN, Jesse 184
FROG LAKE, 203 205-206
FRONTENAC, Comte De 108-109 109 114-115 139 142 Count 52
GAINES, Edward P 187
GENESSEE, 67
GEORGIA, 179-180 184 187 190-191
GLORIOUS REVOLUTION OF 1688, 48
GODYN, Samuel 10
GOHARIS, 97

SAINT ALBERT MOUNTED
   RIFLES, 195-223
SAINT CASTIN, 113 Baron De 108
SAINT CLAIR, Arthur 150
SAINT JOHN'S, Native American
   Band 113 117
SAINT JOHN'S RIVER, 104 113 116-
   117 124
SAINT LAWRENCE RIVER, 43 45-
   46 53 59 68 114 198
SAINT MARKS, 187
SALISBURY, Neal 141
SALMON FALLS, 109
SALTWATER PEOPLE, 6 8 14 27
SANDERSON, Mrs 205
SAULT ST LOUIS, 47
SAUWENARACK, 96 98
SAUWENARO, 98
SAVARD, Jules 223
SCAROYADY, 63
SCHAGHTICOKE, 47 50
SCHAGHTICOKES, 57
SCHENECTADY, New York 50 52 57
   109 Attacked 49
SCHOHARIE CREEK, 68
SCHUYKILL RIVER, 24
SCHUYLER, Peter 48-52 54
SCHUYLKILL, 34
SCOTLAND, 87
SCOTT, Winfield 191
SCRIP COMMISSION, 199
SEMINOLE WAR, First 187-188
   Second 191-192
SEMINOLES, 179-192
SENECAS, 9 39 43 45 54 58 67 106
SEREHOWANE, Peter 66
SESEKEMAS, 97
SESEMUS, 97
SHAWNEES, 66 147-174
SHEPHERD, David 149 153 159-160
SHIRLEY, William 60-61
SHOPTAW, John 161-162
SHUMATOFF, Nicholas Jr 96
SICKONEYSINCK, 9-10 12
SINERONGNIRESE, 49
SINNONQUIRESE, 50
SINQUEES, 23
SINQUEZ, 26
SINTSINGS, 97

SINTSINK, 76
SISIADEGO, 97
SIX NATIONS, 55-57 60-62 64 66-67
SKAHIJOWIO, 63
SKIWIAEN, 97
SKIWIAS, 97-98
SLAUGHTER, Henry 51
SMITH, 135
SMITS, Claes 82
SOUTH BAY, 63
SOUTH BERWICK, Maine 109
SOUTH CAROLINA, 179
SOUTH RIVER, 31
SOUTHOLD, Long Island 99
SPAIN, 187-188
STACKPOLE, Everett S 105
STAMFORD, Connecticut 77 80 82-83
   83 87 91-92 96
STANFORD, 92
STANTFORD, 94
STATEN ISLAND, New York 33-34
   38 80
STOCKBRIDGE, 63
STOUGHTON, William 140
STUYVESANT, Peter 19 21-22 22-26
   32-39 99 Petrus 37
SUPERNANT, Bpt 223
SUSQUEHANNOCKS, 44
SUTHERLAND, 206 John 164
SWAN RIVER, Alberta, Canada 215
SWANENDALE, 22 Destruction of
   10-12
SWANNEKENS, 80
SWANNEKINS, 6 8 21 32
SWEDEN, 26 87
SWEDES, Arrival 1-2 22 Colonial
   Expansion 23-26 Conflict with
   Lenape 22 27-28
SWITS, Claes 79
SWITZERLAND, 88
TAGASHATA, 66
TALLADEGA, 181
TALLAPOOSA RIVER, 181
TALLUSHATCHEE, 180-181
TANECHWANEGE, Cornelius 53
TANKITEKE, 80 97
TAPPAN, 97 New York 13
TAPPAN, Native American Band 76
TAPPEN, Native American Band 38